THE
CATECHUMENAL
PROCESS
~~~~~

THE CATECHUMENAL PROCESS

Adult Initiation & Formation for Christian Life and Ministry

A Resource for Dioceses and Congregations

Office of Evangelism Ministries
The Episcopal Church Center

THE CHURCH HYMNAL CORPORATION • NEW YORK

The Church Hymnal Corporation
800 Second Avenue
New York, NY 10017

10 9 8 7 6 5 4 3

The 1988 General Convention in Detroit called for implementation of the adult catechumenate and parallel rites for the baptized. This publication is a response to that action by The Office of Evangelism Ministries at the Episcopal Church Center in New York City. The Reverend Ann E. P. McElligott, associate rector of St. Paul's church, Indianapolis and a doctoral candidate in religious education at New York University, was commissioned to prepare the basic text for *The Catechumenal Process*.

Contents

Preface

In 1988, the General Convention of the Episcopal Church, meeting in Detroit, focused on the eight Mission Imperatives presented to Convention by the Presiding Bishop and Executive Council, imperatives that were to shape the work of the church in the triennium and beyond. Imperative I reads: "Inspire others by serving them and leading them to seek, follow and serve Jesus Christ through membership in his church." The catechumenal process is a substantive response to that imperative and its call to evangelism. The catechumenal process, in fact, is uniquely suited to the historical, liturgical, pastoral, and socially concerned character of the Episcopal church as it strives to be part of the Body of Christ caught up in God's ongoing transformation of the world.

A publication from The Episcopal Church Center must reflect the variety of applications of the catechumenal process in use throughout the church. It must also be clear. A mandate of Imperative I and Convention makes the revitalization of the catechumenal process a top priority for the whole church and clarity is essential in all the material offered to that end.

The Catechumenal Process:

Adult Initiation and Formation for Christian Ministry honors the commitment to inclusiveness by offering a broadly based overview of all the basic elements of the catechumenal process. Using this book, dioceses and congregations will be able to put these elements together in whatever way suits their specific needs. Plans for the stages of the catechumenal process and discussions of its history and theology are presented with clarity and simplicity. Appendices contain a wealth of material to illustrate approaches to the stages of the catechumenal process and to illuminate the theological and liturgical underpinnings.

Twentieth century use of the catechumenal process presents a challenge unique to our times. Originally, the Catechumenate was developed specifically—and solely—for people seeking baptism. Today, many people who are already baptized—often as infants—seek further preparation for an active, committed role in the church and for more understanding of the Christian path. They are seeking Christian formation like that of the catechumenal process. Other baptized people are looking for ways to be more deeply obedient to their baptismal covenant. Limitations of human "resources" and of space in most congregations have led many to look for ways to include both unbaptized and baptized seekers in one group. When the two groups meet as one, however, there should still be a distinction made between the needs and goals of the two groups and in the choice of rites to accompany their journeys. The fact of baptism must not be overlooked.

Several dioceses and congregations have developed practical approaches for groups in which people who are baptized and those who are not are combined. They have found ways of working that are enriching and fulfilling for everyone concerned. Samples of materials for this kind of mixed group are presented. The diocese of Milwaukee has, for instance, worked out an approach based on both groups working together as have other dioceses and congregations. Examples of a wide variety of single group situations are offered here. We have a lot to learn together.

What this publication does *not* attempt is to offer set, prescribed patterns for the catechumenal process. The effort is to help dioceses and congregations develop their own custom-tailored models so that each may be empowered to form the Christian ministers God wants.

The Catechumenal Process is "user friendly." Some congregational and diocesan groups will need to use only specific chapters. The chapters stand on their own and can be copied and distributed as needed (noting the source is all that is required). The book also offers a wealth of resources that appear in four ways: as footnotes; as planning resources in Chapter 14; by subject; and in a full bibliography. The Evangelism Ministries Office at The Episcopal Church Center will supply a complete set of the catechumenal resources it offers to dioceses on request. Individual congregations may request specific resources. The liturgies for both the unbaptized and the baptized are included in full in Appendix D, with the permission of The Church Hymnal Corporation.

The Program Resources Office through Irene V. Jackson-Brown has guided and expedited the preparation of the manuscript throughout. The Communication Unit through John Ratti has given the work a careful editing. The collaboration of The Church Hymnal Corporation in publishing and distributing the work is invaluable.

Special thanks to Ann Elizabeth Proctor McElligott, who has assembled this wealth of experience and resources and shaped them into a readable, useful, and manageable format. Her long interest in the field, her understanding of reference materials, and her skills as an educator have combined to produce a resource that has long been anticipated and needed. Finally, her diligence and spiritual insight have combined to save the rest of us a great deal of work!

May God lead and empower every diocese and congregation in forming Christian ministers.

A. WAYNE SCHWAB
Evangelism Ministries Coordinator
Education for Mission and Ministry
THE EPISCOPAL CHURCH CENTER

THE
CATECHUMENAL
PROCESS

1

The Catechumenal Process: An Overview

The life and witness of the church faces many challenges in a pluralistic society like our own, with its many complicated human, economic, political, and social issues. One challenge further complicates the situation for the church; a challenge to be faced within its own walls. This challenge is the problem of nominal membership. For many people, church membership and Christian commitment have become peripheral rather than central to their lives. Although it is tempting to say that individuals have the problem and that the solution must be theirs alone, people within the church must seriously confront their responsibility for helping others to form a deep and meaningful commitment to Christ.

In the past, Christians in the United States seemed to rely on the country's culture to form Christian commitment. We often assumed that the institutions and traditions of the national heritage were "Christian" enough to produce and shape Christian commitment and living. Episcopalians "finished off" this process with a confirmation class. Now, Episcopalians are confronted daily with the obvious truth that if this process was ever to any degree effective, it has been far from adequate. Being a good citizen and attending a few confirmation classes has not proved to lead directly to real Christian commitment. If the church is serious about forming Christian commitment in its members, it must approach the task consciously and effectively. The catechumenal process is one way to help people make commitments as Christians.[1] [See Chapter 9 for further discussion of why Evangelism Ministries is involved in the catechumenal process.]

The catechumenal process is an ancient pattern for initiating Christians. It is finding increasing acceptance in modern times. And the process can address the needs of a diverse group of people seeking more mature commitment. Therefore, an effective catechumenal process must be adaptable for use in a variety of settings and with many kinds of people. It must be adaptable to churches of different sizes, from "family–size" with Sunday attendance of up to fifty adults to "corporation–size" with average attendance from 350 to 500, or more.[2] It must offer appropriate liturgical and catechetical experiences, both for people who have never been baptized as Christians and for those baptized and confirmed members of the congregation who want to have a deeper understanding of Christian vocation and ministry. Although the liturgies [see Appendix D] differ for baptized and unbaptized persons, both groups follow a common path of conversion, formation, discovery, and growth.

Today's catechumenal process is modeled after the early church's practice of the "Catechumenate." This was the church's way of preparing adults who converted to Christianity for baptism. Many people who become part of a 20th century catechumenal process are not actual "catechumens" in the old sense of persons preparing for Baptism. Many modern seekers—as many as ninety percent—are already baptized. These participants include—

---

1. A. Wayne Schwab, "Using A Catechumenal Process for Christian Initiation" (The Episcopal Church Center, Evangelism Ministries Office, 815 Second Ave., New York, NY 10017, 1-800-334-7626, June 7, 1987).
2. Arlin J. Rothauge, "Sizing Up A Congregation for New Member Ministry" (The Episcopal Church Center, Office of Congregational Development, c. 1983), introduces these categories of congregational size.

- People baptized as infants, who want to make a mature public affirmation of their faith
- People seeking out the church for marriage or for baptism of a child
- Newcomers from other churches
- Newcomers whose children are newly enrolled in church school
- Newcomers seeking help in time of crisis
- Returnees (for a variety of reasons)
- Active members seeking to deepen their commitment
- Nominal members seeking basic formation
- Lapsed members willing to reconsider Christian commitment

People reaffirming their commitment, renewing their vows, or seeking to deepen their understanding of the faith need formation just as much as those preparing for baptism.

Young people preparing for Confirmation can find a natural place in their congregation's catechumenal process. Provided they are sixteen or older, these young people can make unique contributions to the process and give a clear account of what their participation means to them. Six "pastoral-size" congregations did experiments in the catechumenal process that included young people. [See Schwab, A. Wayne, "A Visit to Three Churches in a Catechumenal Process," June 1987, and Sullivan, Mark, "No Bolts of Lightning," 1985, Evangelism Ministries Office.] A large congregation decided to offer a separate experience for youth when a catechumenal process was introduced. [See Appendix C, Section 13]

The Catechumenal Process: Arena of Conversion and Seedbed for Ministry

Conversion through encounter with the Gospel of Jesus Christ is at the heart of the catechumenal process for both unbaptized and baptized people. The experience of encountering

and responding to the Gospel takes many forms. The catechumenal process creates a place or arena for these experiences
to happen. The process, moreover, provides the time needed.
Conversion is a much longer process than most people imagine.
Few conversions happen in a sudden flash of lightning. And
although one can chart specific, key moments of discovery and
commitment in the conversion experience, no one can predict
exactly when they will happen. The catechumenal process allows a long period of time for initial interest to blossom into
deeper insight into the mysteries and power of the Gospel. The
Gospel speaks of God's reign in all of life. Response is commitment to serve God's reign in all of life—at work, at home, in the
community, through one's citizenship, at leisure, and in the faith
community. Such commitment forms gradually as participants
have time to examine their lives area by area. These areas of life
are discovered to be areas of ministry already carried on. They
begin to see richer ways to serve and find power to carry them
on. The breadth of catechumenal experience allows this examination and growth to occur. [See Appendix A, Section 1 for
further discussion of the variety of encounters and responses to
the Gospel.]

The word *catechumen* comes from a Greek word meaning "to
sound in the ear." Thus, the catechumenal process is not one
of learning by rote. It is the "sounding in the ear" of the Word
of God, the deep hearing of God's will by a believer. The Word
of God reaches its fullest expression in Jesus Christ, "the Word
made flesh." Therefore, the catechumenal process is Word-
centered. At the heart of its study is the Sunday lectionary, the
Word of God. Participants add to and support this deep hearing
of God's Word with a "curriculum of experiences," including
worship, story-sharing, group study, service, working for social
justice, and a "curriculum of knowledge," including specific
material about commitment to and membership in Christian
community.

The heart of the catechumenal process is the participant's
growth from being a hearer of the Word to being a doer of the

Word. The Gospel of Jesus Christ announces the presence of God's "kingdom" (the more familiar word) or reign among us. We are all called to commit ourselves to live in this present realm with our ultimate allegiance in another realm, God's. When we have experienced conversion, we enter a wholly new political, social, and family structure. We go on living in our old political, social, and family structures, but now we seek to conform our life in the old structures to our new-found allegiance to God's realm and family. This is a demanding call. We are not consumers of Christian religious articles. We are ministers of God's reign in our daily places:

- In our daily work (including school for the student and part-time or occasional work for the retired)
- In our homes
- In our communities (local to world)
- In our citizenship (our discussion of the issues of justice and peace with one another, and working in our local, state, and national governments for justice and peace)
- In our leisure
- In our congregations.

  Ministry of this kind calls for a much deeper fellowship than that found in running bazaars and playing in bowling leagues. The catechumenal process introduces us to a kind of community that can support us in the crises that strike everyone, whether in personal ministry at home and at work or in justice ministry in the world. A catechumenal process can also revitalize congregational life for mission. A vital catechumenal process will help to keep a congregation in touch with Jesus Christ and the Holy Spirit, the wellspring for all Christian ministries of love and justice. The catechumenal process is not only an arena for conversion. It is also a fertile seedbed for ministry. All grow in gaining a perspective for making decisions as conscious agents of Christ's reign.

  Further, the heart is involved as well as the head. Louis Weil, a leader in today's revival of the process, emphasizes the fact that growth needs to include the emotions. Therefore, he speaks of the catechumenal process as offering people a chance to make an affective as well as an intellectual response to the Gospel.

The Catechumenal Process and Transformation of Life

The early church was very clear in its belief that conversion is expressed outwardly in transformed lives. Early in its evangelization, the church saw a pattern to conversion. The first hearing of the story of God's coming among us in Jesus Christ, his resurrection, and the gift of the Holy Spirit excited interest in non-Christians. This interest needed to be followed by initial instruction in Christian living, faith, and worship. After this instruction, potential converts had to make a choice: did they want to enter a period of deep Christian formation that could last as long as three years? If the answer was yes, the church had to affirm that decision.

The church's affirmation of seekers was based on signs of growing faith in the individual and signs that growth in faith was beginning to change the convert's way of life. As Origen (185-c.254 AD) wrote, converts could enter the next stage when "the hearers seem to have devoted themselves sufficiently to the desire to live a good life." Dujarier has summarized this period as "the first conversion to Christ that implies a decision to transform one's life, without which none would succeed in being admitted to the catechumenate."[3]

The next stage was the deep formation of the Catechumenate. The "hearers," the catechumens, demonstrated by the way they led their lives that they were among those who "hear the word of God and keep it" (Luke 11:27). Origen described them as those who "desire nothing other than those things of which

---

3. Michael Dujarier, *A History of the Catechumenate* (New York: Sadlier Press, 1979), p. 57.

Christians approve."[4] Hippolytus (c.235 AD) recorded how catechumens were admitted to baptism only on the witness of
church members as to "whether they honored the widows,
whether they visited the sick, whether they have fulfilled every
good work."[5] When baptized, their baptism was what Tertullian
(c.160–c.225 AD) called "the seal of the faith."[6] Augustine (354–
430 AD) wrote an entire treatise "On Faith and Works" to underline the need for changed lives:

> There are certain persons who are of the opinion that ev-
> erybody without exception must be admitted to the font of
> rebirth which is in Christ Jesus our Lord, even those who,
> notorious for their crimes and flagrant vices, are unwilling
> to change their evil and shameful ways, and declare frankly
> (and publicly) that they intend to continue in their state
> of sin . . .
>
> With the help of our Lord God, let us diligently beware
> henceforth of giving men a false confidence by telling them
> that if only they will have been baptized in Christ, no matter
> how they will live in the faith, they will arrive at eternal
> salvation.[7]

Louis Weil tells of the young priest who learned that a business leader in his confirmation class had a reputation for dis-
honest business practices. When the priest confronted the busi-
nessman, he admitted the truth of the accusation, and
commented, "But what has that got to do with being confirmed?"

Changed or transformed living has everything to do with the
baptismal covenant. The early church believed this was true,
looked for signs of that belief in its converts, and built the belief
into its use of the Catechumenate. That same belief underlies

---

4. Dujarier, p. 63.
5. ———. p. 52.
6. ———. p. 31.
7. Dujarier, p. 87.

today's catechumenal process. Readiness for commitment to Christ will show itself in the changed lives that come from true repentance. Participants in today's catechumenal process will begin to seek more opportunity for both private prayer and corporate worship, and will be nourished spiritually by Bible study. Their daily lives will demonstrate growth in love and justice. The development of people in the catechumenal process can be tracked by noting attitudes changed, prejudices acknowledged, and questions asked. These changes in the participants in the catechumenal process will also lead to significant transformation of the life of congregations and of their mission.

Stages and Rites

This resource is entitled *The Catechumenal Process.* However, it really describes three processes. The first process is for unbaptized adults. It has four stages and is outlined in *The Book of Occasional Services* (BOS),[8] as the "Catechumenate" for the "Preparation of Adults for Holy Baptism." The second process is for the baptized adults. It also has four stages, and is outlined in *The Book of Occasional Services* as the "Preparation of Baptized Persons for Reaffirmation of the Baptismal Covenant." The third process is for the "Preparation of Parents and Godparents for the Baptism of Infants and Young Children."[9] Although there are three processes, the primary concern of this resource is with those preparing adults for baptism or for reaffirmation. For clarity, there two processes are described individually, beginning with the first, the process for the unbaptized. It is, in turn, the pattern for the other two. All are shaped by the meaning of adult baptism itself.

As acknowledged in the Preface, most dioceses and congrega-

---

8. *The Book of Occasional Services,* Second Edition (New York: The Church Hymnal Corporation, 1988), pp. 112ff or Appendix D, Section 1.
9. BOS, pp. 132ff or Appendix D, Section 2.

tions will probably combine the unbaptized and baptized in one catechumenal group. Because of this reality, a process or model for combining the two groups is described after the descriptions of separate groups for baptized and unbaptized persons. This "combined" model comes from the diocese of Milwaukee [see Chapter 7] and is outlined here not as the recommended way to proceed, but as an example of one among many ways to go.

Throughout the catechumenal process, the stages must be flexible enough to adapt readily to the individual pace of each participant's journey in faith. Leaders should be careful to encourage individual participants to wait when movement to a next stage seems premature. Participants do not move in "lock step" through a set "program." Movement from one stage to another is marked by a specific liturgy giving shape to the process and providing participants with ways and times to recognize how their faith is changing and growing. Most important, the catechumenal rites themselves help participants move from one stage to the next.

The Catechumenal Process for Those Seeking Baptism

The first stage is called the *Pre-Catechumenal* or *Inquiry Period*. [For a chart of the four parts of the Catechumenate, see Appendix A, Section 2.] During this stage, participants are invited to respond to the call of Christ in their lives and to join a process of inquiry to determine if they wish to move to the next step in becoming Christians. This inquiry is focused, first, on those questions participants have about Christian faith and commitment and, second, on stories they share of their own journeys to date.

Participants move to the second stage when they have had enough questions about the faith answered to make them willing to take the journey further. The promises they will make for admission as catechumens imply that they have already begun to conform their lives more closely to the teachings of the gospel of God's reign among us.

The second stage of the process is called the *Catechumenate*. Participants mark their entrance into this stage by a public liturgical act. The catechumens are presented to the community with their sponsors, who accompany them through their journey to baptism and their new lives as baptized Christians. During this time, participants study the Sunday lectionary, allowing the cycle of Bible texts to help them deal with ministry in their daily lives at work, at home, in the community, in the nation, in leisure time, and in church. In addition to studying salvation history as revealed in Scripture, participants promise to be regularly involved in community worship, to practice Christian living—including service to the poor and neglected, and working for a more just society—and to be engaged in a life of prayer. The length of this stage varies according to the individual's rate of growth. Each catechumen and his or her congregation must discern the individual growth in faith and ministry promised when one became a catechumen.

The third stage begins on the First Sunday in Lent when the catechumens begin a stage called *Candidacy for Baptism*. This stage includes public prayer on Sundays for the candidates and their sponsors. The candidates assume the traditional Christian disciplines of fasting, examination of conscience, and prayer to prepare spiritually and emotionally for their baptisms at the Easter Vigil.

In the fourth stage, the newly baptized persons now experience the full corporate life of the church, and gain a deeper understanding of the sacraments. Those who have reaffirmed their baptismal vows join the newly baptized during this period. *The Book of Occasional Services* does not give this fourth stage a specific name.

The Catechumenal Process for the Baptized Seeking Reaffirmation

The 1988 General Convention approved this four–stage pattern in the rites for "Preparation of Baptized Persons for Reaffirmation of the Baptismal Covenant." [For a chart of the rites, see Appendix A, Section 3.]

A Model Combining Unbaptized and Baptized

Many congregations will choose to combine both unbaptized and baptized persons as they move through the stages. It is important to make clear the full and complete membership of the baptized, who do not share the same rites with the unbaptized. In scheduling the rites, the place of honor is always given to the rites of the catechumens. During meetings, prayers offered for the baptized always acknowledge the fact of their baptism [see Chapter 11]. The pilot project in the diocese of Milwaukee combined both groups. [See Appendix A, Section 4 for a chart of their procedure.] Claiming ancient practice as its guide, the Milwaukee project referred to the procedure as "a catechumenal process" as a further way to avoid treating the baptized as catechumens. The term "Inquiry" was used for both first stages; "Formation in Christ" for both second stages; "Intensive Preparation and the Rites of the Paschal Holy Days" for both third stages; and "Formation in Ministry" for both fourth periods. (An opening stage, "Gathering," was added for the reasons described in Chapter 9.) The full discussion of the stages in Chapter 8 assumes that both groups meet together.

The Catechumenal Process for the Preparation of Parents and Godparents of Infants and Young Children

The 1988 General Convention (also approved) the "Preparation of Parents and Godparents for the Baptism of Infants and

Young Children." [see Appendix D, Section 3.] This pattern is similar, offering three stages, each of which concludes in a rite. A fourth period of formation in salvation history, prayer, worship, and social ministry follows throughout childhood and adolescence until reaffirmation of the baptismal covenant at a mature age. Grace Cathedral in San Francisco has used this model for several years. [For a chart of the preparation of parents and godparents for the baptism of infants and young children, see Appendix A, Section 5.]

History of the Catechumenal Process

The catechumenal process was developed early in the church's history. By the end of the second century, the main stages had been identified, and it was practiced during the period when the state persecuted Christians. An early Christian often took more than three years to complete the catechumenal process, remaining in the second stage for three years before enrolling for Lenten preparation.

The Catechumenate, as an institutionalized practice, began to decline in the fourth century when the Roman Empire recognized Christianity as a religion. The resulting flood of people joining the church made it difficult to maintain previous high standards for initiation. By the fifth century, the process was reduced to a mere formality. Gradually, infant baptism became the usual practice.

The Catechumenate was revived in 1850 in French Equatorial Africa when missionaries sought a means to form Christian faith in new converts. People were baptized tribe by tribe, and a method was needed to help individuals hear the Gospel deeply and develop a Christian perspective on the world. In the mid-twentieth century, European and North American churches, seeking a new way to form mature Christians, began studying the African experience and the initiatory practices of the early church.

Vatican II in the *Constitution on the Sacred Liturgy* established guidelines for revising Roman Catholic initiatory practice and directed restoration of an adult Catechumenate. When provisional texts for the *Rite of Christian Initiation of Adults* were available, Roman Catholic congregations began establishing programs for the Catechumenate. A self-funded support system, the North American Forum on the Catechumenate (5510 Columbia Pike, Suite 310, Arlington, VA 22204, 1-703-671-0330), emerged to provide training and resources to local churches. Other churches began adapting the Roman Catholic catechumenal process to their denominational situations. In the Church of England, a network of congregations used the process. By 1985, about 150 Episcopal congregations in the United States used the catechumenal process. Their work was sustained largely by participating in the support network offered by the North American Forum.

The catechumenal process is important to the Episcopal Church in the twentieth century for several reasons. First, a church that values tradition will obviously look to the early church's model of forming Christian commitment. Second, this process forms people in faith as they live out the basic experiences of Christian life in individual prayer, corporate worship, study, service, and in building a more just society. The process educates the participants by inviting them to reflect on their experience of living as Christians. The process also offers people basic skills for making decisions about living faithfully in their daily lives, at work or at home, in the community or as citizens, in church or at leisure. Third, careful research and a pilot project indicate that the catechumenal process does work. People are touched deeply. Their lives are changed. Congregations are renewed as leaders rise to the task of "making Christians." Finally, the process is being adapted, in both liturgical and catechetical expression, to include both unbaptized and baptized people who want basic Christian formation, deeper conversion, and increased commitment to their ministries.

The Evangelism Ministries Office at The Episcopal Church

Center has been gathering information from the many parishes in the United States that have established a catechumenal process and has been assisting the diocese of Milwaukee with its pilot project in the catechumenal process, called "Living Our Baptismal Covenant." The Evangelism Ministries Office believes that the catechumenal process provides a means to form the kind of faith and living of that faith that evangelism seeks. In this resource, models and guidelines are offered to those wanting to implement a catechumenal process in their diocese. It is informed by the rich experiences of people, both in the Episcopal Church and in other communions, who have helped to make this ancient practice for forming Christians a vital part of the church's work today.

This Resource in Outline

Because interest in the catechumenal process emerged as Christians began to question and renew contemporary initiation practices, this resource begins with a discussion of the issues involved for a community of Christians seriously addressing a call to be a baptizing community. Once a diocese or a congregation has grappled with these basics, it may choose to use a catechumenal process to address formation issues emerging from a serious commitment to evangelism, catechesis, baptism, reaffirmation, and ministry.

After a general discussion of initiation, this resource offers a model for a diocese trying to establish a catechumenal pilot project in its congregations. Early chapters consider the bishop's role in a diocesan catechumenal process; the formation, training, and functions of a diocesan leadership team; and the training and role of congregational leaders in planning and leading a catechumenal process in their local churches. The final chapters discuss the various elements of the catechumenal process: stages of the process; evangelization; rites associated with the catechumenal stages; a suggested curriculum to integrate experience and knowledge, instruction, and reflection; the role of sponsors; and a format for training congregational leaders. A bibliography of resources is also provided.

2

The Catechumenal Process in a Baptizing Community

Churches show signs of coming alive when Christian initiation is taken seriously. Sacramental seriousness is present when baptism is understood as essential and primary, as permanent and nonrepeatable, as operative on several levels of meaning at once, as full inclusion into the Christian household, as open and accessible to persons of all ages and as ordination to the basic order of Christian ministry. Ecclesial or organizational seriousness is present when thoughtful, realistic parish policies are developed and interpreted, when the whole congregation is consciously involved in the initiatory process, when the church year is intentionally related to the baptismal cycle, and when baptism and mission are seen as intimately interrelated. The rich harvest of spiritual food to be gained when parishes begin to work this fertile soil is incalculable.

A. THEODORE EASTMAN[1]

Beyond considering the interest in a restored catechumenal process, the Episcopal Church and other churches are also examining and reconsidering the whole issue of Christian initiation. Questions are being raised about what initiation means, how baptism and confirmation are related, who should be baptized or confirmed, when this should take place, and who should preside over the sacraments. Traditions inherited from the early

---

1. A. Theodore Eastman, *The Baptizing Community: Christian Initiation and the Local Congregation* (New York: The Seabury Press, 1982), p. 42.

church are being studied, as are current ideas emerging from the life of congregations.

The catechumenal project developed by the Evangelism Ministries Office of The Episcopal Church Center emerged from a similar exploration of the larger question of how the twentieth century church can understand and convey the meaning of Christian commitment. This issue also surfaced as Episcopalians worked to revise *The Book of Common Prayer* (BCP).[2] Once the revised initiatory rites of the Prayer Book became a norm for churches, questions arose about the preparation of adults for reception or reaffirmation and of parents and godparents for sponsorship.

These questions led the 1985 General Convention to ask the Standing Liturgical Commission, assisted by the Education and Evangelism Offices of Executive Council, to develop materials and guidelines "for the implementation of a practical adult Catechumenate with experimental use in pilot parishes" and forms for experimental use "for public incorporation of new members transferring into a congregation."[3] The catechumenal process emerged from the discussion in 1985 as a means of providing adequate information for adult initiation and the deepening of commitment, and as a paradigm or model for preparing parents and sponsors for infant baptism. This way of looking at the catechumenal process guided the Standing Liturgical Commission in developing new rites, and the Evangelism Ministries Office in developing appropriate learning models and training techniques to support both the rites and the catechumenal process in congregations.

Just as a catechumenal process was not considered until the whole issue of commitment and initiation was opened for discussion, a diocese or congregation should not adopt such a

---

2. Daniel B. Stevick, *Holy Baptism: Supplement to Prayer Book Studies 26* (New York: The Church Hymnal Corporation, 1973). This foundational document articulates basic principles behind revision of the initiatory rites in *The Book of Common Prayer,* 1979.
3. *Journal of the General Convention, 1985.* (The Episcopal Church Center, 1985.) DO54, p. 195.

process without considering the larger question of what it means to be a gathering of people who seek out and initiate, or baptize, new members into its life and community. For many Episcopal congregations, this question began to emerge, consciously or not, as they experienced the radical changes in the initiatory rites of the 1979 Prayer Book. Daniel Stevick sums up these changes:

> [Baptism] no longer stands first in the life-stage sequence of the pastoral offices (implying that infancy is the expected time for its administration), and it no longer stands complete in itself. It is now placed between the Easter Vigil and the Holy Communion. The organic heart of this Prayer Book and the sacramental system is in this Easter-Baptism-Eucharist center. The two great gospel sacraments are related to one another and to Jesus' death and resurrection. . . . The location of these rites in the Prayer Book emphasizes that all baptisms, no matter when in the year or at what stage of life they are observed, are declarations of and participations in Jesus' death and resurrection; and all are introductions into the eucharistic community.[4]

Now that baptisms are usually held as part of a Sunday service, they are more public. Baptism is associated with certain seasons and festivals of the church year such as Easter, All Saints, or Pentecost. The concept of all Christians being called to renew their baptismal vows—as held up in the 1979 Prayer Book—is integral to the rites. A congregation's role and the responsibilities of all the members are emphasized. Although a congregation's experience of baptism may have undergone a more obvious change, the admission of children to communion has similarly affected the role and meaning of confirmation in the congregation's life. All of this provides ground for examina-

---

4. Daniel B. Stevick, *Adult Baptism: Getting Back to the Beginning* (Cincinnati, OH: Forward Movement Publications, 1984), pp. 19–20.

tion and re-evaluation of initiatory theology, custom, and practice.

The experiences of congregations that start a catechumenal process show that it affects their members' understanding of infant baptism, confirmation, mature profession of faith, sponsorship, membership, education, ministry, and mission. Because a catechumenal process is not just another form of adult education or an elaborate means of leading an inquirer's class, a congregation must prepare its members for these changes and, indeed, might raise questions in these areas as part of introducing a catechumenal process. Various resources might be used for such an inquiry. Bishop Eastman, in *The Baptizing Community*, [5] provides accessible background material and useful models for how congregations might become more intentional about their calling to be baptizing communities. Gail C. Jones, a Christian education consultant in the diocese of Olympia, has written a manual for developing the initiatory process in congregations. She includes models for workshops to consider baptism's role in congregational life. [6]

Beyond considering commitment and initiation, a congregation must ask how becoming more intentional about baptism changes the way its members are called to exercise their ministries and how they should approach evangelism, education, and mission.

A sincere and deliberate attempt by any group to ask how it is called to be a baptizing community raises a variety of related issues. The largest of these issues is consideration of the church's relation to society:

> The processes of Christian initiation are always given their character by the relation that prevails between the Christian community and the society in which it is set.

5. Eastman, *The Baptizing Community*, Ch. 6.
6. Gail C. Jones, *Seeking Life in Christ: A Manual for Developing a Process for Christian Initiation, Including the Catechumenate, in Your Congregation* (Seattle, Resource Center, Diocese of Olympia, 1987), pp. 19–27.

When the society is hostile and it takes courage to identify oneself as a Christian, the church will set up a realistic period of training for converts whereby the church will be shaped as a convinced elite. Hence the formation of the catechumenate by the early church. When the church and the society are virtually the same folk, one becomes a member of the community of faith as one becomes a member of the community of language, culture, social responsibility, and civic competence. It is all gradual, it begins at birth, and much of the process is implicit.

Christian initiation in a highly secularized society will not be dominated by motifs of growth, but by motifs of decision. Becoming a Christian does not embed one in today's culture, but separates one from it. In baptism one joins a community of pilgrims and strangers. If such broad considerations of church and culture do not dictate what we should be doing just now in the administration of the rites of initiation, they at least suggest that we cannot go on doing what we have been doing.[7]

Initiation is a threshold. It is the place where a member is distinguished from a stranger, where hospitality is extended or denied, where an invitation is accepted or refused, and where membership is defined. When a congregation focuses on initiation, it must decide what being a community means: who belongs to it; what the boundaries are between "member" and "visitor," and whether those boundaries may change from case to case; what standards are required for membership; how those defined as "outsider" or "visitor" may be included. Other considerations involve how the congregation educates members and inquirers and how it evangelizes.

Examining how church and society are related leads to a second important issue, that of mission and evangelism. The integral connection between baptism and mission is found at the

---

7. Stevick, *Adult Baptism*, p. 16.

heart of the Gospel. The early church understood Jesus to be calling them to a baptismal mission: "Go therefore and make disciples of all nations, baptizing them in the name of the Father and of the Son and of the Holy Spirit, teaching them to observe all that I have commanded you" (Matthew 28: 19–20a). Further, they understood Jesus to promise that the Holy Spirit would provide power to "be witnesses . . . to the ends of the earth" (Acts 1:5–8). Thus, as Eastman asserts, a connection between initiation and mission is essential in any true baptizing community:

> . . . The church lags and wanders in its mission in direct proportion to the distance that baptism is allowed to stray from the center of ecclesial life. The Matthean formula for mission clearly places baptism at the heart of the matter, for the church is seen as the community that evangelizes and teaches. That vision, that sense of priority, needs to be recaptured today.[8]

Therefore, any serious consideration of how a congregation initiates new members will lead those who are already members to ask how they might serve as Christ's missionaries in the world.

Beyond how the church is related to society, and how its members do mission, a study of Christian initiation raises a third issue: what constitutes membership in a Christian community? The initiation rites themselves, as practiced by each congregation, express and symbolize a universal Christian understanding of salvation, membership, death, rebirth, and new life in Christ. But the rites also convey, within this universal symbolism, both that specific meaning agreed upon and expressed by Episcopalians as they worship according to the rites of the Prayer Book and the particular understandings of membership established by a certain congregation within that larger body.

Part of any serious study of initiation by a congregation en-

---

8. Eastman, *The Baptizing Community*, p. 4.

tails remaining faithful both to the tradition of the universal church and to the call of Jesus Christ in the Gospel. Thus a congregation or a diocese that prepares guidelines for Christian initiation and defines how it understands initiation must ground those guidelines within this larger context of Scripture and tradition.[9]

The final issue raised by a serious study of initiation is that of what constitutes adequate and appropriate Christian formation. William H. Willimon, in "Making Christians in a Secular World," argues for reforming our practice of Christian formation:

> We must be serious about the task of Christian formation. Our youth must come to see themselves in a sort of master-apprentice relationship with older Christians, in which the young look over the shoulders of those who are attempting to be Christian in today's world. Christian education should provide opportunities for developing believers to model their lives upon those of developed believers. It should also encourage all Christians to realize that we have the sacred responsibility to fashion our lives and thoughts upon distinctively Christian conviction.[10]

To be serious about Christian formation means asking ourselves how we educate our children, how we prepare young people for adult profession, how we prepare converts for membership, and how we encourage people in their continuing growth and formation as Christians. A catechumenal process is one model for Christian formation.

At both congregational and diocesan levels, a team or com-

9. See *The Baptizing Community*, pp. 111–123, for models of both congregational and diocesan guidelines. See also "A Parish Customary for Christian Initiation: The Guidelines for Christian Initiation at St. John's Church in Olympia, Washington"; *Water and Fire* (Fall 1985, pp. 1–2); and "Diocesan Guidelines for Christian Initiation and Confirmation," *Open* (June 1984), pp. 6–8.
10. William H. Willimon, "Making Christians in a Secular World," *The Christian Century* (22 October 1986), p. 916.

mission on Christian initiation, composed of laypeople and clergy, should articulate a clear vision of the church as a baptizing community that seeks to carry out Christ's call to evangelize, baptize, and teach. Members of this team should be concerned with liturgy, evangelism, service, social justice, and education. As the baptizing community prepares for this mission, the pattern of Christian formation provided by the catechumenal process is an invaluable tool, one that a bishop and diocese might make available to congregations.

3

The Bishop's Role in the Catechumenal Process

> . . . During the eight days of Easter the bishop stands and interprets all that takes place in Baptism. The newly baptized come and any of the faithful who wish to hear the Mysteries. The bishop relates what has been done, and interprets it, and, as he does so, the applause is so loud that it can be heard outside the church. Indeed the way he expounds the mysteries and interprets them cannot fail to move his hearers.
>
> EGERIA[1]

Egeria, a fourth century Spanish woman on pilgrimage to the Holy Land, wrote this description of a bishop's role in the baptism of new Christians, showing how a bishop of the early church served as chief pastor and teacher. The bishop taught those preparing to be baptized, presided at the Great Vigil of Easter, and taught about the sacraments after Easter. In this simple act of teaching the catechumens, a bishop served as one called to proclaim and interpret the Gospel, to enlighten the minds of the people, and to guard the faith, unity, and discipline of the church.[2] In recovering the catechumenal practices of the early church, we need also to reclaim and adapt the central role of the bishop as teacher, pastor, and leader in the church.

In the instructions concerning the Catechumenate, *The Book*

---

1. *Egeria's Travels to the Holy Land,* trans. John Wilkinson (Jerusalem: Ariel Publishing House, 1981), 47:1–2.
2. *The Book of Common Prayer* (New York: The Church Hymnal Corporation, 1979), "Ordination of a Bishop," p. 518.

of Occasional Services (BOS) clearly states the central or key role played by the bishop in the catechumenal process.

> The systematic instruction and formation of its catechumens is a solemn responsibility of the Christian community. Traditionally, the preparation of catechumens is a responsibility of the bishop, which is shared with the presbyters, deacons, and appointed lay catechists of the diocese.[3]

The Book of Occasional Services also suggests that a bishop might preside at the rites of Admission and Enrollment, as well as at a service in which candidates are confirmed or received or reaffirm their vows.

Because the bishop is the diocese's primary evangelist, a catechumenal process depends on the bishop's leadership. The bishop leads this process both actually and symbolically. In the Milwaukee Pilot Project, the process was related to the bishop's goals for the diocese: building Christian commitment, practicing good stewardship, and developing service and advocacy in the community. The process works best when the bishop makes it part of the diocesan goals. Next, the bishop selects a diocesan support team and invites pilot congregations to participate. The bishop also arranges for, and participates in, training offered by the diocese to orient congregational teams to the process.

The bishop should be visible and vocal in support of the process throughout the diocese. Making this a diocesan program, supported by a team of trained laypeople and clergy, provides greater continuity and support for participating congregations. This support is first experienced by congregations through the bishop's participation in training. The bishop's ongoing role in congregational visits and in diocesan celebrations further expresses that support to people involved in the process

---

3. *BOS*, p. 112 or Appendix D, Sec. 1.

in local congregations and to people planning to implement the process. Finally, the bishop oversees and ensures the highest possible quality of work.

Beyond the organizational task of overseeing the implementation of the process, the bishop also has a symbolic role as teacher or catechist to the diocese. This role is most valuable when the bishop presides at Easter Week liturgies. The bishop's calendar must be cleared during this time for the Laying on of Hands for those who have been baptized or are reaffirming their faith. The bishop might meet with these people for regional services throughout the diocese. Gatherings like these also give the bishop an opportunity to "catechize" those who have come for reaffirmation. There should be time, beyond the liturgy itself, for the bishop to join in teaching the candidates. The bishop might also re-examine the format of parish visits with participating congregations. With confirmation at regional services during Easter season, these visits by the bishop should include time to meet the candidates and to share in or teach one of their sessions.

4

Diocesan Leadership for the Catechumenal Process

How to Begin

Establishing a catechumenal process in a diocese begins with the bishop. The bishop gathers a support group of several people to meet and consider the process and to support a decision to undertake it. These persons should be advisors who are familiar with the diocese and its congregations. The bishop might include concerned members of the diocesan staff and those in the diocese who are familiar with the catechumenal process and interested in a diocesan project. Some bishops have included spiritual formation, liturgical, social service and justice ministry people in the support group. The Evangelism Ministries Office at The Episcopal Church Center offers diocesan bishops print resources and consultants. A consultant's initial presentation to the bishop and support group usually takes at least a day.

The support group's first task is to help the bishop decide whether to implement a pilot project in the diocese. Once this decision is made, the bishop and support group pick a convener and recruit a team to lead the project; the size and makeup of the diocesan team depends on the diocese's size and the needs and number of congregations expected to participate. A leadership team should include people who are willing both to participate in training as learners and to serve as trainers and consultants to congregational teams. Other members might assist with publicity, scheduling, or other organizational details of the project. Members should represent a cross-section of the diocese, and have the interest, time, and skills necessary to implement it. Again, some bishops have included spirituality, liturgy, service and justice people in their leadership team.

Once a diocese decides to implement a project, the bishop and members of the leadership team can arrange, through the Coordinator of Evangelism Ministries at the Church Center, to attend a training conference. An ecumenical project to offer five-day training events for teams from dioceses and congregations is being sponsored by the Joint Committee on Christian Initiation of the Episcopal Church and the Congregational Life Division of the Evangelical Lutheran Church in America. The first training will be offered in the spring of 1991. In addition, training is available through the North American Forum on the Catechumenate, a volunteer Roman Catholic agency supporting development of the catechumenal process in that communion. Although designed for Roman Catholic congregations implementing the *Rite of Christian Initiation of Adults* in their churches, this conference, the Beginnings and Beyond Institute, provides an invaluable orientation to the history and current practice of the catechumenal process in congregational settings.

Dioceses considering a pilot project in the catechumenal process will also find conferences and newsletters that are useful as resources. For instance, in February 1988, Grace Cathedral in San Francisco, the Lay Academy of California, the Church Divinity School of the Pacific, the Association of Diocesan Music and Liturgy Commissions, and Associated Parishes sponsored a four-day gathering of Episcopal leaders, workers, and interested people at Grace Cathedral. The subject of this gathering was "The Baptismal Mystery and the Catechumenate." A newsletter, *Water and Fire,* edited by the Reverend Charles Kiblinger, St. James' Church, 3921 Oak Ridge Drive, Jackson, MS 39216, has been circulated occasionally. In the Church of England, the

Reverend Canon Peter Ball edits a newsletter distributed by Catechumenate Network, 1 Amen Court, London, BC4M 7BU, England, for $12-13. [See Chapter XV for further discussion of recruitment, orientation and training for the diocesan team.]

The Role of a Diocesan Leadership Team and Some Basic Decisions

A leadership team's primary function is to provide initial and ongoing training for congregational teams and to be available to them for consultation. Skills in communication and training are essential for team members. After completing national training, a team schedules a suitable orientation and training event. The Evangelism Ministries Office can recommend trainers for these events. Events of this kind help in team building, give an overview of catechumenal stages, introduce liturgical rites developed for Episcopal congregations, and prepare teams to use and train others in various models of experiential learning.

During this kind of training session, the team makes some basic decisions. It decides whether to suggest that unbaptized and baptized participants be separated or included in the same group. The team chooses the basic format and the names of the stages of the process it will recommend to the congregations— names that might express the individual style or flavor of the diocese. The team will also decide on the scheduling of reaffirmation rites with the bishop.

Diocesan teams offer similar orientation to congregational groups involved in planning local catechumenal processes. Diocesan teams also assist in ongoing training and provide ways for congregations to reflect on their experiences with the process, and to plan for the future.

A team convener coordinates arrangements for team meetings, sets up consultation and team training (with the help of the

Evangelism Ministries Office, if needed), and oversees prepara-
tions for diocesan training events. A convener also maintains the
budget and provides necessary reports to the diocese. This person consults with the bishop and the diocesan staff to coordinate
events with the diocesan schedule and arranges for the bishop's
participation. The convener also has a key role in explaining
the process to the congregation—both active and potential
members.

The Role of a Diocesan Catechist or Staff Person

The role of a diocesan staff person, or volunteer diocesan
catechist in small dioceses, is to expedite the work of a bishop's
appointed leadership team. This role includes being general
liaison for the leadership team and participating congregations;
assisting in arranging and publicizing meetings, training sessions, and retreats; coordinating the entire process with the
bishop's schedule; and serving as a center of communications
for the process. This volunteer or staff person might also maintain a supply of print resources for congregations and plan to
visit participating congregations to affirm their work and to con-
nect their experiences with those of others. These activities
would require a commitment of one day a week for a process
involving twelve congregations.

Recruiting Participating Congregations

When a leadership team has been organized and has completed training, it consults with the bishop, who designates congregational leaders to be invited to participate in the diocese's
project and to attend the team's first training session. Ideally, a
pilot project would include five to eight healthy congregations,
representing a variety of locations, sizes, leadership styles, and

memberships. Invitations to participate in the pilot are extended to congregational leaders.

One diocese has developed a three-hour presentation for team members to use in congregations considering the diocesan project. The presentation begins with an overview of the cate-chumenal process followed by some story-sharing. After a cele-bration of the Eucharist, the group has Bible study, using one of the models of Scripture study for "breaking open the Word." For mission congregations in this diocese, in order to encourage participation in the diocesan catechumenal process, the presen-tation follows the bishop's visit.

A diocesan team completing its orientation and training in the spring might be ready to recruit congregations during the fall and to offer training after the first of the year. With adequate consultation and assistance, these congregations might recruit participants to begin the process the next fall.

Ongoing Support for Participating Congregations

As the work begins, the diocesan team will begin to sense the need for ongoing support. Congregations in their second year need to reflect on their experience and receive further orienta-tion and training. Congregations in their third year need an annual gathering for fresh insight and vision, and continuing training. [See Appendix B, Sections 7 and 8, for results of a sample reflection session and a proposal for ongoing support.]

5

Congregational Leadership for the Catechumenal Process

How to Begin

Congregations participating in a diocesan pilot project are chosen by the bishop and diocesan team to represent as many facets or aspects of diocesan life as possible. When pilot congregations have completed their first year, new congregations may be added, either at their request or at the bishop's invitation.

An initial invitation is extended to a congregation through its rector or vicar, or, in the case of a vacancy, through its designated leader—a senior warden, for instance. In clustered or yoked congregations, the cluster leader extends the invitation to some or all member churches.

As the bishop does at the diocesan level, the congregational leader's first task in initiating consideration of the catechumenal process is to create an advisory group to help the congregation weigh its options. This advisory group should have two, three, four, or more members depending on the congregation's size. It does not include all those leaders who would eventually share in implementing the process. The group should include leaders who understand the congregation's history, current situation and potential, and who can serve as perceptive and discriminating advisors to a congregational leader, either a priest or layperson. When congregations consider participating in a diocesan project, they need information about the catechumenal process to help them make their decision. To provide this assistance, a bishop and diocesan leadership team might gather the advisory groups of several congregations [1] to describe the catechumenal process; [2] to discuss its function for the diocese, especially its relation to diocesan goals and planning; and [3] to provide resources for leaders to introduce the process to their advisory groups. Members of a diocesan team also visit congregations to discuss the process with advisory groups or other leaders in presentations such as those outlined in Chapter 3.

The Role of a Congregation's Advisory Group

With information about the catechumenal process from the diocese, a leader and advisory group can discuss the process in light of the congregation's goals and priorities. Questions to consider are:

1. What form of adult catechesis is offered now to people entering the congregation or seeking to make adult reaffirmation of their baptismal vows?

2. What are the evangelism goals of this congregation? How might the catechumenal process express them?

3. What are this congregation's goals for developing lay ministry? How might the catechumenal process help?

4. How are we helping people to recognize, reflect on, and live out their ministries, not just their ministries in church, but especially their ministries in their daily places?

5. How would the catechumenal process enrich our lives as they are now? What changes and accommodations might be needed?

6. Has the congregation adequate resources, including people, to undertake such a process effectively?

When a congregational leader and advisory group have agreed to implement the process, they should report to the vestry or other governing body. A clear presentation about the catechumenal process and its value to the congregation's plans and goals will help the leaders in seeing that it is carried out.

Forming a Congregation's Leadership Team

The final task for a congregational leader's advisory group is to choose a convener for the process and recruit any additional members to form a leadership team for the catechumenal process. As with a diocesan team, the size of this team depends on the congregation's size and needs. The personnel chart in Appendix B, Section 6, suggests how the team size might vary with the congregation's size alone. As a team gathers information for planning, it may need to re-evaluate team size and recruit others, either as team members or for specified tasks in the process.

The leadership team is important. Great care should be taken with issues of team formation and group support. Members being recruited should be given clear information about the extent of their commitment. In most congregations, team members should expect at least six months for evaluation and planning, and at least one year with the first group of people entering the process. Members should also anticipate how often the leaders and participants will meet as a group—probably weekly—and how often the leaders alone will meet for team building and planning. Also, attendance at training events offered by the diocese should be required of all team members because this training helps in team formation and provides information and skill.

When organizing a team, recruiters should recognize that certain abilities are valuable for all members:

1. Ability to understand and respond to people with diverse approaches to Christian faith and living: for example, those who are trusting and desire clear direction; or those who question and prefer self-direction; or those whose primary interest is in spirituality; or those whose interest is in action.

2. Ability to understand and value learning by experience.

3. Ability to understand the demands and value of teamwork, such as team building by story-sharing; time requirements for group decision-making; candor in group reflection on activities and team interaction. People new to teamwork usually underestimate the time required for actual work together.

A congregation's leadership or catechumenal team plans, provides much of the initial leadership, and is a resource for explaining and supporting the process in a congregation. The leadership team need not include all the people involved in the catechumenal process. In a family–size congregation, all leaders will probably serve on the leadership team. In larger congregations, the leadership team would be limited to about seven people, including convener, evangelist, catechist, liturgist, sponsor coordinator, hospitality coordinator, and a clergy person. Others are also needed for specific tasks: providing rides or child care, or planning and assisting in the liturgies.

The congregation's leadership team provides or arranges for certain functions. Some roles, such as convener or liturgist, are specific leadership tasks for team members. Other roles, such as sponsor or table leader, may be filled by persons recruited for that task alone. Although more than one person may be involved in each of these roles, and some responsibilities may overlap, provision must be made for all of the following functions:

Convener: This layperson takes primary responsibility for gathering and leading the team. He or she is liaison between the diocese and the local team, passing on information from the diocese to team members, including training arrangements. The convener, working with the clergy, communicates with the congregation as a whole and with the vestry or bishop's committee in particular about the catechumenal process. The convener, depending on team size and number of participants, might also assist in leading sessions. The convener has a primary role in the liturgies, presenting candidates to the congregation at rites marking the stages of the catechumenal process.

Evangelizer: The heart of evangelism lies in recognizing and responding to those seeking faith in Jesus Christ and commitment to God's presence in human life. Although this responsibility belongs to all members of the team, and ultimately to the whole congregation, the evangelizer takes the responsibility for training both the team and the members of the congregation for this work. This responsibility begins with training those who help gather people for the Inquiry stage. The evangelizer leads in planning and conducting any sessions offered before the Inquiry, or Pre-catechumenal, stage to help potential inquirers consider the catechumenal process. Evangelizers are trained in story-sharing and group process, and are willing to talk about their personal faith journeys and witness to the place of Christ and the community in their lives.

Gatherers: A gatherer is simply one person who contacts another and invites that person to join the Inquiry stage. Although gatherers may initially be team members, any member of a congregation could serve as a gatherer. Gatherers should be able to describe the process to prospective participants so that they can decide whether or not to join in Inquiry stage sessions. Gatherers may choose to share the Inquiry stage with those they invite.

Catechist: This person (or group of persons in a larger congregation) takes primary responsibility for designing and leading the catechumenal sessions. The catechist receives training in the various models for Bible study, story-sharing, and session planning, and makes these resources available to other members.

Liturgist: The liturgist is responsible for the rites marking the stages of the catechumenal process and for any special prayers or services associated with the group sessions. The liturgist, with the clergy, arranges celebrations of the catechumenal rites. He or she is familiar with all of the rites for both unbaptized and baptized participants. In addition to helping plan these services, the liturgist is liaison to other groups involved in the congregation's worship, including lay leaders, altar guild members, ushers and greeters, and those responsible for coffee hour hospitality.

Coordinator of Sponsors: This team member is responsible for recruiting and training sponsors of catechumens and candidates, and for assisting them in their ministry.

Sponsors: Each person entering the catechumenal process is sponsored through all four stages by a member of the congregation. A sponsor is a guide, friend, and fellow pilgrim to one person in the process. Beginning with the Rites of Admission or Welcome, a sponsor offers support to a candidate by [1] sharing all activities with the candidate; [2] sharing in liturgies with the candidate; [3] meeting occasionally with the candidate to reflect on the experience; and [4] sharing with the team a sense of the candidate's experience in the process, particularly when it is time to decide about moving to the next stage. Sponsors present their candidates to the congregation at the public rites. Sponsors are active members of the congregation who are willing to be trained for their role and to attend sessions with their candidates. Some congregations have chosen to call these people "companions."

Small Group/Table Leaders: Throughout the catechumenal process, participants join in various small group activities for discussion and Bible study. Leaders help these small groups to work effectively by making procedures clear and holding the group to standards, such as ensuring that all members have a chance to participate. These leaders share in planning and evaluating activities, and in discerning the experience of participants.

Hospitality: These people welcome participants, talk with them, and supply refreshments for the sessions, beginning with the Inquiry stage. They might also plan receptions or parties for those services in which the rites of the process are celebrated.

Clergy: The main role for clergy in the catechumenal process is acting as spiritual director to all of the participants. Clergy usually train the congregational leadership team rather than leading group sessions themselves. The clergy use the various learning models to help lay catechists plan group sessions. The clergy also help catechists in providing participants with settings for service and social justice ministries. A priest presides at those rites at which the bishop cannot be present. The clergy preach, teach, and prepare the congregation to serve as an evangelizing and baptizing community. The clergy remind the community of the miracle of God's presence in the midst of all those taking part in the catechumenal process.

When the congregation's leadership team members have been named, their roles can be recognized before the congregation by commissioning them for their ministries. *The Book of Occasional Services* has a form for the Commissioning for Lay Ministries in the Church[1] with options for such ministries as catechists or teachers, evangelists, parish visitors, officers of church organizations, or other lay ministries. Commissioning members for their various roles recognizes them for their commitment and provides an opportunity for the team to share information about the catechumenal process with the congregation. Most important, commissioning increases the prayer support for the team and the team's sense of the Spirit's work among them. As other persons are recruited for their roles—

---

1. BOS, p. 175.

sponsors or table leaders, for instance—they, too, may be commissioned.

The next chapter outlines a four-phase planning procedure for a team developing a catechumenal process for its congregation: [1] information gathering; [2] group formation and purpose setting; [3] plan development; and [4] evaluation and re-planning.

Team Training

Training is essential for the work of a congregation's team. Teams from congregations joining a pilot or an existing diocesan project should be required to attend training events sponsored by their diocese. As it does for a diocesan team, this training assists with team building, gives an overview of catechumenal stages, introduces liturgical rites, and teaches useful learning designs such as models for Bible study. It also helps people new to group work to learn about the time and dynamics needed for teams to work together. In the four-phase planning procedure outlined in the following chapter, a congregation should complete the first information-gathering phase before diocesan training. Training is likewise essential to the second phase of group formation and purpose setting, and to the third phase of developing the plan. Such training will include the following:

- Story-telling and other team-building methods
- Evaluation of the last session and planning for the next one
- Standards and procedures for effective group work
- Identification of work-styles using the Myers-Briggs Typology Inventory, or a similar procedure
- Group leadership
- Group decision making
- Working with conflict
- Giving and receiving feedback

Diocesan teams can acquire the skills to plan and lead this training through opportunities available around the country under both church and secular sponsorship. To help congregations in their work, diocesan teams must offer events at times and locations that are convenient for the congregations. In addition, a congregation's team might invite a member of their diocesan team to consult with them on either team formation or planning.

6

Planning the Catechumenal Process

Initially, the catechumenal process may seem to be rigidly structured in shape and content. In fact, the process does have set stages, particular liturgies, and a specified purpose and outcome. But its design can be easily adapted to a particular congregation's needs. Its stages suggest a model for Christian growth and transition. People are drawn to a community in which they may explore their questions about Christian faith and life. This inquiry leads to a desire for a deeper formation that includes scriptural study, corporate worship, the life of prayer, and service and justice ministry.

Deeper formation is followed by intense preparation for commitment, and experience of the sacraments leads people to further reflection on Christian faith and life. Therefore, a catechumenal process is *not* a curriculum, although planning its process of formation might include identifying curricula of experiences and of knowledge. A catechumenal process is *not* an educational program. It is a journey through which people move into deeper relationships with Christ, and find power for their ministries. It is a process of growing theologically, of growing in response to life with God.

Planning is a critical task for a leadership team. A catechumenal process designed for a congregation's needs, suited to its

demographics, and structured for its members requires perceptive analysis and careful planning. [See samples of materials
resulting from careful planning in corporation-size St. Paul's
Church, Indianapolis. In Appendix C, Section 13.] The first
planning step is gathering information about the congregation,
its current and prospective members, its history, and its future
goals.

Phase One: Information Gathering

1. *Study the demographics of the congregation and its context.* The first
   task is gathering accurate information about the size and
   membership of the congregation. Information of this sort
   helps the team anticipate how a catechumenal process might
   be received, who might share in its work, and who might
   participate. Counting entries in a church directory may not be
   enough. The team must determine how many people in the
   congregation are working actively toward congregational life;
   how many simply take what is offered them; and how many
   are loosely connected with the life of the congregation and
   become more seriously involved only in time of crisis and/or
   for special occasions. After these groups and their relative
   sizes have been estimated, the team should define who the
   people are in each category, where they live, where they work,
   what their ages are, how long they have belonged to the
   church, how they relate to one another, how they organize
   themselves, and what needs they have.

   Next, there should be a realistic assessment made of the
   broader community in which the congregation lives. Who are
   the people who are not church members? What are the demographic characteristics and cultural groups represented in the
   broader community? How do church members meet or relate
   to other people in the community? Can the team pinpoint
   outside groups that might produce new members? The team
   should then try to define these potential members using the

same questions of where they live, where they work, what their ages are, how long they have lived in the community, how they relate to one another, how they organize themselves, and what needs they have. If the congregation is in a community that is in transition, the team should consider how current members may differ from potential members.

2. *Analyze the congregation.* The Evangelism Ministries Office suggests three resources for further analyzing a congregation's demographics: *Handbook for Evangelism, Sizing Up a Congregation for New Member Ministry,* and *Reshaping a Congregation for a New Future.*

An important part of the catechumenal process is including new members. *Handbook for Evangelism* outlines activities that lead to the newcomers' integration into the life of the congregation from their first visit on. *Sizing up a Congregation* gives useful models for determining the effect church size has on congregational dynamics, and how the size of the congregation affects the dynamics of absorbing new people. Because congregations are not static bodies, *Reshaping a Congregation* examines a congregation's transitions—such as change in size, movement through their life cycle, or change in the broader community.

A thoughtful analysis of a congregation in these terms helps in planning a catechumenal process. Those people who will be formed by this process are being equipped for membership and ministry. As they become members of the Body of Christ, they also join a specific church community to which they look for strength and guidance for their ministries in the broader community and in the world. A team must learn about the new people coming into the church, the church community that they join, and what that church community actually does to bring them into its life.

3. *Survey congregation members about how they understand ministry and the formation of adults for ministry.* To discover how members of a congregation understand their ministries and view their own formation, a team might ask all members to fill out ques-

tionnaires or use another appropriate survey process. The team might begin this survey by inviting people to consider the congregation's ministry and their individual roles as ministers. The survey would ask them to describe how they were prepared for this ministry when they made an adult faith commitment—either at confirmation or when they were received into the church as adults. The survey would ask members if this preparation were adequate or, if not, to describe what was lacking and might be added to it. The survey might raise these issues:

- What should the church's ministry be?
- What part do you take as your responsibility?
- Would you take more responsibility?
- Describe how you were prepared for making an adult commitment to Christ, either when confirmed, or when received into the church.
- Did this prepare you for your ministry?
- How could this preparation have been more effective?

4. *Identify potential leaders and support people.* A catechumenal process requires leaders in various roles. In addition to those leaders who teach and lead small groups, a sponsor is needed for each candidate in the process. People providing support or leadership in other settings—from prayer groups to child care, from office workers to worship leaders—are also needed. A team's assessment of congregational leadership should look beneath the surface and identify people with leadership potential beyond the congregation's already identified leaders. The team should consider how the leadership capacity of these other members of the congregation might be nurtured by being included in the catechumenal process.

5. *Plan organizational details and support structures.* A team must see to various organizational details for the catechumenal process to run smoothly. These details include:

- Budget—determine expenses and sources of funds
- Space requirements
- Schedule—consider other congregational activities
- Notification of other church components or organizations—worship or education committees, adult social or study groups, the hospitality committee
- Publicity—make the process known to people in the congregation and in the broader community who might want to participate
- Communication—keep the whole congregation informed about and included in the catechumenal process
- Resources—determine what print materials must be purchased or duplicated for both the team and the participants

6. *Complete readiness for training.* As noted, much of the information gathering phase should be completed before a team goes to a diocesan training event. With the congregation analyzed and surveyed, leaders identified, and some organizational details planned, a team is ready for more intensive formation and preparation for their catechumenal work.

Phase Two: Group Formation and Purpose Setting

At diocesan training sessions, leadership teams from the congregations are helped in learning to work together effectively through the use of basic training techniques such as story-sharing. Teams also learn to apply those techniques to the catechumenal process they plan for their congregations.

Diocesan training also asks each team to state a purpose to guide the process they plan for their own congregation. A stated purpose of a catechumenal process might be:

To enable participants to respond to the Gospel with both mind and emotion, and to help them to live as Christians in their daily places (at work, at home, in the community, as citizens of a nation, at leisure, and at church).

Each congregation's leadership team must carefully consider its purpose and state it in its own way. If a catechumenal process is to help people live in the world as Christians, a leadership team must know where participants actually live and work, the nature of the communities in which they live, and how they spend their free time. This is where the demographic information gathered in advance by congregations takes on deeper importance. The needs of current members of a congregation, as well as those people who may choose to become members, shape a congregation's catechumenal process and affect how a leadership team defines its purpose.

Phase Three: Plan Development

The final task diocesan training must accomplish is to provide information and suggest models for planning the stages that mark the catechumenal process and for planning the rites and designing the formation appropriate for each stage of the catechumenal process. With these models and a clear statement of purpose, a congregational leadership team is ready to develop its own plan.

Elements of such a plan would include:

1. An outline of the stages of a congregation's process, including a purpose statement for each stage, pertinent dates, and useful resources (see Appendix C, Sections 10 and 11 for initial outlines from a small and a large congregation).
2. Plans for the rites marking the stages of the process, taking into account that rites would differ for catechumens and for baptized persons reaffirming their baptismal vows.
3. Clear statements of what goals and objectives should be met in each stage of the process, including elements of both experience and knowledge; what constitutes completion of each stage; and ways to determine what has been accomplished in each stage, and at what depth.

4. Plans for getting the whole congregation involved in evangelization and in recruiting participants in the catechumenal process.
5. A statement about the role of, and the minimum participation required by, a sponsor, and a plan for recruiting and training sponsors.
6. A description of leadership roles, including minimum training requirements for identified leaders, and plans for recruiting additional leaders to support each stage of the process.
7. Resources needed for the process—whether print, human, physical, or monetary—and plans for obtaining them.
8. Plans for telling the congregation about the catechumenal process, both its leaders and its members, including a schedule of all meetings and where they will take place, and when all rites will be observed.
9. Plans for gathering feedback from participants and leaders for evaluation of the process.

Although a leadership team should be attentive to the needs of the participants and prepared to adapt its plan to those needs, a clearly defined plan allows necessary changes to be made without sacrificing the integrity of the process. Such a plan also provides clear standards to people entering the process by explaining its purpose, the place of each stage in achieving that purpose, and the minimum expected of leaders, participants, and sponsors.

Phase Four: Evaluation and Replanning

A clearly defined or stated plan has a further advantage: it provides standards and measures by which the process can be evaluated. When a team defines a purpose for its congregation's process and purposes for each stage of that process, it also establishes the basis for its evaluation. A team must evaluate both the success of its plan in achieving its stated purpose, and the adequacy of the purpose statement itself. A team must ask what worked and what did not; what should be repeated; and what should be changed. It would also be wise to evaluate the quality of the leadership. Information should be obtained from both participants and leaders. A team should also determine the impact of the catechumenal process on other members of the congregation, on its leaders, and on other congregational activities and goals. With clear evaluation information, a team can continually adapt the process it offers. (See Appendix C, Section 12, Designing and Evaluating Short– and Long–Range Plans, for further help.)

Although a full catechumenal process cannot be confined to the framework of an academic program year, some of the participants will complete the process during each Easter season. Because evaluation and planning should be scheduled regularly, the beginning of Pentecost is an appropriate season for an annual evaluation. This is also an appropriate time for a congregation's leadership team to include new members and for diocesan consultants to offer in-service training. A diocesan team might hold an annual retreat to encourage this evaluation and provide a forum in which participating congregations might trade their experiences with the catechumenal process.

Schedule: Process not Program

One important warning must be sounded here: the catechumenal process is just that, a *process:* a process is *not* a program. As a process of growth, conversion, and awakening to new life, it will burst out of the constraints of any carefully programmed calendar. In literature about the process, experienced pastors and catechists repeatedly warn that conversion takes place in God's time, not ours—on sacred time and in sacred space. [See especially the literature of the North American Forum on the Catechumenate, 5510 Columbia Pike, Suite 310,

Arlington, VA 22204, 1-703-671-0330. Also, James B. Dunning, *New Wine: New Wineskins: Pastoral Implications of the Rite of Christian Initiation of Adults* (New York: Sadlier Press, 1981); Raymond B. Kemp, *A Journey in Faith: An Experience of the Catechumenate* (New York: Sadlier Press, 1979).]

This idea of unpredictability may seem to contradict the emphasis on planning and goal setting described here. But actually the element of the unknown in this process makes clarity of purpose at each stage even more important. These stated goals form the yardstick by which both participants and leaders are able to measure their growth in the process.

The church year itself provides a rhythm and shape to the life of the whole congregation, a pattern that is also vital to the experience of people involved in the catechumenal process. Each year, Lent provides a special and appropriate setting for adults who are prepared for and willing to undertake the intense preparation of the catechumenal process for Easter baptism or renewal of baptismal vows. Each Easter season calls for those people who have been so cleansed, fed, and renewed, to reflect again on the experience of dying and rising to new life in Christ Jesus. But the catechesis and formation that leads to the witness, initiation, and reflection of Easter cannot be determined by simply counting out "enough" meeting dates on a calendar. That formation is shaped by the people involved, by their needs, by their stories and histories, and by the continued and ever-present converting action of God in their lives.

Although a specific schedule seems to be suggested by the pilot project the diocese of Milwaukee described in this resource, the project has worked itself out with much more flexibility. During the first year, congregations did tend to follow a schedule. Participants began the Inquiry stage in September and were initiated the following Easter. But within those parameters, each congregation actually adapted the calendar to suit its needs. Congregations in their second year are already experimenting with greater freedom from the calendar. Although this one-year schedule was valuable for this pilot project, other calendars might also be considered.

The Inquiry stage might begin during Eastertide so that inquirers might hear firsthand the experience of those members of the congregation who were baptized or renewed their baptismal vows at Easter. This Inquiry stage might continue with some informal sessions during the summer, and with a more regular meeting schedule in the fall. In Advent, inquirers would be asked to decide if they were ready to commit themselves further and be enrolled as catechumens, or be welcomed to the community as baptized members. This formation stage might last for a year, from January to January. After spending a year with the lectionary, people would be invited during Epiphany to decide if they were ready for the intense preparation that leads to baptism or the renewal of baptismal vows. Those ready to witness to their growth in faith and living would proclaim this growth to the congregation in a rite held at the beginning of Lent. Baptized persons would commit themselves to special disciplines on Ash Wednesday, and the unbaptized would enroll for baptism on the First Sunday of Lent. After Easter, they would join the congregation in witness and evangelization with the next group of participants in the catechumenal process.

An even more flexible schedule, one that would work best in a large congregation, would have ongoing groups involved in both pre-catechumenal inquiry and catechumenal formation, with the rites for entering the second stage, Admission of Catechumens or Welcoming of Baptized Christians to a Community, taking place several times during the year. Each Lent, those persons who, regardless of the length of their involvement in the process, were seen as being ready for intensive preparation for baptism or for renewal of baptismal vows, would come forward. Following the rites, these people would reflect on where they were and would begin to move toward some ongoing support group for their faith and ministry. Here, conversion expressed in transformed living and deeper spirituality in the individual's journey are the true criteria for movement through the process.

Any schedule is appropriate if it unites the community's journey with the individual's journey and enriches it, and if the individual's journey, shaped by God's converting and transforming action, renews the life of the community.

7

The Story of a Diocesan Pilot Project

The Evangelism Ministries Office has been working closely with the diocese of Milwaukee on a pilot project to implement the catechumenal process. This experience is the background for many of the recommendations in this resource. To further clarify the process recommended for dioceses and for congregations, a summary of this experience may be helpful.

The Milwaukee Pilot Project, later named "Living Our Baptismal Covenant," began in spring 1985 when Bishop Roger White offered his diocese as the site of a pilot. In June 1985, a planning team including the Reverend Louis Weil, STD, professor of Music and Liturgy at Nashotah House, and representatives of the Evangelism Ministries Office met to design the basic format, information collection procedures, and training required. The Evangelism Ministries members included two people from the Ministry Development Network who had responded to the call for collaboration. The planning team reviewed its work with Bishop White and reached agreement for the next steps.

Bishop White invited eight congregations to participate in the pilot project. Six agreed. Five went the full cycle; and the sixth began with the next group of churches during the second year. Throughout the planning and training phases of the pilot project, Bishop White prepared the Milwaukee congregations for the process by what he taught and preached in the diocese and in how he organized and described the program and planned the diocesan budget. He preached about the baptismal covenant at every opportunity, and the covenant provided the theological guidelines for the diocesan budget.

The Evangelism Ministries team supervising the pilot project met in October 1985 with clergy from interested congregations to introduce them to the pilot project. In December, the team met with clergy and lay leaders for a training session.

Between those two meetings, the Milwaukee clergy and selected lay leaders participated in a phone survey of clergy and lay leaders of the catechumenal process in eighteen Episcopal congregations across the country. Each congregational leader considering the pilot project talked with people from three congregations who had experience with the process. The interviewees discussed its impact on the participants and on their congregations, the strengths and weaknesses of their particular approach, and any observations that would help others in planning. The enthusiasm of these interviewees and the things they had learned from their experience guided the Milwaukee congregations in considering such issues as the role of sponsors, the importance of lay participation, the tendency to rework the old confirmation class, and the need to emphasize ministry formation, mission, and service in planning their processes.

When five congregations had committed themselves to the pilot project, a working calendar was drawn up. All the churches agreed to follow the same general schedule in order to foster mutual support in participating congregations. Between January and June 1986, they explained the process to their members, recruited and trained leaders, selected resources, and developed plans for each stage of the process. September was designated for the evangelization aspect of the pre-catechumenate, which they named "Gathering." The pre-catechumenate stage, or Inquiry, culminated during the fall, with the rite of Admission of Catechumens and the recognition of the baptized participants. The longer formation stage, "Formation in Christ," began during either Advent or Epiphany and was completed before Ash Wednesday. "Intensive Preparation" took place during Lent. Catechumens were baptized in their own congregations at the Easter Vigil. Bishop White presided at regional services for the Laying on of Hands during Easter Week for those baptized at the Vigil and those seeking confirmation, reception, or reaffirmation. The sacramental catechesis stage of the process, "Formation in Ministry," was held during the Great Fifty Days of Easter.

Training sessions preceded each stage of the process, allowing the congregations to come together to reflect on the stage just completed, to prepare for the next stage, and to improve their skills in working together. (The liturgies for baptized persons being produced by the Standing Liturgical Commission were not yet available for their use.)

At the December 1985 planning meeting, the five congregations agreed on a basic purpose statement for the pilot project and on statements to guide each stage of the process. With this document in hand, each congregation then designed its own variation on the process. The general purpose statement for "Living Our Baptismal Covenant" and the plans developed by the five congregations are included in Appendix B. A sample plan[1] was also prepared and distributed to assist congregations in developing their own individual plans. Although the congregations used the basic shape and outline of the process, each developed a plan appropriate to its own needs and unique character. The ways in which congregations made the process their own is evident in the variety of plans; the common shape and purpose of the catechumenal process is evident in the similarity of their plans. Also included in Appendix B, Section 4 and Section 5, are the calendars for the first two groups of congregations.

The five congregations in the Milwaukee Pilot Project are

---

1. "Resources for Planning": available through Evangelism Ministries Office, The Episcopal Church Center.

essentially different, one from the other. Three congregations are in diverse Milwaukee suburbs; one Madison congregation is suburban; the other is in an area adjacent to the large University of Wisconsin. The congregations represent relatively affluent professionals, young suburban middle-class families, blue-collar families, and university professors and students.

Just as the congregations vary, so did the character of their catechumenal processes. The two congregations in Madison joined for some of the Inquiry stage meetings. In one congregation, lay catechists led all meetings. In others, clergy were more involved in both planning and leading sessions. Some emphasized the rites and the liturgical aspects of the process. Some emphasized experiential learning and models of biblical reflection. Others followed a more academic style of presentation. Some included sponsors in their group at the beginning of the process. In other groups, sponsors joined later. Despite the variations, each congregation spoke with enthusiasm about the success of the catechumenal process for both participants and leaders, and about its powerful effect on all members of the congregation.

The plans developed in these five congregations for their first year were revised substantively for their second year. Thus, these plans are simply examples of how the catechumenal process came to life in five congregations of one diocese, congregations that are continuing to grow and to adapt the process to their needs.

8

Elements of the Catechumenal Process

> The catechumenate is a period of training and instruction in Christian understandings about God, human relationships, and the meaning of life, which culminates in reception of the Sacraments of Christian Initiation.[1]

The rites for the Preparation of Adults for Baptism in *The Book of Occasional Services*[2] (BOS) and the rites for Preparation of Baptized Persons for Reaffirmation of the Baptismal Covenant[3] provide detailed descriptions of the formation process that should accompany the rites. Neither the rites nor the formation stand alone. The rites, taking place within the context of the whole gathered community, act out in prayer, praise, oblation, and thanksgiving what God has done and is doing in formation. If the congregation and the participants in the catechumenal process have been properly formed, the rites will have a profound meaning for all who experience them. The formation, or catechesis, enables the participants' growth in faith and living. It is that growth, made visible in the rites, that helps the participants to reflect on their experience after the rites are completed.

The catechumenal process is, at one level, a process for training and instruction. Surrounding this formation is a cycle of liturgies which mark and shape the stages of that formation. These liturgies communicate the essential meaning of the

---

1. BOS, p. 112 or Appendix D, Sec. 1.
2. BOS, pp. 112–114 or Appendix D, Sec. 1.
3. BOS, pp. 132–134 or Appendix D, Sec. 2.

stages, both for the participants and for the community. Further, surrounding the formation and liturgies of the catechumenal process is a larger vision of the Christian journey or pilgrimage in God and through Christ, expressed for and shared by the whole community in the essential Christian rites of baptism and eucharist. The witness of the people in the catechumenal process, shared with the whole congregation, can make the reality of the Christian pilgrimage come clear to everyone. In turn, the vision comes clearer to the people in the process when they experience its impact on the whole congregation—their Christian family. The congregation rediscovers its pilgrimage and thereby gives back to the participants the vision of the journey of the whole people of God in history.

Much has been written about the stages of the catechumenal process, especially about the process as set forth in the Roman Catholic *Rite of Christian Initiation of Adults.* This experience with and reflection on the process is invaluable. Three books are particularly important resources for any congregation planning a catechumenal process: *A History of the Catechumenate,* by Michael Dujarier, examines the historical development of the process; *New Wine: New Wineskins,* by James B. Dunning, discusses the pastoral implications of the process and examines the liturgies, catechesis, and ministries related to each stage; *A Journey in Faith,* by Raymond Kemp, tells the story of one Roman Catholic congregation's experience with the rite. No summary of the history of the catechumenal process, nor description of it, currently exists to match these resources.

Although these three publications are invaluable, the catechumenal process practiced in Episcopal congregations has been changed significantly from Roman Catholic practice by the particular liturgical expression of the Episcopal rites, by the kind of formation designed to accompany those rites, and by the way baptism and membership in a congregation are defined by Episcopalians, both sacramentally and canonically. Of particular note are the new rites for baptized persons preparing for Reaffirmation of the Baptismal Covenant. These rites clearly state that Christian initiation is completed in baptism.

The following chapters are a commentary on the stages of the catechumenal process, placed within the context of the rites and practice of the Episcopal Church. These descriptions of liturgies and stages, however, are not neatly organized blueprints that must be followed. Each chapter discusses one element of the catechumenal process: stages of the process; evangelization; liturgies for the unbaptized; liturgies for the baptized; sponsorship; and models for catechetical formation. Drawing from these elements, each congregation can design its own process, assembling those elements that help and support participants in their catechumenal journey.

9

Stages of the Catechumenal Process

The heart of the catechumenal process is the journey of growth and formation embarked on by people seeking to discover how God is calling them and how God is acting in their lives and ministries in the world. As their insight into God's call and God's work grows, participants themselves grow and change. Sometimes growth occurs in the catechumenal group. Sometimes growth occurs as participants cope with issues in their daily lives.

A *stage* in the catechumenal process is not a grade or status that participants achieve. Participants do not "graduate" from the catechumenal process. Rites do not confer status, but allow journeyers a way of acknowledging publicly their deepening level of commitment and living. In this way, a catechumenal process is not an education program, but a formation process. As one educator notes, it is "a method of formation, not just in doctrinal purity, but in the re-imagined self, with a redirected affect and restructured patterns of life."[1] From the beginning, the emphasis of catechumenal formation has been on how par-

---

1. Michael Warren, "Religious Formation in the Context of Social Formation," *Religious Education* (Fall 1987): 82, no. 4: p. 526.

ticipants live their lives and on how they are called by God to restructure the commitments of those lives."

The following discussion of the stages assumes that both unbaptized and baptized participants are in the same group. Congregations using separate groups for each are asked to determine where comments may apply to one group but not to the other.

The catechumenal process, as described here, has four stages. However, a congregation engaging in this process must also prepare for an additional element, a particularly important aspect of the first stage, that of identifying and inviting potential participants. This work is shared by laity and clergy. Potential participants are invited into a setting where they can freely ask questions and explore the possibility of entering the process for deeper formation. Those people making the invitation to participate would, themselves, have received some preparation. They need an overview of the whole catechumenal process and how to work with the questions interested people will ask. Among those questions will be: "What *is* the Christian message?", "What is the shape of the Christian life?" and, "What is the purpose of the Church?"

During this preparation stage, the people welcoming inquirers become explicit evangelists; they need training to do the job well. The Milwaukee Pilot Project designed this time of training, finding, and inviting as a separate stage called "Gathering." Evangelization and the Gathering stage is discussed in the next chapter.

Stage 1: Pre-Catechumenate and Inquiry

The first stage of the process is a period of inquiry and exploration. For an unbaptized person, this stage is called the Pre-catechumenal Period:

To this stage belong inquirers' classes with sufficient preparation to enable persons to determine that they wish to become Christians. It is a time during which those who have been initially attracted to the Christian community are guided to examine and test their motives, in order that they may freely commit themselves to pursue a disciplined exploration of the implications of Christian living.[2]

For a baptized person, this stage is called the Inquiry period:

A period of inquiry designed for story sharing and to give persons enough information about Christian faith and practice and the life of the local community so they may determine if they wish to enter a disciplined period of mature formation in the story of God's saving deeds, prayer, worship and service.[3]

Both baptized and unbaptized persons approach this stage with questions as they prepare to decide whether or not to enter into a process of deeper formation and commitment. Although the final step, baptism or reaffirmation, differs for the two groups, they share the common experience of questioning and discernment.

The first stage of a catechumenal process should include four key elements: [1] hospitality; [2] story-sharing; [3] open inquiry; and [4] discernment. Although these elements are not confined to the first stage, including them at the beginning of the catechumenal journey takes into account the integrity of the participants and helps them open themselves still more to God's call and to conversion.

Hospitality: Whether the inquirer is baptized or unbaptized, the catechumenal team should first be ready to offer hospitality and

---

2. BOS, p. 113 or Appendix D, Sec. 1.
3. BOS, p. 133 or Appendix D, Sec. 2.

welcome. In addition to an open door and a warm greeting, this hospitality includes an offer to make room for inquirers in the community. By this act, the team represents the whole congregation in extending a welcome to those seeking a community where they may open themselves to God.

> The purposefulness and the warmth of the pre-catechumenate must come from a parish that knows itself and is confident enough to open itself to new members without fear. . . . The parish and its [catechumenal process] are of a pilgrim nature, of a journey in faith, redeemed sinners all and sure in the saving power of Christ. The pre-catechumenate is the parish's way of introducing itself.[4]

The community is obliged to give inquirers enough preparation and information to start them on their way to serious formation. Thus, a catechumenal team opens all aspects of a congregation's life to inquirers and presents adequate information and an atmosphere of trust in which they may freely decide whether or not to enter a "disciplined period of mature formation."[5]

This hospitality might have a very "homey" flavor. It may be as simple as giving a tour of the church, visiting all the building's nooks and crannies. This may also be a time to examine the "things" of the church that have liturgical meaning and use, such as vestments and church furnishings, or to introduce newcomers to the ceremonial customs of the congregation. People from the congregation's many ministries might visit sessions to discuss how they themselves support the life of the congregation, and what this means to them. A history of the congregation may help inquirers better understand their church home, telling when and how it was founded, how it has changed during its life, and the impact of local, national, and world events on its life.

An introduction to *The Book of Common Prayer* may help those

---

4. Raymond B. Kemp, *A Journey in Faith: An Experience of the Catechumenate* (New York: Sadlier Press, 1979), p. 63.
5. BOS, p. 133 or Appendix D, Sec. 2.

people who are less familiar with Episcopal worship feel welcome. Beyond discussing corporate worship, this is an opportunity to present the Prayer Book as a resource for private devotions and study, including the daily offices and lectionary, the psalter, the section of special prayers and thanksgivings, and the catechism and historical documents. Participants should be encouraged to make their own decisions about how they will use the Prayer Book in corporate worship—from following every word to using it only during parts of the service that are different each Sunday, such as psalms and intercessions.

Story-sharing and Open Inquiry: All persons entering a catechumenal process bring at least two things to it: "their own stories and their questions about those stories."[6] The hospitality offered to inquirers helps support these two central elements of the first stage. Thus, in an atmosphere of hospitality and trust, people are honored for the stories they bring and are allowed to freely ask any questions about them they choose. This is the primary work of the first stage of the process. The inquirers are met by people who have found their own stories to be honored and loved by God and to have been given special meaning in the story of Jesus Christ.

Writing about the catechumenal process in *New Wine: New Wineskins,* James Dunning says that its central theme is "does my personal story find meaning in the story of Jesus so that my story becomes God's story."[7] If the response is "Yes!" or "I begin to believe so," the inquirer is ready to embark on the next stage of the journey; a stage of transformation and commitment.

At the practical level, this means that participants in the inquiry phase should be encouraged to tell stories about how they came to know God in their lives and what brought them to the catechumenal process. Warm–up and activities that help or encourage people to tell their stories have a place here. Further,

---

6. James B. Dunning, *New Wine: New Wineskins: Pastoral Implications of the Rite of Christian Initiation of Adults* (New York: Sadlier Press, 1981), p. 42.
7. ———. p. 31.

all questions should, if possible, be honored so that participants
are free to discuss any concern and trust that they will find an
adequate response. The meeting does not allow participants to
become *passive* listeners. The church has its story to tell, but it
is most effectively—and enduringly—told in response to the
questions of inquirers. The inquiry stage is a dialogue, a time
when the story of the Christian community meets with, and
celebrates, the personal stories of inquirers.

Discernment: The first stage culminates with a decision. The
inquirer must decide whether to engage in an additional period
of formation leading to an act of commitment to Christ and the
church. For the people who are not baptized, this is whether or
not to prepare for baptism. For the baptized, the decision is
whether or not to renew the baptismal covenant. Thus, an important element of this first stage is discerning whether or not
the inquirer is ready to be involved in this kind of formation and
commitment. Competent spiritual direction should be available
to inquirers to help them understand the nature of the commitment and to hear, see, and respond to God's transforming activity in their lives. In the stories they have told and the questions
they have asked, inquirers have openly dealt with their journeys
to this point. Now, they must decide whether or not they are
willing to "risk the conversion process."[8] At the same time, the
community or congregation must acknowledge its willingness to
stand by and participate in the inquirers' risky journey of transformation and growth.

As in the early centuries of Christianity, today's catechumenal
teams should be able to see some growth in faith and living
already under way in the inquirers who wish to enter the second
stage. The questions asked and the experiences discussed by
inquirers will be indicators of spiritual growth to discerning
members of the community. When both the inquirers and the
community see readiness for the journey together, the commu-

---

8. Robert J. Brooks, "Imaging the Story," *The Living Church* (11 January 1981), p. 7.

nity ratifies or accepts that decision by admitting the inquirers to the second stage of the process.

Aidan Kavanagh, a Roman Catholic leader in the recovery of baptism, refers to the catechumenal process as "conversion therapy." It is a good term because it acknowledges the need for change and the healing that comes with turning toward God.

Stage 2: Catechumenate and Deeper Formation

The second stage for the unbaptized is the Catechumenate. Beginning with the rite of Admission of Catechumens, it is described as follows:

> To this stage belong regular associations with the worshiping community, the practice of life in accordance with the Gospel [including service to the poor and neglected], encouragement and instruction in the life of prayer, and basic instruction in the history of salvation as revealed in the Holy Scriptures of the Old and New Testaments.[9]

Although the rites for baptized persons do not name this second stage, its theme is "deeper exploration of faith and ministry." In the Milwaukee Pilot Project it was called "Formation in Christ." It follows a rite at which inquirers are welcomed as members of the community, sign the register of baptized persons, and commit themselves to a disciplined exploration of Christian living. The rites describe this stage of formation:

> This is a longer period during which those being formed, along with sponsors, catechists and other members of the community engage in deeper exploration of faith and ministry.
>
> This formation period is based on a pattern of experi-

---

9. BOS, p. 113 or Appendix D, Sec. 1.

ence followed by reflection. The baptized persons explore the meanings of baptism and the baptismal covenant, while discerning the type of service to which God calls them in the context of the local community. The sponsors and catechists in turn train and support them in that service and help them to reflect theologically on their experience of ministry through the study of Scripture, in prayer and worship. Substantial periods of time are spent doing ministry and reflecting on it with catechists and sponsors.[10]

The rites do not specify the duration of this stage. *The Book of Occasional Services* states that it may vary according to the individual participant's needs and previous understanding of the Christian religion. One goal of this period might be that it allows participants to have a year with the lectionary. Based on the church year, the lectionary includes lessons that set forth the biblical bases for the major Christian doctrines involved in each season.

For those who "already possess an understanding and appreciation of the Christian religion, [this second stage] might be relatively short."[11] Careful listening to newcomers will indicate whether or not they have a working Christian faith and have already made an affective response to the Gospel. This can be true of unbaptized as well as baptized people.

Although the length of this stage may vary, the content of the formation for this stage is very clear and involves a combination of practice and reflection. This stage includes four essential components:

• Regular participation in corporate worship
• Development and enrichment of personal devotional life
• Practice of Christian living, including involvement in social service and in social justice ministry

---

10. BOS, p. 133 or Appendix D, Sec. 2.
11. BOS, p. 113 or Appendix D, Sec. 1.

- Instruction in the history of salvation as revealed in Scripture and the exploration of one's own history in the light of that salvation history.

Although some may question the inclusion of work for social justice, one cannot give service to the poor and neglected without working to change the social conditions that contribute to poverty and neglect. The Milwaukee Pilot Project also included among its essential components exploring proportionate giving, with a serious consideration given to tithing. When we consider the fascination with the dollar in the United States, part of humanity's inclination to greed, it is especially important to begin to raise questions about faith's claim on one's material resources early in an exploration of the Christian way.

Further, the method for instruction in the four components of this period is clearly stated in the rites. Formation emerges from a pattern of experience followed by reflection. Time is devoted to active ministry followed by time to reflect theologically on that experience, in community, with sponsors and catechists. In the context of a small group, people are encouraged to reflect on what God is doing in their daily lives, in their work, in their homes, in their communities, in their citizenship, in their leisure time, and in their church life. Through this reflection, participants discover how they are accountable for Christian conduct in every aspect of their daily lives and how they might draw on the support of their fellow Christians, especially those with whom they share the trusting relationship of the catechumenal group.

The basic text of this second stage of formation is the Bible. But rather than being limited to Bible study, the catechumenal process calls participants to explore how their own stories are touched and informed by the salvation history as recorded and revealed in Scripture. More than study *about* Scripture, this is study *through* Scripture to see how God's truth is being revealed. This kind of study demands personal engagement with the stories of Hebrew and Christian Scripture, the majestic sweep of salvation history culminating in the life and ministry of Jesus. Issues of church history, theology, social justice, service, ethics, evangelism, ministry, stewardship, worship, and education can also be explored from the perspective of this formative story. Here the importance of the participants' year with the lectionary, a liturgical year of formation in Christian life, becomes clear.

In the course of a year, the lectionary presents the story of Jesus' life, his birth and ministry, his death and resurrection. The other two lessons are related themes from the Old Testament and the story of the church. During the year, all of the major Christian doctrines are presented. Through the lectionary, doctrines and life come together as the lessons call up similar experiences in the participant's daily life for reflection, and for careful listening for God's word.

Finally, during this stage participants are plunged into the fullness of Christian living. They learn to pray. They join in corporate worship. They minister to others by choosing or being assigned to works of social service and social justice. They are able to see how their growing Christian commitment shapes and transforms the way they function in their daily places. Again, they are not learning *about* being Christians. They are learning *through* their own experience of living as Christians.

Involvement in ministries of social service and social justice is critical. The formation for catechumens calls for them to be active in "service to the poor and neglected" and to "work for justice and peace."[12] Formation for the baptized requires that they "explore the meanings of baptism and the baptismal covenant, while discerning the type of service to which God calls them"[13] and suggests that "substantial periods of time are spent doing ministry."[14] They also commit themselves to "the building up of God's reign of peace and justice."[15] This apostolic

12. BOS, pp. 112–113 or Appendix D, Sec. 1.
13. BOS, p. 133 or Appendix D, Sec. 2.
14. BOS, p. 133 or Appendix D, Sec. 2.
15. BOS, p. 136, or Appendix D, Sec 2.

service is not an option or an ideal. Rather, this formation invites participants to redirect and restructure the patterns of their lives—from now on. From their experience of this ministry of service to the poor and neglected, they come to a renewed hearing of God's Word. That Word has always called the faithful to relieve the poor and to remove injustice and oppression. Jesus stands squarely in the tradition of the prophets and their call to let "justice flow like water" (Amos 5:24). When the participants come to terms with the call to justice, they begin to understand the costly nature of true discipleship.

As with the first stage, the completion of this second stage requires participants to decide if they are ready to commit themselves to the intense preparation required for public commitment. Here again, catechists and sponsors should offer spiritual direction and support. The community also has an important role in this process. As the individual participants state their readiness to be baptized or to reaffirm the baptismal covenant, the community testifies to the conversion they find evident in the participants' lives and invites them to be witnesses of God's transforming and renewing action during the ninety days of Lent and Easter. This long second period will produce many indications of what is happening in the participants' faith and living—in their talk of prayer, in their response to worship, in their love, in their involvement in service and in justice ministries. All those involved look carefully at these indicators.

The integrity of this process must be maintained, both for the sake of the individual participants and for the community. This is where the fluidity of the catechumenal process becomes crucial. Although each Lent calls forth those people who are willing to represent the congregation in their witness of special discipline in preparation for the Paschal season, this does not mean that every person engaged in the second stage of the process has had sufficient formation to make that commitment. All are encouraged to search their own consciences, to seek counsel, and to make the decision prayerfully, with God's guidance. Further, participants offer evidence to the community of the seriousness of their commitment and of the growth and conversion manifest in their lives.

Stage 3: Candidacy and Immediate Preparation

The second stage culminates for catechumens in the Rite of Enrollment for Baptism and for the baptized in an Ash Wednesday rite. The most appropriate time for candidacy for baptism or reaffirmation is the Lenten season, although *The Book of Occasional Services* suggests alternative times for catechumens preparing for baptism. However, the fundamental meanings of both candidacy and the fourth stage of reflection on living the sacramental life in one's daily places are so tied to Lent and Easter that they not only draw from but also bring vital significance to the whole congregation's liturgical celebration of these seasons.

At this third stage, the catechumenal process becomes much more public. Its public role is set forth on Ash Wednesday when the celebrant invites the people to observe a holy Lent, saying:

> The first Christians observed with great devotion the days of our Lord's passion and resurrection, and it became the custom of the Church to prepare for them by a season of penitence and fasting. This season of Lent provided a time in which converts to the faith were prepared for Holy Baptism. It was also a time when those who, because of notorious sins, had been separated from the body of the faithful were reconciled by penitence and forgiveness, and restored to the fellowship of the Church. Thereby, the whole congregation was put in mind of the message of pardon and absolution set forth in the Gospel of our Savior, and of the need which all Christians continually have to renew their repentance and faith.[16]

---

16. BCP, pp. 264–265.

Catechumens and people preparing to reaffirm their baptismal covenant bear the sign of this repentance and renewal for the whole community. Just as candidates need the example of the faithful to support their catechumenal journeys during this final time of preparation, so the community needs these candidates as examples of disciplined prayer, fasting, and self-examination in order to prepare for the renewal of their own baptismal covenant at Easter.

A congregation with people engaged in both catechumenal formation and in preparation to reaffirm the baptismal covenant would celebrate two distinct rites. The witness of candidates for reaffirmation is on Ash Wednesday at the Calling of the Baptized to Continuing Conversion. Catechumens enroll for baptism on the First Sunday of Lent. The liturgies and formation of candidates for baptism are described as follows:

> To this stage belongs a series of liturgical acts leading to baptism. These ordinarily take place on a series of Sundays preceding one of the stated days for baptism and involve public prayer for the candidates, who are present at the services as a group, accompanied by their sponsors. . . . In addition to these public acts, this stage involves the private disciplines of fasting, examination of conscience, and prayer, in order that the candidates will be spiritually and emotionally ready for baptism. It is appropriate that, in accordance with ancient custom, the sponsors support their candidates by joining them in prayer and fasting.[17]

The formation for persons reaffirming their baptismal covenant is set forth in the rites:

> The candidates focus on the Lenten disciplines and their role in ministry to others. In their group meetings, candidates for reaffirmation share their on-going experience of

---

17. BOS, p. 114 or Appendix D, Sec. 1.

conversion—especially with those catechumens that are preparing for baptism—and explore more deeply the life of prayer and ministry.[18]

These candidates are promising to take part in the same activities to which the whole congregation is called in keeping Lent. Again the celebrant's call to the congregation on Ash Wednesday sets forth disciplines to be observed by all Christians:

> I invite you, therefore, in the name of the Church, to the observance of a holy Lent, by self-examination and repentance; by prayer and fasting, and self-denial; and by reading and meditating on God's holy Word.[19]

Thus, at its core, the third stage of the catechumenal process is a forty–day baptismal retreat kept through the observance of a holy Lent. This retreat consists of three elements: [1] meditating on God's holy Word; [2] prayer, fasting, and self-denial; and [3] self-examination and repentance.

Again, one focus of the Lenten disciplines is on daily life. What do this Sunday's readings say about my daily work? What prayers reflect the quality of my home now? What fasting does my life in my community ask of me? What self-denial does Christian citizenship require? What should be examined in my use of leisure time? Where do I need to turn around in my life, in my congregation? The Lenten period is a time to concentrate our ethical awareness of the costly issues of Christian living in today's world. The other focus of the Lenten disciplines is the promise and power available in the resurrection life lived in the Christian community. The risen Lord is present to lead, forgive, and empower us for ministry in these same daily places.

At this stage, the Scripture study should center on the Sunday Gospel. The Standing Liturgical Commission recommends that

---

18. BOS, p. 133 or Appendix D, Sec. 2.
19. BCP, p. 265.

the Year A lections for Lent always be used when a congregation has candidates for baptism. These readings as established in the Gelasian Sacramentary, the earliest source of liturgical texts arranged according to the church year, and are particularly appropriate for baptismal candidates. The readings from the Gospel of John on the four Sundays of Lent after catechumens are enrolled provide a rich source for meditations on those central symbols that will be powerfully present at the Easter Vigil: being born anew (Jesus and Nicodemus, John 3:1–17); living water (the woman at the well, John 4:5–42); blindness and light (the man born blind, John 9:1–38); and life eternal (the raising of Lazarus, John 11:1–44).

The disciplines of prayer, fasting, and self-denial are encouraged for both candidates and their sponsors during Lent. In addition, as they grow in their personal prayer lives, candidates and their sponsors are called forward for special prayers and blessings on the Third, Fourth, and Fifth Sundays of Lent.

As during all previous stages, spiritual direction is important for the candidates' growth and preparation and to assist them with their Lenten disciplines and prayer life. Further, during this stage, they should have counsel in self-examination available to them as they prepare to renounce their former ways of life and enter into renewed lives as Christians. Spiritual direction can be offered in a group or individually by sponsors or members of the catechumenal team.

Those persons preparing to reaffirm their baptismal covenants offer the congregation special witness of their commitment to Christian servanthood at the Maundy Thursday rite, and renew their covenant at the Great Easter Vigil when the catechumens are baptized.

These rites complete the third stage of the catechumenal process. Frequently, literature on the catechumenal process recommends that these rites be celebrated with all the rich visual, tactile, and auditory beauty that Christian initiatory symbols provide. The movement from dark to light, the plunge into the deep cleansing and living waters of baptism, the vivid scents of fire and incense and oil, the sounds of cheers and alleluias, the taste of bread and wine—all of these symbols should imprint themselves on the senses in celebration of Christ's victory over death and the renewal of all life in and through Christ. This celebration is the very raising of Christ in the midst of the congregation through the witness of people who have "risked the conversion process." Descriptions of how congregations, using a catechumenal process, prepare for and celebrate their Great Vigil of Easter suggest ways these rich symbols can be fully appropriated.[20]

Stage 4: Understanding Sacramental Living

The fourth stage completes the ninety-day cycle of preparation and celebration of the Paschal Mystery. The Great Fifty Days following Easter are "The Lord's Day" of the Christian Year. They comprise one seventh of a year, just as Sunday is the Lord's Day of the Week. Throughout Lent, Christian people are called "to become." Easter says: "You are! You are the people of God. See the ones dressed in white, the ones who died and rose to new life before your very eyes in the waters of baptism. The Risen One is among you, and you too are risen ones. You are Easter people!"

In the early centuries, this Easter period was dedicated to teaching about the sacraments of baptism and the Eucharist. The catechumens did not witness these sacraments until their own initiation. The ancient form of Christian initiation was baptism, laying of hands by the bishop, and Eucharist. Thus, the weekly Eucharist became the weekly repetition of one's baptism. The basilicas were packed to the doors as Cyril, Ambrose, and Augustine expounded the meanings of the sacraments. The newly baptized were in front, in the seats of honor. The rest of

---

20. Brooks, "Imaging the Story," pp. 8–9; and Brooks, "Faith of Our Fathers," *The Living Church* (11 January 1981), pp. 9–10.

the places were taken by the faithful eager to deepen their understanding of sacramental living. The period's original name, *mystagogia,* means study of the "mysteries," the other name for the sacraments.

Even after Constantine, catechumens left after the Ministry of the Word for special instruction. Their teachers did not avoid reference to what happens at baptism and Eucharist, but rather assumed that the catechumens could not really understand them until they had experienced them. Accordingly, full teaching about baptism became the usual practice during Eastertide. As infant baptism became the usual practice, this teaching of the mysteries or *mystagogia* during Eastertide fell into disuse.

Today, baptism and Eucharist are not secret but public. However, our use of this last stage is similar in that we reflect on the meaning of the sacraments in our daily lives. The Milwaukee Pilot Project called it "Formation in Ministry."

This Easter period may therefore be best explained as:

> [the] time to reflect upon our experience of the mysteries of dying and rising in the sacraments, and . . . the time when the new Christian determined how to extend those mysteries of dying and rising by offering his/her gifts in service or ministry.[21]

This is the stage of the process that most forcefully flies in the face of contemporary cultural expectations. It shows clearly that baptism is not graduation *from* but entrance *into* a community for which formation, growth, and transition are ongoing processes. It says we do not go home when the party is over, but stay and join a family that celebrates again and again the central experience of dying and rising to new life.

As with the forty days of Lent, the Great Fifty Days of Easter find essential meaning in the presence of the newly baptized, the neophytes, the newly enlightened ones.

---

21. Dunning, *New Wine: New Wineskins,* p. 71.

These ninety days, one fourth of the calendar year, beginning with Ash Wednesday or the First Sunday of Lent and concluding with Pentecost, is the Church's short course to itself on the nature and meaning of Christian life. In a very direct way the pre-catechumenate and the catechumenate phases are valuable only as the preparation for these ninety days of corporate dying and rising experience with the Lord.[22]

Just as the Sunday lections during Lent are preparation for initiation, so the readings appointed for the Sundays of Easter highlight the experience of the Great Easter Vigil. The readings from the Book of Acts are stories of the disciples. The disciples continued in the work Jesus had done, and Christians today continue "in the apostles' teaching and fellowship."[23]

The Gospel readings are a commentary on the sacraments of baptism and the Eucharist, and form the basis for the sacramental catechesis. For example, in the Gospel for the Second Sunday of Easter, which recounts the Risen Lord's appearance to the disciples and Thomas' outburst of praise and recognition, there is a commentary on the very human response of mingled fear and awe and joy at the presence of Christ in the waters of baptism. The lections on succeeding Sundays have reflections on the Eucharist, Christian ministry, the Holy Spirit, and the church. Finally, the seal is placed on the Great Fifty Days with the revelation of the Holy Spirit to the community on the Day of Pentecost.[24]

Easter is also the season for great festivity. *The Book of Occasional Services* suggests it is customary for a parish priest to visit parishioners' homes during the Fifty Days of Easter and provides a form for house blessings during this season.[25] This is

22. Kemp, *A Journey in Faith,* p. 164.
23. BCP, p. 304.
24. Michael W. Merriman, "The Liturgy in the Easter Season," *Open* (March 1987), pp. 16–19.
25. BOS, pp. 97–100.

part of the celebration of Christ's presence with us; Christ lives in our homes, in ourselves, in our lives. The Risen Lord is made flesh in the people. This atmosphere of celebration surrounds and enriches the catechesis of those who have been initiated into, or who have renewed, the covenant of their relationship with the community. Now the Christian community has become their home. Now Christ is at home in them.

As in the earlier stages of formation, catechesis during Eastertide follows the distinctively Christian pattern of reflection on experience. Rather than being taught about the sacraments before initiation, those who are newly washed and fed are invited to reflect on and try to understand the meaning of those experiences. Most sacramental catechesis should wait until the newly initiated are "surrounded with water, burning candle, white garment, oil, bread and wine, alleluia, and a risen people."[26]

From that reflection, participants can then consider how they might live in response to their experience of the sacraments. This is a question about ministry. The design for the catechumenal process in the Milwaukee Pilot Project described the following goals for the fourth stage:

> Following initiation or reaffirmation, participants will reflect on the meaning of the rites for their ministry in the world and in the church. By this time, their experience in all of the foregoing has already built capacity to, in company with their fellow pilgrims, use the lections to discern God's presence and call in their daily places and in the Christian Community and give and receive support in responding to God's presence and call. They, probably, already desire an ongoing support group for ministry for the rest of their lives. The task of this period is then to help the participants get settled in such an ongoing group. Frequent use of the Celebration of a New Ministry in some form will

26. Dunning, *New Wine: New Wineskins*, p. 97.

express their sense of vocation in their daily places year by year.

As the Scripture readings of the Easter season reflect on Christian vocation and ministry, participants in this stage should consider their own gifts for ministry and how they might best exercise them both in the congregation and in their daily lives. Participants should spend a week on each of their daily places, asking "What difference has my baptism or my reaffirmation made for my ministry *here?*" Their call to ministry in the world is echoed in the story of the disciples on the Day of Pentecost, when they moved into the world with the power of the Holy Spirit.

A continuing problem of the catechumenal process is the letdown that follows the end of the weekly sessions with fellow Christians. Because of this, special attention is given to bridging participants into ongoing support groups. Some will want task groups such as outreach ministries or the altar guild, Christian education, or choir. Others will want groups that are built around biblical reflection, prayer, and ministry support. One member of the catechumenal team in a family size church, three or more in a larger church, can take on this responsibility.

At some time during the Easter season, preferably either immediately after Easter or at Pentecost, the newly baptized and those who reaffirmed their baptismal covenants are presented to the bishop for the Laying on of Hands.

10

Evangelization

So I came to Milan, to Ambrose. . . . All unknowingly I was
brought by God to him that knowing I should be brought by
him to God. That man of God received me as a father, and
as bishop welcomed my coming. I came to love him, not at
first as a teacher of the truth . . . but for his kindness toward
me. . . . His words I listened to with greatest care; his matter
I held quite unworthy of attention. . . . Ambrose taught the
doctrine of salvation most profitably. But salvation is far from
sinners, of the sort that I then was. Yet little by little I was
drawing closer, though I did not yet realize it.

AUGUSTINE, *Confessions*, 5. 13[1]

Evangelization is the sharing of the Christian story with another
person and the forming of people in the Christian faith. For
Augustine, it was Ambrose, the famous teacher, preacher, and
bishop, who was able to reach him in his search for truth and
open him to know and love God. But it was not Ambrose's
eloquence in preaching or even the truth of what he taught that
most touched Augustine. Rather, Ambrose welcomed him and
showed him great kindness. That kind of meeting can be offered
by every person in a congregation. This work is not the special
province of clergy, or even of a bishop.

Augustine's experience also shows another dimension of how
Christians meet and invite people to know God. God had always
been at work in Augustine's life. He did not yet know the truth
about himself, but Ambrose saw it, honored it, and welcomed
it. That same reality is present in every person who comes to
Christ. The catechumenal process "is not bringing God to peo-

---

1. *The Confessions of St. Augustine,* trans. F. J. Sheed (New York: Sheed and Ward, 1943)
pp. 100ff.

ple but helping them to discern a presence that always has been."[2] Members of the community then offer hospitality to others so that those others might also recognize the truth of God's presence in their lives as well.

Evangelization as Encounter and Formation

The evangelization of Augustine began long before his encounter with Ambrose. Monica, his mother, had told him of Jesus Christ while he was a child. His search for truth had led him through Manichaeism (a dualism of good and evil) to Neoplatonism (a philosophy of ideas as the source of all that exists) to the preaching of Ambrose. His evangelization came to a climax with the news of unlearned men in Egypt taking up the celibate life, going into the desert with Anthony, and putting away the temptations of sexual gratification that Augustine was, at that point, powerless to resist. His evangelization continued as he received further instruction as a catechumen and disciplined his appetites and trained his intellect. His baptism was a seal upon a changed life that would continue to change.

Augustine is thus an example of the breadth of evangelization. It begins in all encounters with Christians along life's way. These encounters are both *dialogical* (involving a frank and open verbal exchange) and formative. News of Jesus Christ is shared in open inquiry. These encounters continue through close contact with the Christian community in a catechumenal–like formation until one sees and takes up the whole of one's life in the world as a conscious agent, or steward, of God's reign.

Evangelization in the Catechumenal Community

Evangelization describes the way a congregation acts out its mission as a baptizing and catechumenal community. A baptiz-

---

2. Dunning, *New Wine: New Wineskins,* p. 29.

ing community is one that takes seriously its mission to preach and baptize in the name of Jesus Christ. A catechumenal community is the Church continually coming into being. Such a community honors those it invites with time and a place to explore their experience of God; and it offers companionship and support for that process.

James Dunning, writing about evangelization, says we should think of it as being like Alcoholics Anonymous (AA):

> Would anyone suggest that lectures, classes, instructions could convey Good News to alcoholics on Skid Row? Think AA. Think of sponsors scooping a drunk off the floor . . . Think of peers who have "been there," who are "every man and woman you meet" sharing stories about a God who accepts us in our brokenness and heals our fear, panic, and self-hatred. Think doctrine; think of the Twelve Steps of AA, not as abstract theory but lived truth about our total dependence on a Power beyond us. Think of passing through stages of deepening conversion and commitment. Think of the alcoholic's bible, what they call the Big Book, full of stories of their people who have journeyed from stupor to sobriety. Think of the commitment of the twelfth step of bringing the message of recovery to practicing alcoholics. Think of conversion in and through a community. Then think—evangelization of catechumens![3]

This is a vision that underlies all evangelization. All members of a congregation are members of the fellowship. Some have been broken and are being healed by the power of God. Some have been searching for meaning and are finding it in the Gospel of God's presence and saving work among us. All are witnesses to the Good News of God in Jesus Christ. All have stories of their spiritual journeys to tell. Then, through the witness of partici-

---

3. James B. Dunning, "Dynamics of Evangelization in the Catechumenate," c. 1982, p. 2. Also see reprints of these articles from the North American Forum on the Catechumenate: "What Happens After 'Christ Among Us'?" 1984; and "Words of the Word: Evangelization, Catechists, and the Catechumenate," c. 1983.

pants in the catechumenal process and the growth and commitment they express in public rites and shared stories, congregation members are given the energy to continue in their work of evangelization.

A congregation serious about serving as a catechumenal community should demonstrate certain qualities and characteristics. Such a congregation should be:

1. A community of hospitality, friendship, and communion
2. A community in a process of ongoing conversion
3. A community in search of meaning
4. A community that is attentive to God's Word—shared and interpreted with honesty
5. A community that celebrates and worships in praise and thanksgiving
6. A community that witnesses in the world and shares in the pastoral, prophetic, and priestly ministry of the church
7. A community where all members are partners in ministry.[4]

Essentially, this kind of community calls for an atmosphere and a language in which such activities in a congregation can come to life. Although an atmosphere and a language may seem to be intangible elements, they lie at the heart of Christian life. One commentator on the catechumenal process suggests that being a catechumenal community means being intentional about how we preach and share our experience of the Paschal Mystery, the mystery of the dying and rising Christ:

> . . . the paschal mystery is, to most people, a near abstraction. The dying and rising of Christ is perceived more as a past event than as a present reality. If we are going to do any real initiating, we are going to have to become comfortable with God-talk, gospel-talk, Jesus-talk, and Spirit-talk,

---

4. Dunning, *New Wine: New Wineskins,* pp. 62–63. Adapted by Dunning from presentations by Christiane Brusselmans.

which is both convinced and convincing. . . . We are baptized not simply into a human community, but into the
risen Christ and the indwelling Spirit. We are, most of us,
horribly inept at communicating this, and horribly embar-
rassed by it, (so much so that the homiletic and catechetical
Christ is usually presented as an abstract lawgiver and
teacher and example). Unless we can learn to speak of God
as a living and present reality, we are doomed (and the
word is appropriate) to failure.[5]

Thus, the language is one that proclaims the presence of the
Paschal Mystery, the dying and rising Christ, in the congregation. The atmosphere is one in which members openly proclaim
this presence, with joy and conviction.

There are three ways to prepare congregations for evangelizing encounters: (1) preaching to, communicating with, and
training a congregation so that members are nurtured in their
abilities to recognize God's activity in the lives of others and to
share their own stories when that time comes; (2) making the
catechumenal process a vital part of a congregation's life
through robust, lively celebrations of its rites and through the
witness of participants, so that members can understand the
process and talk about it enthusiastically with others; and (3)
offering training that provides practical skills and encouragement to members who invite people to consider the process.
These three activities offer people a vision and the skills to
become evangelizers for a catechumenal or evangelizing community.

Adding a Gathering Stage

Finding and inviting people from outside the church community to participate in a catechumenal process is a challenge in

---

5. Ralph A. Keifer, "Christian Initiation: The State of the Question," in *Made, Not Born*
(South Bend, IN: University of Notre Dame Press, 1976), p. 150.

many ways. Some possible participants easily come to mind. They are "seekers" who have made themselves known in a variety of ways. Other potential participants are friends, colleagues, or neighbors of church members who the members believe might be challenged by and respond to an invitation to explore the Christian faith in depth. Members may well have sensed the readiness of the outsiders, but may not have actually discussed it with them. The mere existence of the catechumenal process in a congregation sets the stage for an invitation. In either case, members will need help in preparing to offer such invitations.

The Milwaukee Pilot Project decided to give explicit attention to this finding and inviting process by including a separate first stage called "Gathering." During this stage, team members were prepared to recognize and invite potential participants, and to bring them together for sessions introducing the process. Ultimately, all members of a congregation might share in this gathering process as they begin to form a true catechumenal community—the church continually in the process of coming into being; the story of the Gospel meeting the stories of people.

In congregations beginning a catechumenal process, attention to and training for gathering and bringing together prospective members is important for the leadership team and for other members of the congregation. A Mississippi congregation that has worked with the catechumenal process involved its members in a six-month gathering period before Inquiry:

> During this period a special emphasis is placed on bringing new church members into the church. The people are exhorted in church, in classes, and in written communications to seek out the un-churched in the community and to bring them to church and then to the meeting of the catechumenal group in September. Frequently those who bring inquirers become sponsors if the new person decides to be admitted as a catechumen or candidate. Newspaper advertisement is also used during August and September to an-

nounce the beginning of the group which is referred to as "A Journey into Faith."[6]

As noted, the Milwaukee Pilot Project made gathering a separate stage in its process because recruiting prospective members was considered an integral and necessary step for its congregations' first experience with the process. The Milwaukee Pilot Project described this activity as follows:

Laity and clergy will be involved in contacting and inviting adults to consider or re-examine Christian commitment. The gathering will be an ongoing process. Those contacted will include:
• Non–church adults and youth (sixteen and over), whether baptized or not
• Those sixteen years or older who were baptized as infants
• New participants:
—who have entered their children in church school education programs
—who are adults returning to church participation
—who have sought out the church in time of crisis or for sacramental ministries
—regular members and/or communicants who are seeking further formation
—baptized members of other churches seeking membership in the Episcopal Church
—those lapsed members considering reaffirmation of their faith.
This purpose statement sets out three activities for a team:

[1] seeking out people without church affiliation; [2] identifying potential participants already related to the congrega-

6. "The Process of the Catechumenate at St. James' Church, Jackson, MS" p. 1. Available through St. James' Church, 3921 Oak Ridge Drive, Jackson, MS, 39216.

tion or to its members; [3] developing strategies for approaching those people and interesting them in the process.

Clergy and lay leaders share the task of seeking out and identifying potential participants. Although clergy could easily designate many such people, especially newcomers or those who have sought the church's sacramental ministry such as baptism or marriage, this is not their responsibility alone. In addition to newcomers, some longtime members of the congregation may be ready to deepen and strengthen their Christian commitment. Some members, both adults and young people, may be ready to consider making an adult reaffirmation of their baptismal covenant. Lay team members share in approaching these people to discuss the process with them.

To identify people and offer them the catechumenal process, a congregation's leadership team can prepare itself and others to recruit, and it can design group sessions to introduce the catechumenal process to those it recruits.

Training for Inviting

To prepare for gathering, members of the leadership team and other designated leaders in the congregation receive training in ways and means of inviting people to join the catechumenal process. Because this training is similar to training for evangelism or new member ministry, resources that offer experiential exercises for these ministries are appropriate. *Proclamation as Offering Story and Choice*[7] is one such resource. With this resource, a team can plan a training program of one to three sessions that combines designs for reflecting on the Bible as story, on the Anglican heritage, and on story-sharing with practice in how to approach people and offer them an opportunity

---

7. Schwab and Yon, p. 123.

to consider the Christian way. Among the designs in *Proclamation* that might be adapted for this training are the following:

- "Offering Consideration of the Christian Way."
  A design for practicing inviting a friend who is not affiliated with the church to consider the Christian Way through partici- pating in the catechumenal process.
- "The Bible as Story: The Drama of Redemption."
  A session to help people see the Bible as the Story of the Faith and to use its dramatic framework to understand and communicate the story.
- "Sharing Our Own Spiritual Pilgrimage."
  Practice in sharing one's story with others.
- "Identifying the Foundations of One's Faith and Stating the Gospel in Our own Words."
  A session to develop brief ways to summarize our own faith and the Gospel in our own words.
- "The Drama of Anglicanism" and "The Characteristics of Anglicanism."
  Sessions to develop a realistic understanding of the distinc- tive characteristics of the Episcopal Church.
- "Working with Joys and Concerns."
  A session to develop sensitivity to the depths of people's joys and concerns through practice in sharing and responding to these joys and concerns in their fellow Christians.
- "Entering a New Congregation."
  A session to explore the variety of experiences people have in entering a new congregation and to develop greater flexi- bility in responding to new people.
- "Discussing the Purpose of the Congregation."
  Practice in identifying and talking about the purpose of a congregation with newcomers or people who are not con- nected with a church.
- "Talking with Persons Different from Yourself."
  A session to enable people to talk more easily with people different from themselves.

• "Individual and Corporate Motives for Evangelism."
    A session to identify motives for evangelism and inviting people to consider the Christian way.

Whatever the design and content of these sessions, the purpose is to enable team members to identify people they might ask to consider the catechumenal process and to develop skills in approaching them.

As with other ministries related to the catechumenal process, people completing training should be commissioned for their work on behalf of the entire congregation. Using the form for Commissioning for Lay Ministries in the Church, these people might be commissioned as gatherers.[8] This also provides opportunity for the congregation to recognize and support the ministry of some of its members and for the team to share information about its work.

Designs for Introductory Sessions

When team members, clergy, and other church members have invited people to consider the process, introductory sessions might be planned to welcome people and give them information about the process and the congregation. However these sessions are organized, they should be an extension and expression of the hospitality central to the first or Inquiry stage of the process. In addition to members of the leadership team, members of the congregation who have invited potential inquirers should accompany them to the initial sessions.

Introductory sessions may either be very deliberately organized, scheduled, and advertised, or may be ongoing gatherings of people dedicated to sharing with, and including, inquirers. In

---

8. BOS, pp. 175–191.

designing such meetings, congregations might consider formats as varied as the following:

1. A single introductory meeting in which inquirers meet with members of the team and with the congregation. After the introductions, the catechumenal process is described, individual story-sharing takes place, there is a summary of the Gospel story, and then there is informal hospitality. Potential candidates, contacted by team members or clergy, are accompanied at the meeting by people who will follow up with them, answer their questions, and determine if they wish to proceed with the process. The first sessions of the Inquiry stage would follow.

2. A more formal plan includes three sessions providing a comprehensive introduction to Anglican Christianity (the Gospel, the Church, Anglicanism, and the Christian life) and group experiences to help people decide if they are ready to commit themselves to more disciplined inquiry. A congregation beginning its catechumenal process might plan and schedule such introductory sessions to precede the Inquiry stage.

3. In a more flexible format, a team member gathers other members of the congregation to meet regularly for Bible study and story-sharing. This group meets potential participants, offers hospitality, and provides information. A newcomer to the congregation expressing interest in the church might also be directed to this group. Also, members of the congregation might bring friends to the group as a way of introducing them to the congregation and the catechumenal process.

   Congregation members interested in reaffirming their baptismal covenant would also attend this group while deciding whether or not to enter the process. Meeting throughout the year, part of the group's charge would be introducing the catechumenal process. Its larger task would be to provide welcome, encouragement, and Christian fellowship to people whenever they come seeking it.

The design of sessions to introduce the catechumenal process depends on the overall design of the process, the resources of the congregation, and the schedule of the process itself. A more formal design may be most appropriate for a church implementing the process for the first time. A group that meets weekly for study and sharing, and that undertakes a ministry of greeting and including participants, may develop later as the process becomes an ongoing activity in the life of a congregation.

11

Liturgies for the Unbaptized

The catechumenal process and accompanying liturgies were first made available for Episcopal congregations when *The Book of Occasional Services* appeared initially in 1979. This book, prepared by The Standing Liturgical Commission at the direction of General Convention, provides selected rites, prayers, and blessings, many of a seasonal nature, and various optional pastoral and episcopal services. Among the pastoral services are rites for Preparation of Adults for Holy Baptism.

Preparation for baptism consists of two rites, Admission of Catechumens and Enrollment of Candidates for Baptism, and prayers for use during two of the stages, catechumenate and candidacy. The rite of Holy Baptism in *The Book of Common Prayer* completes the process. The rubrics provide guidelines for when and how the rites are to be used. The preface to the rites describes the catechumenal process and explains how the rites are related to and mark the progress of its stages. This process "culminates in the reception of the Sacraments of Christian Initiation."[1] The preface states clearly that only unbaptized people can be catechumens, just as only unbaptized people can be candidates for baptism.[2]

---

1. BOS, p. 112, or Appendix D, Sec. 1.
2. BOS, 112 and 130, or Appendix D, Sec. 1, and Sec. 2.

The following discussion of the rites and prayers for preparation for baptism is keyed to *The Book of Occasional Services* and refers both to the rubrics and to the commentary on the formation process in the preface to the rites. A careful reading of the rites in *The Book of Occasional Services* is necessary. For your convenience, these rites are printed in full in Appendix D by permission of The Church Hymnal Corporation. [See Appendix C, Section 8 for methods of preparation for these rites and reflections on them.]

Admission of Catechumens

The first rite marks completion of the pre-Catechumenate stage. It is the first public liturgical act of the catechumenal process, as well as the first public recognition of the journey to which these people are committing themselves. The rite can take place at any time during the year and is made public by being "within a principal Sunday liturgy."[3]

Those to be admitted come forward with their sponsors. They are asked, "What do you seek?" and they answer, "Life in Christ." By becoming catechumens, they do not commit themselves to being baptized. They commit themselves to a journey toward Christ that *may* end in full Christian initiation. Still, catechumens are seen as part of the Christian community. For example, a person who dies as a catechumen can receive a Christian burial.

At this stage, catechumens vow to obey the Great Commandment (Mark 12:29–31), to worship regularly, to receive instruction, and to open their ears to hear the Word of God, and their hearts and minds to receive the Lord Jesus.[4] Each person is presented by a sponsor who promises to accompany and support the catechumen throughout this journey. Those admitted

---

3. BOS, p. 115, or Appendix D, Sec. 1.
4. BOS, p. 116, Appendix D, Sec. 1.

are marked with the sign of the cross, first by the celebrant and then by their sponsors.

During the Catechumenate

Prayers suggested for the Catechumenate are not for public worship, but for catechetical sessions, or "formal instruction." In these sessions, catechumens pray in silence for themselves and for one another. Sponsors and other baptized people offer prayers for them. If sessions include people preparing for reaffirmation or reception, they, too, offer prayers for the catechumens. The instructor offers a suitable prayer and concludes by laying a hand on the head of each catechumen in silence. This act is to be performed by the instructor, whether that person is lay catechist, deacon, priest, or bishop.

Enrollment of Candidates for Baptism

This rite marks passage from the Catechumenate to Candidacy for Baptism. During this rite, catechumens express their desire to be baptized and are enrolled as candidates for baptism by signing their names in a "large book"[5] or register. This public liturgical act takes place at a congregation's principal liturgy.

Because most candidates are baptized at the Great Vigil of Easter, enrollment usually takes place on the First Sunday of Lent. *The Book of Occasional Services* offers an option of enrolling candidates on the First Sunday of Advent if baptism is to be administered on the Feast of Our Lord's Baptism.

At enrollment, candidates come forward with their sponsors and are presented by their catechist or other lay representative of the congregation. The sponsors are asked to certify that the

---

5. BOS, p. 120–124 Appendix D, Sec. 1.

catechumens have kept the promises they made when they were admitted. They are accepted as candidates and sign the book. Their sponsors may also sign. A special form of the Prayers of the People is offered with petitions for the candidates, their sponsors, their families and friends, and the congregation. The celebrant, hands extended over the candidates, prays for them.

During Candidacy

After Enrollment, public prayers are offered on Sundays for the candidates and their sponsors. They are prayed for by name in the Prayers of the People or in the Eucharistic Prayer if Prayer D is used. Candidates and their sponsors worship together during this time. Special prayers and blessings are suggested for use before the Prayers for the People, especially on the Third, Fourth, and Fifth Sundays in Lent (or on the Second, Third, and Fourth Sundays of Advent). When these special prayers and blessings are used, candidates come forward and kneel or bow their heads. Sponsors place a hand on the shoulder of their candidates while the celebrant calls the people to prayer for them. All pray in silence. Then the celebrant prays aloud for all the candidates, lays a hand on the head of each in silence, blesses them, and all return to their places.

Holy Baptism

The candidates are baptized and begin the next stage of reflection on sacramental living. Catechumens are customarily baptized at the Great Vigil of Easter.

Those planning the Great Vigil for the first time may find Dr. Louis Weil's suggestions helpful. He notes that the Great Vigil has four basic parts: [1] the lighting of the Paschal candle; [2] the Liturgy of the Word; [3] baptism; and [4] the Eucharist. The creation story, the Red Sea, Isaiah 55, and the two Ezekiel passages are sufficient if there is desire to reduce the number of readings. The baptism follows the homily in the Eucharist. This procedure combines the Old Testament and New Testament readings and announces that the candidates are being baptized into this resurrection faith. Immediately after baptism, the Eucharist completes the initiation. The Eucharist then becomes the weekly repetition of our baptism.

12

Liturgies for
the Baptized

The 1988 General Convention approved a set of rites for Preparation of Baptized Persons for Reaffirmation of the Baptismal Covenant. These rites are printed, by permission of The Church Hymnal Corporation, in Appendix D, Section 2 of this resource.

These rites are for mature baptized persons preparing to reaffirm their baptism, for previously confirmed members seeking to undertake a time of disciplined renewal of their baptismal covenant, or for people transferring into a congregation. The rites of the catechumens are not appropriate for this group. Although limited resources may require these baptized people to attend sessions with catechumens, the distinction between baptized people and catechumens should be maintained. To maintain this distinction, Emmanuel Church in Houston, TX is considering using "Reaffirmation Process" or "Reaffirmation Catechesis" for its work with the baptized.

Three rites are provided: the Welcoming of Baptized Christians Into a Community; the Calling of the Baptized to Continuing Conversion; and the Maundy Thursday Rite of Preparation for the Paschal Holy Days [see Appendix D, Section 2]. As with the rites for the unbaptized, the rubrics offer guidelines for how and when the rites should be used. The preface describes how the rites are related to the stages of a formation process. Some of the rites need adaptation. For example, the Welcoming rite must be adapted for current members seeking a deepening of their faith. The bishop must approve such adaptations. See Appendix C, Section 9 for methods of preparation for these rites and reflections on them.

The Welcoming of Baptized Christians Into a Community

Used at a principal Sunday Eucharist, this rite, like the Admission of Catechumens, concludes the Inquiry stage. Here, those wishing to pursue "a disciplined exploration of the implications of Christian living are recognized by the community and welcomed to begin this process."[1] These people vow to study and to strive to keep the promises made at their baptism, to attend worship regularly, to join others "in the life of service to those who are poor, outcast, or powerless," and "to strive to recognize the gifts that God has given [them] and discern how they are to be used in the building up of God's reign of peace and justice."[2]

Sponsors, chosen by the community to serve as companions to these people promise to support them by prayer and example. As the celebrant offers a prayer on behalf of the new members, their sponsors place a hand on their shoulders. Then, as a deacon or their sponsor calls out their names, the baptized sign the church's register of baptized persons. Some of these new members might read the lessons, present the Bread and Wine, or perform other liturgical functions for which they are qualified.

---

1. BOS, p. 135, or Appendix D, Sec. 2.
2. BOS, p. 136 or Appendix D, Sec. 2.

During the Formation Stage

Baptized candidates take part in the Eucharist, including receiving Holy Communion, unless prevented by penitential discipline. If they attend sessions with the unbaptized, prayers offered for them should acknowledge their baptism. Suggested examples are the weekday collects for the Great Fifty Days of Easter from *Lesser Feasts and Fasts* (pp. 57–67).

The Calling of the Baptized to Continuing Conversion

This rite is used at the principal service on Ash Wednesday. People who previously committed themselves to explore the implications of their baptismal covenant and are preparing to reaffirm that covenant at the Easter Vigil "are recognized as examples of conversion for the congregation in its journey towards Easter."[3]

After the Blessing of the Ashes, these people are presented to the celebrant. Confirming that they have fulfilled their vows of study, worship, service, and social justice ministry, they promise to "strive to set an example . . . of that turning towards Jesus Christ which marks true conversion."[4] Candidates kneel or bow their heads, and sponsors place a hand on their shoulders. The celebrant then prays for them and the witness they will offer.

Having agreed to the period of intense preparation to reaffirm their baptismal covenants, the candidates are addressed: "Receive ashes as a symbol of repentance and conversion and show us by your example how to turn to Christ."[5] After the celebrant has imposed ashes on the candidates, they join the celebrant in imposing ashes on the congregation.

---

3. See BOS, p. 138, or Appendix D, Sec. 2.
4. See BOS, p. 138, or Appendix D, Sec. 2.
5. See BOS, p. 139, or Appendix D, Sec. 2.

During the Lenten Season

Candidates are prayed for by name, separately from any cate-chumens, at the Prayers of the People.

Maundy Thursday Rite of Preparation for the Paschal Holy Days

This rite is used at the principal service on Maundy Thursday. During this rite, those persons "who have been preparing for reaffirmation of their baptismal covenant at the Easter Vigil are further recognized as members so they may join the community in its Paschal celebration."[6]

After the Liturgy of the Word, before the foot-washing cere-mony, candidates for reaffirmation stand before the celebrant with their sponsors. The celebrant welcomes them to the com-munity which they are joining as disciples of Christ by imitating his example and by dedicating themselves to service. The cele-brant then asks the candidates if they are prepared to join the life of service. After signifying their readiness, they join the congregation in a rite of reconciliation (*The Book of Common Prayer,* p. 450) omitting the confession of particular sins. The celebrant lays a hand on each candidate while pronouncing the absolution. The celebrant washes the candidates' feet. Then, as a sign of the servanthood of Christ to which all are called, the candidates are given basins, ewers, and towels so they can wash the feet of other members of the congregation. The service continues with the Peace.

The baptized reaffirm their baptismal covenant at the Easter Vigil. If a bishop is not at this service, the baptized are presented to a bishop during the Great Fifty Days for the Laying on of Hands, Reception, or Commitment to Christian Service, as ap-propriate.

---

6. BOS, p. 140, or Appendix D, Sec. 2.

13

Sponsors

> Before there was a catechumenate, there were sponsors—a sponsoring, welcoming community of people who were convinced that Jesus was Good News for them and that he might be Good News for others. From the year 30 to 180, there was no catechumenal institution as such . . . There were only Christians, sharing their lives, sharing both the stories of Jesus and their own faith stories with other people.
>
> JAMES B. DUNNING[1]

In Chapter 5 of this resource, sponsors were described as those who befriend, guide, and support participants, beginning with the rites of Admission or Welcome, by [1] sharing all activities with the candidates; [2] sharing in liturgies with the candidates; [3] meeting occasionally with the candidates to reflect on the experience; and [4] sharing with the team a sense of the candidates' experience in the process.

The sponsor's public role begins with the rite of Admission of Catechumens or the rite of Welcoming Baptized Christians to a Community. In these rites, inquirers come before the congregation with their sponsors and commit themselves to a process of formation and study. Sponsors promise to support the inquirers by acting as companions to them, representing the congregation, and to also support them through prayer and example.

> You have been chosen by this community to serve as companions to these persons. Will you support them by prayer and example and help them to grow in the knowledge and love of God?[2]

---

1. *New Wine: New Wineskins,* p. 15.
2. BOS p. 136 or Appendix D, Sec. 2.

The Book of Occasional Services notes that this sponsor "normally accompanies the catechumen through the process of candidacy and serves as sponsor at Holy Baptism."[3] A sponsor attests to a candidate's attendance at worship, diligence in prayer and study during formation, and readiness for the intense formation of the third stage. Sponsors present those being baptized and those reaffirming their baptismal covenant to the bishop.

The sponsor's role is a very serious and significant ministry in the catechumenal process. This ministry is offered on behalf of the congregation for the person being sponsored. The rite of Welcoming says the sponsors "have been chosen by this community"[4] and thereby acknowledge that a sponsor is related both to the candidate and to the congregation. James Dunning describes a sponsor as being a witness in two ways: "witness to the catechumen of what it means to be possessed by the Lord in faith, and witness for the catechumen before
the community."[5] In their witness to the community, sponsors also remind all members of their call to continuing sponsorship.

Although the first public recognition of this role comes in the rites of Admission or Welcoming, the relationship may begin informally when congregation members first invite potential candidates to an introductory or inquiry meeting. Although accompanying them to these initial meetings may have established a meaningful bond, thoughtful appraisal of the relationship by the leadership team, the sponsor, and the candidate is important in building a formal sponsoring relationship.

Upon deciding to enter the second stage of the process, the inquirer, with the leadership team's counsel, considers carefully who is to serve as his or her sponsor. Sponsorship is far more than a ceremonial role. The sponsor has a serious task to fulfill in walking through the rest of the catechumenal process beside

---

3. BOS, p. 113 or Appendix D, Sec. 1.
4. BOS, p. 136, or Appendix D, Sec. 2.
5. *New Wine: New Wineskins*, p. 64.

the candidate, helping the candidate assess his or her readiness for each stage, and attesting before the congregation to the candidate's growth and commitment to a Christian life. The sponsor makes a serious commitment because a sponsor may well be closer to the individual candidate than anyone else in the process.

> The sponsor attends formal sessions. The more important moments, however, are those informal times in conversation on the way home, or in prayer together, or in journeying through times of dying and rising together when in communion they experience the Lord. In those times, the sponsor witnesses to what the Lord means to him/her. In those times, the sponsor helps the catechumen discern what the Lord is doing in his/her life, assists the catechumen to make decisions about membership in the community, and gives public witness to the community in the liturgical rites about what the Lord is doing in the life of the new Christian.[6]

Clearly, a role of this importance deserves careful attention from candidate and congregation, both in recruiting sponsors and providing them with adequate training.

Depending on the number of participants and the congregation's resources, some team members may want to sponsor a candidate. Sponsors may also want to assist in other capacities, such as being a table or small group leader, providing hospitality for meetings, or being a catechist. The sponsor and the team must determine the individual sponsor's level of involvement.

---

6. *New Wine: New Wineskins,* p. 64.

Characteristics of a Helpful Sponsor

According to John Westerhoff's presentation, helpful sponsors:[7]

- Are able to share intimately and to risk vulnerability; are able to tell of their own pain and sorrow
- Believe God is present and active in the lives of all people, not that one "has it" and another does not; rather some have not yet named God's presence and activities in their lives
- Are affirming persons who can see the image of God in every human being
- Are communal persons who do not see themselves as other than part of a community; that is, they are those who save souls for Christ and for the church
- Do not see the world as being split between the physical and the spiritual, between the rational and the instinctive
- Feel good about themselves as:
  first, children of God and members of the human family
  second, members of Christ
  third, members of the Anglican Communion
  fourth, members of a particular congregation
- Cannot be shocked and are willing to know both the violence in themselves and their reliance on God
- Are clear about their convictions and can name them, but do not need to have others accept them
- Have varied experiences in their lives as Christians and can tell stories about these experiences
- Have a love/hate relationship with the church and can be honest about it
- Are caring and hospitable; they can give people what they want rather than what they need, yet can confront others when confrontation is needed

---

7. "Characteristics of a Helpful Sponsor," Evangelism Ministries Office (February 1986).

These characteristics have a great deal more to do with self-knowledge than with "book learning." Sponsors give of themselves and of their time to build relationships with their candidates. They arrange to meet their candidates over coffee or for a walk—in whatever setting a candidate is likely to feel free to raise questions or concerns. Sponsors are storytellers. They are willing to reveal themselves and tell their stories to others. Sponsors are fellow pilgrims. They are ready to listen to another person's story without being judgmental, and to journey with another through joy as well as sorrow. Sponsors are representatives. In knowing themselves to be loved by God in Christ, to be part of Christ's gathered church made up of other human beings, and to have found their identity in that community, they can both *present* and *represent* the congregation and the wider church to those exploring their own identities and relationships.

Recruiting Sponsors

As part of its planning, a leadership team designates persons in the congregation who might sponsor candidates. The team considers a number of factors in choosing sponsors. Some sponsors may have been trained to do evangelization and, by their invitation to an interested person, may have already begun a sponsor-like relationship with that person. This should be made clear in their training. Other participants may already have formed a meaningful companionship with a member of the congregation, making that person an appropriate sponsor. Thus, designating sponsors requires a team to be attentive to the identities of potential candidates.

The leadership team is appropriately cautious about a spouse, a fiance, a dating partner, a parent, or a sibling serving as a sponsor. Confusion between the faith–journey relationship and the family relationship can arise, especially if the latter has some problematic elements.

The responsibilities of this role are made clear to a sponsor when recruited, especially if the sponsor is required specifically by an inquirer. Both candidates and sponsors must be helped to understand the special nature of the sponsor's role, the relationship, and the commitment being requested. One church in the Milwaukee Pilot Project wrote guidelines for sponsors, including standards for their selection and the expectations for their role. A congregation in the diocese of Olympia wrote combined guidelines for sponsors of adults and sponsors of infants and children being baptized.[8] Such guidelines assist sponsors and aid a team in recruiting. (Guidelines for sponsors from a congregation in the Milwaukee Pilot Project are included in Appendix B, Section 3.)

A leadership team must decide when sponsors should begin attending the sessions with candidates. At the latest, sponsors should begin attending sessions after the rites of Admission or Welcoming that begin the second stage of the process. It is also appropriate, however, to recruit sponsors before the inquiry stage and ask them to participate during this stage. Those members of the congregation being trained in inviting people to an introductory or inquiry meeting, might also be urged to attend these meetings with their invitees. A congregation in the Milwaukee Pilot Project included both sponsors and candidates in all meetings held during the Inquiry stage. At the end of this stage, the team used information and observations from all who attended to assign a sponsor to each candidate. Another congregation recruited sponsors during the second stage and discussed their choices with the candidates. In each of these models, the sponsors were an important part of the catechumenal group through most of the process.

As with other ministries related to the catechumenal process, a congregation may commission those persons serving as sponsors. Using the form of Commissioning for Lay Ministries in the church in *The Book of Occasional Services,*[9] this public recognition

---

8. Martha Liska, "A Companion in Christ," *Water and Fire* (Fall 1986), p. 5. These sample guidelines are from St. John's Episcopal Church, Olympia, WA.
9. BOS, pp. 175–191. See the options for the Commissioning of Evangelists (p. 182),

of their ministry can also serve to further remind the congregation of its role as a baptizing and catechumenal community.

Preparing Sponsors

Because sponsorship is so important to the process, sponsors
deserve adequate training and support. Some training comes
from the catechumenal meetings they attend. In sharing the
experience of the process with their candidates, they, too, are
formed by their year with the lectionary. Like the candidates,
sponsors need spiritual direction to support their own Christian
journeys, journeys they are talking about with those they sponsor. Sponsors need to know that they have access to support and
direction from team members and clergy throughout the process.

In addition to support and spiritual direction, the coordinator
of sponsors on the leadership team should offer training for
sponsors [1] to describe the catechumenal process, including its
history, purpose, stages, and rites; [2] to explain the role of
sponsors, including their public role as defined in the rites; [3]
to discuss the "Characteristics of a Helpful Sponsor" as a way
to understand the relationship between a sponsor and a candidate; and [4] to practice techniques of listening and story-sharing to develop necessary skills in those areas. A list of guidelines,
including standards for participation both in catechetical sessions and liturgies, and other expectations, can be reviewed with
sponsors. Participation in training may be one of these standards. If sponsors are to be commissioned, arrangements
should be made for a commissioning service. These elements
could be combined into a one-day workshop for sponsors or
into two or three short meetings.

---

and Other Lay Ministries (p. 190).

14

Catechesis

Tertullian wrote, "Christians are made, not born," and the process by which Christians are made was identified as 'catechesis.' I like [the word] precisely because it is a church word . . . to indicate all intentional learning within a community of Christian faith and life. We are made a Christian at our baptism. We spend the rest of our lives involved in a process of becoming more Christian. That life long process is one of catechesis.

JOHN WESTERHOFF[1]

At the heart of the catechumenal process is an experience of nurture, enculturation, growth, and learning. Whatever one names it, this is an activity of education, of "catechesis." Westerhoff, in reclaiming the term "catechesis," suggests that it consists of three activities: Christian formation, Christian education, and Christian instruction. Christian formation is a process of "experiencing Christian faith and life." Christian education is a process of "reflecting on experience in the light of Christian faith and life." Christian instruction is the process of "acquiring knowledge and skills necessary for and useful to Christian living." (An outline of these three processes, with definition, outcomes, and components of each, is in Appendix C, Section 1.)

Most church teaching programs, whether for adults or children, have emphasized only one portion of one of these processes—the portion of Christian instruction described as "acquiring knowledge." The traditional Inquirers' class has followed this model. The catechumenal process seeks to incor-

---

1. "Formation, Education, Instruction," *Religious Education,* 82, no. 4, (Fall 1987), p. 580.

porate all three aspects of catechesis: formation, education, and instruction.

The catechesis for the second stage, as prescribed in the rites for both catechumens and baptized, calls for this same combination of experience, reflection, and instruction.

Participants are to practice a Christian life of worship and ministry. The people in the formation process are incorporated into a community in which they can practice living as Christians and can turn to others as role models and for support. Formation for ministry includes experience in ministry, especially in service to the poor and neglected and in work for a more just society. Participants are to explore faith and ministry through a pattern of experience followed by reflection. Instruction in the life of prayer and history of salvation shapes and informs both experience and reflection.

A closer examination of Westerhoff's paradigm or model will show that all three elements of formation, education, and instruction have a place in catechesis for the catechumenal process. Differentiating these three types of teaching activities also distinguishes the various methods needed to accomplish the whole task.

Formation: This aspect of catechesis, defined as "experiencing Christian faith and life," refers to learning by being incorporated into a practicing community, encultured by the traditions of that community, and apprenticed by its members. In the catechumenal process, formation takes place as participants worship with the community, develop their personal prayer lives, and practice living according to the Gospel, especially in service to the poor and neglected and in work for a more just society. The church environment and the gathered community both play a part in this formation.

The congregation, the leadership team, and the sponsors all serve as role models—mentors to whom participants are apprenticed as they "observe and imitate ways of Christian living." They are initiated into the community's tradition, that of both the local church and twenty centuries of practicing Christians. Through their apprenticeship to members of a local community, they also discover what it means to be apprenticed to their true mentor and guide, what it means to be a servant of Christ.

Education: Defined as "reflecting on experience in the light of Christian faith and life," this aspect of catechesis is learning through a creative process of criticism and discovery. In the catechumenal process, participants are "to reflect theologically on their experience of ministry through the study of Scripture, in prayer and in worship" and are to spend "substantial periods of time . . . doing ministry and reflecting on it."[2] As participants name and describe their experiences in worship, prayer, and ministry, they can explore them in the light of Scripture, tradition, and reason, and evaluate their consequences. This critical process allows participants to recognize the ways in which they are called to grow and change in their ministries.

Instruction: Defined as "acquiring knowledge and skills considered necessary and useful to Christian life," this final aspect of catechesis is not confined to book learning. Although part of this learning involves becoming knowledgeable in Scripture, tradition, theology, and Christian history, instruction also takes place as persons interpret and reflect on this knowledge. An equally important part of instruction is acquired through doing—that is, by practicing skills for Christian living.

In the catechumenal process, instruction involves studying Scripture, learning about theology, history, customs of worship, and beginning to reflect morally on the implications of this knowledge. It also includes learning basic skills: how to pray; how to take part in community worship; how to discover the theological and ethical issues in one's daily work; how to offer Christian support and guidance in one's home and with one's friends; how to be a minister in the community and for the community in service to others in need; how to discern God's

---

2. BOS, p. 133, or Appendix D, Sec. 2.

work for justice in the local, national, and world community; how to approach leisure time as God's gift; and how to work for change in one's congregation, diocese, and national church.

The formation process or catechesis for each stage varies according to the stated purpose for that stage and the content of the experience/reflection process. In the first stage, participants reflect on the story (their own stories and the Christian story). In the second stage, they reflect on the Christian life (worship, service, prayer, ministry, and community), on Scripture, and on the tradition. In the third stage, they reflect on preparing to be disciples, on practicing the disciplines of the Christian life. In the fourth stage, they reflect on the sacramental life (baptism and Eucharist), on the Paschal Mystery, and how these shape their lives and call, guide, and empower them to and for ministry. In each stage, formation is accomplished through the process of experience followed by reflection. In experiencing the mystery of what Christ has accomplished and is accomplishing for them, Christians are drawn to reflect on the meaning of that experience in their lives.

Planning the Catechetical Formation

The experience of others is a good foundation for planning catechetical formation for the catechumenal process. Resources available from Roman Catholic pastors and catechists using the *Rite of Christian Initiation of Adults* are invaluable here. Both *New Wine: New Wineskins,* by James Dunning, and *A Journey in Faith,* by Raymond Kemp, describe formation models in the framework of the four stages of the process as practiced in Roman Catholic congregations. Although the content must be adapted to accommodate Episcopal tradition, doctrine, interpretation, and polity, these resources present a valuable basic shape for formation and methodology.

In addition, reprints of articles available from the North

American Forum on the Catechumenate, or from the Evangelism Ministries Office at The Episcopal Church Center, will supplement other resources with theory and method for catechumenal formation.[3] There is no substitute for such resources. They break open the traditional inquirers' class model and place formation in the context of a faithful journey in community toward deeper commitment to Christ.

Designing a Plan

As noted in Chapter 5, the first step in planning the catechumenal process is to develop purpose statements for the whole process and for each stage of the process. This involves studying the purpose of each stage and adapting that purpose to the congregation's needs. The purpose and thesis statements [See Appendix B, Section 1] that guided the Milwaukee Pilot Project are an example of a general purpose statement. Working from this, each Milwaukee congregation adapted and restated the purpose statement for each stage to develop an outline of the stages of its own process [see Appendix B, Section 2].

With a purpose established for each stage of the process, a number of approaches might then be used to plan the formation or catechesis to best accomplish that purpose. Because the process is always one of experience followed by reflection, the following three approaches are among the possibilities for organizing and planning the catechetical formation:

3. Among available reprints in photocopied form are the following: James Dunning's "Dynamics of Evangelization in the Catechumenate" (c. 1982); "Words of the Word: Evangelization, Catechesis, and the Catechumenate" (c. 1982); "Method is the Medium is the Message: Catechetical Method in the RCIA" (1982); "The RCIA Journey: From Emmaus to South Carolina to San Antonio," p. 14 (Winona, MN: St. Mary's Press, 1983–84); and Karen M. Hinman, "Catechetical Method: A Model for Sunday Catechumenal Sessions" (1983). Normally, these reprints are part of a set of resources given by the Evangelism Ministries Office of The Episcopal Church Center (815 Second Ave., New York, 10017, 1-800-334-7626 or 1-212-867-8400), to a diocese beginning to develop or already using a catechetical process.

1. Following Westerhoff's model, determine how formation, education, and instruction will be included in each stage.
2. Name what would constitute a "curriculum of experiences" and "a curriculum of knowledge" for each stage and design a plan that balances experience, reflection, and instruction.
3. Name the content called for at each stage, both the experiences and the knowledge, and choose models for reflection appropriate to that content.

Based on one of these models, a session planning document might be prepared that includes the following:[4]

1. Purpose for the stage
2. Resources for leaders to use in designing sessions
3. Proposed session design, or method(s) appropriate to the stage to be used by leaders for planning.

In addition to fulfilling the purpose of each stage and finding appropriate resources and learning methods, planners should attend to several additional concerns. They need to help participants in developing their practice of "life in accordance with the Gospel,"[5] that is, assigning them to apostolic works of social service and justice, and fostering personal devotional practices. Sessions should allow participants to reflect on these practices, as well as on experiences of worship and the catechumenal rites.

The Elements of Catechumenal Formation

In planning catechumenal formation, some general guidelines will help to balance the key elements of the process. James

4. A planning document like this was prepared for the Milwaukee Pilot Project by Rev. A. Wayne Schwab of the Evangelism Ministries Office and is available from The Episcopal Church Center. The document is called "Resources for Planning," (February 1986).
5. BOS, p. 113, or Appendix D, Sec. 1.

Dunning proposes that seven "imperatives" or principles constitute the key elements of the process. These principles are:[6]

1. *Let there be story-telling.* All people have stories to tell, especially those embarking on a journey of faith, conversion, and healing.
2. *Let there be questions.* All people come to the process with questions about the meaning and purpose of life, about God and human beings and how they are related to each other, about the church and the community. Such questions are the windows through which our own stories and questions are connected to the Christian story and to God.
3. *Let there be a community of faith.* Stories and questions are shared in a community of peers—sponsors, congregation members—who share their faith and prayer companions. Further, there is a community of faith that gathers for worship.
4. *Let there be tradition.* Tradition is the story the community has to tell, accounts of personal journeys with God from Abraham and Moses to Bishop Tutu and Mother Theresa. We hand on this tradition first through the lectionary, the great story of our faith, and then through the lives and written records of Christians over the centuries.
5. *Let there be conversion.* At the very center of the process is the story of Jesus, the one who was crucified, died and rose again. The catechumenal process allows space and time for this dying and rising, this transformation so familiar in our lives, to be given new meaning. In Christ, people can share their brokenness and find healing and new life. In Christ they can "risk the conversion process."
6. *Let there be celebration.* The catechumenal process "restores the integral ties between catechesis and liturgy, word and rite." These rites need to be celebrated with lively signs, with colorful sights, and with the smells and sounds of liturgy.

6. Dunning, "Dynamics of Evangelization in the Catechumenate," pp. 7–8.

7. *Let there be mission.* "At rock bottom, the Catechumenate journey is the Church's way of forming people for mission." The
Great Commission is acted out in the lives of candidates as
they dare to journey to the font; but it is also lived out as they
begin their own ministries of service in Christ's name.

Resources for Planning Catechesis

The following is a brief review of the formation process for
each stage and of the resources for designing catechumenal
sessions. This is not an exhaustive list. It does not set forth
"curriculum" one must follow in the catechumenal process.
Rather, it provides planning guidelines and resources to be
mined for further ideas. As has been emphasized throughout
this resource, flexibility and attention to the unique needs of
participants remain key factors for planning all aspects of the
process—including catechesis! Appendices B and C offer a sample of planning resources, methods for Bible study and for small
group reflection, lesson plans, and a description of the formation process as currently practiced in some congregations. Resources included here are chosen primarily for the methodology
they present, rather than for their content. Additional resources,
especially on the Episcopal Church and the Anglican tradition,
are in the bibliography. Catechists should consult these resources, both for planning and for their own continued study.

The general outline of the process from congregations in the
Milwaukee Pilot Project (Appendix B, Section 2), some session
plans from these congregations (Appendix C, Section 7), and
the outline of weekly meetings and description of the process at
St. James', Jackson, Mississippi (Appendix C, Section 6), may be
helpful in considering the process as a whole and the stages in
relation to one another.

During orientation sessions in Milwaukee, congregational
teams preparing for the catechumenal process used the following analysis of learning in considering planning. In any learning

situation, a combination of three modes, or ways of learning, all of which are important, must be balanced:

Attitude: In this phase, we consider the positions the person holds about any given subject or idea. This is an area that touches on emotions, and can include such elements as prejudice, ways of doing certain bits of work, politics, confidence in our own ability, and so forth. A person usually holds a given position or attitude because, for whatever reason, no other choices seem open.

Teacher Goal: Exploration and experimentation are called for. The hope is that the learner will discover new options, more options, and more attractive options than those usually held.

Knowledge: The world's body of knowledge is comprised of all the things that people have experienced, developed, learned, and discovered.

Teacher Goal: To convey the right information and the right amount of information to the student, in the most effective way possible. Lectures, videos, demonstrations, readings, and dialogue are ways of doing this.

Experience: We learn to read, write, paint, swim, ride a bicycle, for instance, by doing these activities, under the supervision of skilled people.

Teacher Goal: To teach students how to practice a given skill so that they may continue to practice it on their own in the absence of the teacher.

None of these ways of learning constitutes a "method." The emphasis may be on a particular way in any given learning time, but the other ways will always be present. For example, when learning to ride a bicycle, one's attitude about riding will change, and one will collect knowledge about riding, even though the principal effort will be in pedaling and steering.

A teacher can be aware of the ways or modes of learning and use them to achieve the best possible learning environment. The balance may shift in any session as the participants move through the process.

Various approaches to planning and evaluating are available. Congregational catechumenal teams are encouraged to find the one that works best for them. [See Appendix C, Section 12, for one such approach.]

Stage 1: Pre-Catechumenate and Inquiry

The primary ingredients in catechesis at this stage are story-telling, Bible study, and questioning. Dunning describes the storytelling as follows:

> I suggest that the period of the *catechumenate* is the time to ponder in depth on *past Tradition,* the living faith of dead people. To help the inquirer decide whether or not to join a Church of fellow travelers, the *pre-catechumenate* might expose inquirers to *living people* and their experiences of dying and rising. . . . The question continues to be "Do the stories of these fellow travelers bring meaning to my experiences of death and life, so much so that I want to join their company?"[7]

These individual stories, the stories of the inquirers and the stories of team members, are held up to the light of the Christian story or Gospel, which is offered early in this period. The community has a story to tell of the history and common life of its members. Inquirers bring questions and try to find meaning for their lives. They are invited to determine whether or not to make their religious pilgrimage in fellowship with this community.

---

7. *New Wine: New Wineskins* p. 51.

General Resources:

- Michael Merriman, ed., *The Baptismal Mystery and the Catechumenate* (New York: The Church Hymnal Corporation).
- James B. Dunning, *New Wine: New Wineskins,* pp. 39–54.
- James B. Dunning, *The Dynamics of Evangelization in the Catechumenate* and "Words of the Word: Evangelization, Catechesis, and the Catechumenate" (North American Forum on the Catechumenate).
- Raymond B. Kemp, *A Journey in Faith,* pp. 31–63.
- Ron Lewinski, *Welcoming the New Catholic* (Chicago: Liturgy Training Publications).
- Anne Rowthorn, *The Liberation of the Laity* (Wilton CT: Morehouse-Barlow).
- Louis Weil, *Christian Initiation and Ministry* (Evangelism Ministries, The Episcopal Church Center, 815 Second Avenue, NY, NY 10017 (800) 334-7626).

Resources for Session Planning:

- "Sharing Our Spiritual Journey," Appendix C, Section 4.
- "Choosing To Be Christian Ministers" (Evangelism Ministries Office, The Episcopal Church Center).
- Ann E.P. McElligott, from *Faith Development and Evangelism:* "The Unfolding Tapestry of My Life: A Reflection Exercise" in the *Participant's Handbook,* pp. 3–5; and Session Two of *The Leader's Guide,* pp. 21–24, has an exercise for story-sharing using James Fowler's model for doing a faith interview. (Parish Services, The Episcopal Church Center.)
- Gail C. Jones, *Seeking Life in Christ* (Resource Center, Diocese of Olympia).
- *Do This for the Remembrance of Me,* a film/video of a Sunday Eucharist and its participants (Communication Unit, The Episcopal Church Center).

- Arlin J. Rothauge, *Reshaping a Congregation for a New Future* (Congregational Development, The Episcopal Church Center). Helps participants to understand the impact of the community, the life cycle, and the size of the congregation on the congregation's way of doing things and on some of the issues it faces.

Resources for Bible Study:

- "Methods for Bible Study and Reflection," Appendix C, Section 2. The African Model for Bible Study is offered in two forms in Appendix C: *An African Model for Bible Study,* and a more detailed description of the model as practiced in RCIA, *African Model.*
- Adult Lectionary Curriculum available from Living the Good News, P.O. Box 18345, Denver, CO 80218, 1-800-824-1813. Published quarterly.
- "Catechetical Methods for Sunday Morning Sessions," Appendix C, Section 3.
- *In Dialogue: An Episcopal Guide for Adult Bible Study,* Joseph P. Russell and John D. Vogelsang (The Episcopal Church Center).

Resources in Anglicanism:

- "An Outline of Faith," *The Book of Common Prayer.*
- John Booty, "The Drama of Anglicanism" (Forward Movement).
- Arlin J. Rothauge, *Catechism: The Outline of the Faith We Profess* (Evangelism Ministries Office).
- Beverly D. Tucker and William H. Swatos Jr., *Questions on the Way: A Catechism Based on the Book of Common Prayer* (Forward Movement).

Stage 2: Catechumenate and Deeper Exploration

The second stage of formation is generally the longest. During this stage the basic text is Scripture, the Christian story as it unfolds through the church year in the weekly lectionary. Formation takes place as participants [1] join the worshiping community; [2] seek to live according to the Gospel through a ministry of social service and social justice; [3] discover how being Christian shapes who they are in all facets of their daily lives; and [4] develop a practice of personal prayer and devotion.

Some congregations may begin a process of naming one's gifts for ministry. Other congregations may also begin to explore stewardship of money. They reflect on stories of these experiences in light of Scripture, theology, and tradition. Different models for studying Scripture and for doing critical reflection are valuable. Resources that present theology, church history, worship, or approaches to Bible study should inform leaders as they augment group discussion, especially as leaders respond to the issues raised by participants' experiences or by the weekly lectionary. Attending to all aspects of learning—formation, education, and instruction—will balance the learning experience.

The time of catechetical sessions shapes their design. One decision a team needs to make is whether the participants are to stay through the Sunday liturgy or are to be dismissed with a blessing after the Liturgy of the Word and the homily. Models for breaking open the Word are included among the Bible study resources and are particularly appropriate when Sunday dismissal is practiced. Most congregations probably include participants throughout the Sunday liturgy. Although Bible study will not immediately follow the Liturgy of the Word, it will still make its impact. Sessions held on Sundays will probably use the day's lessons. Sessions held from Monday on may use lessons for the coming Sunday.

General Resources:

- Conrad Boerma, *The Rich, the Poor and the Bible* (Westminster Press).
- James B. Dunning, *New Wine: New Wineskins: Pastoral Implications of the Rite of Christian Initiation of Adults,* 1981 pp. 55–73.
- Raymond B. Kemp, *A Journey in Faith: An Experience of the Catechumentate,* 1979 pp. 65–120.
- Ron Lewinski, *A Guide for Sponsors* (Chicago: Liturgy Training Publications).

Resources from the North American Forum on the Catechumenate:

- James B. Dunning, "Method in Religious Education and Ministry"; "Method is the Medium is the Message: Catechetical Method in the RCIA"; "What Happens After 'Christ Among Us?' "
- Karen Hinman, "Cathechetical Method: A Model for Sunday Catechumenate Sessions."

Resources from the Evangelism Ministries Office:

- Charles Kiblinger, "The Process of the Catechumenate at St. James' Church, Jackson, Mississippi."
- Ann E. P. McElligott, *Evangelism with the Poor; Faith Development and Evangelism.*
- Jerry Ryle, "The Catechumenate in Story and Experience: A Roman Catholic Setting."
- A. Wayne Schwab, *Handbook for Evangelism,* Rev. ed. pp. 22–27.
- A. Wayne Schwab and William A. Yon, *Proclamation as Offering Story and Choice.*

Resources for Session Planning:

- Thomas H. Groome, *Christian Religious Education* (Harper & Row).
- Gail C. Jones, *Seeking Life in Christ* (Resource Center, Diocese of Olympia).
- Frederick Wolf, *Journey in Faith* (Morehouse-Barlow).
- "Methods for Bible Study and Reflection," Appendix C, Sec. 2.
- "Methods for Sunday Morning Catechetical Sessions," Appendix C, Sec. 3.
- "Methods for Story-Sharing," Appendix C, Sec. 4.
- "Methods for Critical Reflection," Appendix C, Sec. 5.
- "Session Plans: Jackson, Mississippi," Appendix C, Sec. 6.
- "Session Plans: Milwaukee Pilot Project," Appendix C, Sec. 7.

Resources on Bible Study:

[See suggested resources for Stage 1.]

- Kenneth Bailey, *Jesus, the Theologian; New Testament Themes; Jesus Interprets His Own Cross; A Clear View of Jesus' Birth; Inauguration;* and *Inspiration in the Bible;* Harvest Communications, 900 George Washington Blvd., Wichita, KS 67211, 316-652-9900. Videotapes.
- Raymond E. Brown, *The Churches the Apostles Left Behind* (New York: Paulist Press).
- Lyman Coleman, *The Serendipity Bible Study Book* (Zondervan).
- Verna Dozier, *Equipping the Saints* (Alban Institute).
- Karen M. Hinman and Joseph P. Sinwell, Cycles A, B and C, *Breaking Open the Word of God* (New York: Paulist Press).
- Eugene LeVerdiere, *The Infancy Narratives* (National Catholic

Reporter Publishing Co., Box 281 Kansas City, MO 64141).
Audio cassettes.

* *The Prayerbook Guide to Christian Education* (Morehouse-Barlow).
* *Proclamation 3 and 4: Series A, B and C* (Philadelphia: Fortress Press).
* Joseph P. Russell, *Sharing Our Biblical Story* (Winston Press).
* Minka Shura Sprague, *One To Watch, One To Pray: A Devotional Introduction to the Gospels* (Morehouse-Barlow).
* Hans-Reudi Weber, *Experiments With Bible Study* (Geneva: World Council of Churches).
* Walter Wink, *Transforming Bible Study* (Abingdon Press).

Resources on Anglicanism:

[See suggested resources for Stage 1 and additional resources listed in the bibliography.]

* The Church's Teaching Series (The Seabury Press). This seven-volume set includes study guides. Especially valuable are:
    Price and Weil, *Liturgy for Living*
    Norris, *Understanding the Faith of the Church*
    Bennett and Edwards, *The Bible for Today's Church*
* Verna Dozier, "What Anglicans Believe." Videotape.

Resources for Prayer and Spirituality:

* Elizabeth Canham, *Praying the Bible* (Cowley Publications).
* Tilden Edwards, *Spiritual Friend: Reclaiming the Gift of Spiritual Direction* (Paulist Press).
* James C. Fenhagen, *More Than Wanderers: Spiritual Discipline for Christian Ministry* (The Seabury Press).
* Louis Weil, *Gathered to Pray: Understanding Liturgical Prayer* (Cowley Publications).

Resources on Proportionate Giving:

- *In God's Image,* twelve sessions on stewardship, Department of Stewardship, Diocese of Atlanta 2744 Peachtree Road, N.W., Atlanta, GA 30363.
- Terence Kelshaw, *Three Streams, One River: A Biblical Understanding of Stewardship;* and Terence McCabe, *A Leader's Manual,* Office of Stewardship Development, The Episcopal Church Center.
- Ronald Reed, *The Steward's Count: A Theological Essay on Stewardship,* Office of Stewardship Development, The Episcopal Church Center.

Stage 3: Candidacy and Immediate Preparation

The third stage, intensive preparation for the rites of initiation, is shaped by the Lenten season and by the rites associated with preparation for initiation. The rites for the baptized on Ash Wednesday and Maundy Thursday and the enrollment of candidates for baptism on the First Sunday of Lent are visible symbols of their preparation to all members of the congregation. Candidates for baptism are also visible as they present themselves with their sponsors for special prayer and blessings on the Third, Fourth, and Fifth Sundays of Lent. The baptized can be prayed for by name as part of the Prayers for the Church.

In preparation for baptism, candidates may want to reflect on the renunciation and the vows they will be asked to make at that rite. A pre-baptismal retreat may also be planned.

The lectionary continues to be the primary text, especially the readings appointed for Year A of the three-year lectionary. Candidates are drawn to reflect on the symbols that will be visible at the Easter celebration of the Paschal Mystery—symbols of light and sight, water and rebirth, death and life.

The disciplines of spirituality and ministry that have been

fostered in candidates during the preceding stages continue to be the source of reflection during this period. Now, however, the reflection is done in the shadow of the cross, in a period of intense preparation and self-control. Methods for Bible study, theological reflection, and story-sharing continue to be resources for this stage.

General Resources:

• James B. Dunning, *New Wine: New Wineskins,* pp. 75–88.
• Raymond B. Kemp, *A Journey in Faith,* pp. 122–156.

Resources from the Evangelism Ministries Office:

• Kathryn M. Cayler, "Living Out Our Baptismal Vows."

Resources for Session Planning and Bible Study:

[See suggestions from Stage 1 and Stage 2]

• Catechumenate Retreat Schedule, Appendix C, Sec. 7. *From Ashes to Easter,* (the Liturgical Conference)

Resources on Liturgy:

• *The Book of Occasional Services,* Second Edition, The Church Hymnal Corporation.
• *Celebrating Redemption—the Liturgies of Lent, Holy Week and the Great Fifty Days.* Associated Parishes.
• *The Great Vigil of Easter: A Commentary,* Associated Parishes.

Stage 4: Sacramental Living

The final stage of Sacramental living—mystagogia, or study of the mysteries as noted on pp. 73–75—is shaped by the lectionary of the Easter Season. The emphasis is on examining and understanding the symbols of Easter and preparing those people who were baptized and who reaffirmed their baptismal vows for their mission in the world. This is the time for sacramental catechesis. The sacraments are studied in light of the Paschal, or Easter, Mystery, as being shaped by the central Christian pattern of dying and rising. Baptism and Eucharist, the pastoral offices, all the sacraments are given meaning in that central Easter image.

> The period of mystagogia is jammed with this kind of liturgy-catechesis. Let the symbols speak, and then reflect together on their response . . . [S]ome sacramental catechesis will have to be done during the catechumenate. But for most sacramental reflection, we would wait until the neophytes at Easter and paschal time are surrounded with water, burning candle, white garment, oil, bread and wine, alleluia, and a risen people.[8]

This final stage, this time leading to Pentecost and, perhaps, into the fall, is also a time for further exploring how sharing in the sacraments is connected with the ministry to which each person is called. Throughout the process, participants have reflected on their ministries in the world and developed their skills for Christian service and pursuit of justice in and on behalf of the congregation. They have learned how to find support for those ministries with others committed to discipleship. Rooted in this experience and reflection, and born anew in their Easter faith, they can further discern the shape of their ministries.

> Once celebrated, Easter is a gift that has to be given . . . We do what we do because of Easter. And because of Easter we

---

8. *New Wine: New Wineskins,* p. 97.

encourage one another to keep doing for the sake of the new creation.[9]

Bible reflection on the lectionary, story-sharing, and group reflection continue during this stage. In addition, models for discerning or identifying gifts for ministry are valuable resources if they have not already been used in the second stage.

The end of this fourth stage can be a severe letdown for all the participants. They have been richly sustained by their weekly gatherings. They need a bridge to ongoing small group life of some kind. Some will find this need met in a task group such as a choir, a committee, or work with an educational program. Others will prefer a small face-to-face group that meets regularly for Bible reflection, supportive discussion, and prayer concerning ministries in their daily places. The catechumenal team is wise to continue its guidance for the participants until they are a part of the ongoing small group which reflects their interests and needs.

General Resources:

- James B. Dunning, *New Wine: New Wineskins,* pp. 89–99.
- Raymond B. Kemp, *A Journey in Faith,* pp. 157–167.
- Mahaffey, "The Identification of Gifts for Ministry."

Resources from the Evangelism Ministries Office:

- Anne Harrison, "Giftedness Conference."
- George Plattenburg and Sherrill Akyol, "A Workshop for Discerning and Empowering Our Gifts for Ministry."
- Evangelism Ministries Office "Six Weekly Sessions in Ministry Formation."

---

9. Kemp, *A Journey in Faith: An Experience of the Catechumenate.*

Resources on Ministry Development:

- James Dunning, *Ministries: Sharing God's Gifts* (St. Mary's Press).
- V. N. Goetchius and Charles P. Price, *The Gifts of God* (Wilton, CT: Morehouse-Barlow).
- Nelvin Vos, *Seven Days a Week: Faith in Action* (Fortress Press).
- "Windows on Gifts: A Review of Ten Resource Materials," researched by Jean Haldane (Ministry Development Office, The Episcopal Church Center).

Resources on the Sacraments:

- Michael W. Merriman, "The Liturgy in the Easter Season," *Open.*
- Leonel L. Mitchell, *Praying Shapes Believing: A Theological Commentary on the Book of Common Prayer* (Morehouse–Barlow).
- Price and Weil, *Liturgy for Living* (The Seabury Press).

Resources for Small Groups:

- "Building Community Through Small Groups," Dr. Roberta Hestenes, Media Services, Fuller Theological Seminary, Pasadena, CA 91182. Videotape.
- "Conference on Growing the Church Through Small Groups," offered twice a year by the Berry Institute, Fuller Theological Seminary, Pasadena, CA 91182, (800) 235-2222 Ext. 5315.
- Neighborhood Bible Studies Inc.; Small group study guides; Box 222, Dobbs Ferry, NY 10522.
- *Powerhouse of Prayer,* workshop leading to small prayer groups, Anglican Fellowship of Prayer, P.O. Box M, Winter Park, FL 32790, (407) 628-4330.

• Serendipity House; Current catalogue. Box 1012, Littleton, CO 80160 (800) 525-9563.

An observation by the Reverend Walter L. Guettsche of Emmanuel Church, Houston, Texas, closes this chapter on catechesis and planning. He distinguishes "pastoral" from "program" catechesis. Pastoral catechesis centers on the life journeys of participants. Caring, compassion, and focus on the journeys of the participants characterize the catechesis. The catechesis looks different each year or each time the participants change. Program catechesis occurs by default when the catechists become accustomed to the security of the notebook of lesson plans or when the content and structure become the dominant priority.

15

Leadership Development for the Catechumenal Process

Well-trained leaders are needed for the catechumenal process, both in dioceses and in congregations. When recruiting leadership teams, dioceses and congregations should search for people who have an outgoing nature and who want to work as leaders in a group process for learning in which skills are acquired and developed. People with these skills are especially valuable if they have themselves been through the catechumenal process. Keeping in mind that by being inclusive it is possible to raise up the gifts of all people, it is also important to find people who are committed to the vision and the work of the catechumenal process. Growth and good learning take time. Leaders need to know before they begin how much will be required of them.

Ideally, a diocese developing the catechumenal process in its congregations will start with a team of at least six persons to consult with and train leaders for congregations. When those people with the necessary gifts and commitment have been identified and the team has been formed, the team members will, on a permanent basis, need further preparation for their roles.

The Episcopal Church Center offers orientation and training for diocesan teams on a partnership basis. The bishop has a key role in the diocese's catechumenal process and will be involved in the contract for training and consulting, as well as in the training itself. A diocese sponsors workshops to prepare a diocesan leadership team. Workshop trainers, consultants, and team consultations can all be arranged through the Evangelism Ministries Office. The actual format and goals are adapted to the needs and capacities of the diocese. The cost of the training and consultation is shared and varies with the need.

Orientation for a diocesan team includes two major areas of work. Team members read *The Catechumenal Process* in preparation for the orientation session. The first major area introduced by the consultant is a discussion of the major issues that a diocese and a congregation face in establishing an effective catechumenal process. These issues include experiential education, enabling participants to move at their own pace, team-building for the leaders, provision for experience in service and justice ministries, focus on Christian living in one's daily places, and discerning growth in Christian living and attitudes. The other major area for orientation is working out a time chart of what steps need to be taken to result in both baptized and reaffirmed adults who live out their lives as conscious agents of God's reign in Jesus Christ. Appendix B, Section 4 is the time chart developed for the Milwaukee pilot.

Training for a diocesan team is built on a process of modeling. The members of the diocesan team are trained with the same training format they will use with congregational teams. In addition, they are taught basics of training design that allow them to be flexible in designing events for congregations. After the diocesan pilot is under way, team members are offered an additional consulting workshop to help them work with congregational leadership teams on an ongoing basis.

The national training team will continue to consult and to coach a diocesan leadership team as long as necessary. The initial workshop for training a diocesan team usually lasts for five days and includes six basic elements: learning theory, group process awareness, team building, training skills, design skills, and catechumenal process overview.

The following sections outline the decisions made by trainers in designing a diocesan training event. This process, and the planning decisions that were made, would be duplicated by a diocesan team when designing a workshop for congregational teams.

Planning Issues

The first step in planning is determining workshop attendance and the conditions under which the work will be done. The following are among the issues to be considered:

1. How many members will attend? This determines how many staff members are needed and how experienced they need to be.
2. Can the workshop be held in a residential setting in which all participants can stay without going home at night?
3. How much time can be expected of both participants and staff? Is it enough to accomplish the workshop purpose and goals?
4. How much time does the staff need to learn to work together to prepare and rehearse each session and to set purpose statements? Is this adequate time for the staff to be well prepared and ready for the workshop?
5. How committed are both leaders and participants? Commitment is important both for those attending a workshop and for those who staff it. The work is demanding and time consuming.
6. What supplies and resources are needed? Are all supplies on hand and ready to use? Can we print materials for distribution to those who attend?

Group Standards

Another important issue the team must address when it begins planning is the group standards by which the staff members operate. Such standards facilitate planning and leading the workshop. Standards might include:

We are present, full time, for every staff meeting.

We take time to make decisions about what we want to accomplish and put them in the form of purpose statements before we begin any other kind of work.

We take turns at various group maintenance tasks: convening meetings, checking for feelings, writing on newsprint-size paper, preparing presentations, making presentations, etc.

When we have written a presentation, we discuss it with the rest of the staff and make needed revisions before presenting it in a workshop. All staff members attend presentations to offer support and give feedback.

We assess the response to the training event as it unfolds by keeping in touch with the reactions and feelings of the participants. We are ready to alter the format to meet emerging needs or conflicts. To do so, we meet regularly throughout the training event.

We collect information from participants as we go, to help improve the design for the future.

Components of the Workshop

When the team knows the group for whom it is planning and has established standards for its work, it can decide what to include in the workshop. A workshop for a diocesan team would include the following components as learning exercises of models a team might use in congregations:

Spiritual History or Story-Sharing: This valuable process can be used in many ways. It will help to build trust, build the team, encourage openness and involvement, foster understanding and appreciation of the group experience, and more.

Overview of the Catechumenal Process: This introduction discusses the history and theology of the process, its stages, the rationale for using it today, ways in which it can be adapted to the church's current needs, and ways of determining where participants are in their journeys.

Bible Study: This presents creative and interesting models for using Scripture in the learning process.

Theory of Learning: This includes discussion of environments that foster the most effective learning; how to help others to grow in knowing their own spirituality; and how best to use available time and resources for learning.

Liturgy: The catechumenal process involves a number of liturgical rites, rooted in early church practice. Participants will study, experience, and reflect on contemporary adaptations of these rites, as well as consider how to prepare others for these liturgies. There will also be discussion of the nature of liturgy itself and its role in shaping and expressing the experience of the participants in a catechumenal process.

Leadership: This includes discussion of various individual styles of leadership (authoritarian, shared, etc.), the functions needed for efficient group leadership, and the ways in which leaders can adapt to the needs of the individual and the performance of a task.[1] It also includes a summary of the roles or functions needed [See Chapters 4 and 5].

Standards: The model of the workshop itself will clarify the importance of working standards for a training staff. Other standards will also be considered: for example, any educational event will work better if attention is given to preparation and

---

1. "Leadership Style and the Catechumenal Process," presentation by L. E. May, IV, Evangelism Ministries Office, Episcopal Church Center, 815 Second Avenue, New York City, NY, 10017, 800-334-7626, 1987.

rehearsal details; when the staff members support each other; and when time limits are carefully set and maintained. Any skill practice sessions should allow enough time for practice, feedback, more practice, and identifying learnings.

Setting a Purpose and Planning: The key to successful planning is allowing enough time to work out and agree on its purpose. A purpose statement tells potential learners what they can expect if they participate. The statement expresses for the staff, "This is what we hope to have happen." Gathering and carefully analyzing information helps the staff formulate their purpose. Plans work well when the staff understands its purpose. Evaluation is also based on the purpose and asks, "Did it happen the way we wanted? If not, why not? If yes, what made it work?"

Simulation: This is an important skill and is, in some way, included in every practice session. Practice with forms of simulation will show how they work.

As noted earlier, the team adapts the general approach to a form suitable for the diocese.

Schedule and Assignment of Roles:

The final task is planning the daily schedule (including adequate time for breaks, meals, and recreation) and assigning team members to leadership roles for each segment. The assigned leader is responsible for knowing that segment's content and design, and for having the necessary supplies.

The following is a working schedule for the opening and first day of a diocesan workshop.

A Sample of a Diocesan Workshop

This workshop is designed for the mid-sized diocese. The diocesan leadership team has seven members, including six lay-people—three men, three women—and one priest. All are appointed by the bishop. The team members and the bishop attend the workshop. The workshop lasts from Sunday evening to Friday noon. All participants stay at a diocesan conference center. The bishop participates in the entire workshop. The staff consists of two trainers, Peter and Mary.

SUNDAY

4:00 PM - Registration.
6:00 PM - Supper.
7:00 PM - Opening Session. Led by Mary.

Welcome and information about the workshop. Ask everyone to tell who they are, where they are from, and their expectations of this workshop.

Introduce an exercise for sharing spiritual journeys; allow each person twenty minutes to share his/her story. All, including the trainers, will share their stories. Sharing will continue during the morning session.

8:00 PM - Story-sharing session with whole group. Share stories from three persons, beginning with one of the trainers to model the process.
9:00 PM - Compline. Read by participants.
9:15 PM - Social hour.

MONDAY

8:00 AM - Breakfast.
9:00 AM - Session. Continue story-sharing in small groups of eight.
10:30 AM - Break.

10:45 AM - Session. Complete story-sharing
11:45 AM - Theory and discussion for a demonstration liturgy this evening; have them rehearse with Mary after lunch.
12:30 PM - Lunch.
 2:00 PM - Session. Led by Peter.
           Introduce Bible study.
 2:10 PM - Introduce the African model for Bible study. Break into small groups—groups of four.
 2:20 PM - Small groups.
 3:15 PM - Break.
 3:30 PM - Session. Share learnings from Bible study exercise with whole group.
 4:00 PM - Session. Present and discuss a "Theory of the Learning Process," how we learn.
 5:00 PM - Free time.
 6:00 PM - Supper.
 7:00 PM - Liturgy—The rite of Welcoming Baptized Christians into a Community. Led by Mary.
 8:00 PM - Share reactions to the rite; make presentation about all the rites of the catechumenal process.
 9:00 PM - Social time.

(The format continues with the essential elements for training the particular team in the time available.)

Congregational Training by a Diocesan Team

When a diocesan leadership team leads a training event for teams working with congregations, it uses the same set of goals and the same model it used in the nationally sponsored training. The team members should keep the same standards and address the same planning considerations as the team that trained them. The congregational teams will probably need more time than the diocesan team to react to and assimilate what is being offered and to initially plan the process for their congregations. Time for this work can be offered each day.

Time and commitment will be the most common challenges that the team will address. In many congregations, people are not used to giving the large blocks of time required to provide the high educational quality demanded by this process. When designing training events, the team may have to settle for the longest period of time they can negotiate and ask participants to be present for the whole event.

A training event must have five days to allow enough time for all parts of the training. A five-day workshop, from Sunday evening to Friday noon, provides the following blocks of working time:

	Morning	*Afternoon*	*Evening*
Sunday	—	—	2
Monday	3	3	2
Tuesday	3	3	2
Wednesday	3	3	free
Thursday	3	3	2
Friday	3	—	—

This design includes eight three-hour blocks of time between Monday and Thursday; these periods are the most productive. Evenings are shorter and call for less energetic work. Sunday is devoted to getting settled and making introductions. One night off is needed. Friday morning is for winding up last details. During the first hour, teams assess what needs to be done when they return home. Consultation with the diocesan liaison, as plans are developed, is scheduled, and specific appointments are made. An overview of the team's work through the completion of the first full cycle helps in this assessment [See Appendix B, Section 5, "Planning Outline for Congregations . . ."]. The last two hours, a brief retreat with meditation, silence, and the Eucharist, lifts up the spiritual dimensions of the event.

Although continuous training provides for better attendance and continuity of design, training can be adapted to time constraints. If shorter periods of training are offered, solid blocks of time should be included. All participants should be committed to attend all parts of the training.

APPENDIX A

Supplementary Resources

Sections

Section 1

Encounter with and Response to the Gospel

Conversion is encounter with the Gospel and response to it. The variety of encounter and response is wide. The following examples illustrate this variety.

One form, *confrontation,* is described by Robert Brooks, an Episcopal priest and liturgist, as having three stages.[1] The first is *separation,* a shattering feeling that one's world has disintegrated, rendering as worthless everything that was meaningful in the past. The second stage, called the *liminal* or in-between stage, is marked by disorientation and disillusionment, restlessness and insecurity, and an intense desire for something that remains distant and unknown. The third stage is marked by *transformation:* disorientation is replaced by assurance, and disillusionment by acceptance; and restlessness becomes a journey. One experiences rebirth and finds new life and renewed purpose. In this new life, one recovers hope and begins to rebuild a world of meaning. This phenomenon of separation, disillusionment, and renewal, of death, burial, and resurrection, lies at the heart of human experience and at the heart of the Christian experience. Christ endured all this in his crucifixion, death, and resurrection. We, too, endure it when we are plunged into the water of baptism and raised to new life in Christ. Baptism, and the promises we make in our baptismal vows, form the heart of the transformation and conversion of the catechumenal process.

The encounter in *confrontation* sometimes awaits those in

---

[1] Robert J. Brooks, "Imaging the Story of Jesus Through Baptism," *The Christian Ministry* (July 1987), pp. 5–10.

search of the meaning of human existence. People are shaken to their roots when they discover that the meanings they have lived by are too weak to sustain them in crisis. Further, confrontation is often the experience of those encountering Jesus' call to befriend the poor and the outcast, to understand how the social order contributes to their lot in life, and to correct injustice in the society.

Another form of encounter with the Gospel is *acceptance.* Those people who carry heavy burdens of guilt suddenly find the accepting, forgiving arms of God's love for us in Jesus Christ. Sometimes the guilt is real. Sometimes the guilt has been imposed by others. Sorting out which is which will occupy these persons' Christian journeys for some time. Nevertheless, encounter with the accepting, empowering love of God in Jesus Christ will have turned their lives around and set them on a new path.

Affirmation is still another form of encounter with the Gospel. Those who rejoice in the goodness of human life—the ability to love, to create, to reason, and to work for a more just society—find that these gifts are God's work in them. What these people value and hope for proves to be rooted in the ultimate reality, God. This discovery occurs in their encounter with Jesus Christ. In him, the order, harmony, love, and justice that we all sense instinctively to be the core of the universe take on flesh, and nurture and lead us.

Empowerment is often the experience of the oppressed and the outcast when they encounter the Good News of Jesus Christ. They find in him one who knows their lot from inside and who gives them power to mobilize themselves to secure the justice they deserve. And the story is often the same for the searchers, those who look for meanings in the world and have seen through the pretensions of limited human systems. These people find in the Gospel the "pearl of great price" that lends value to and makes sense of all the rest of life.

All forms of *encounter* are caught up in the energy of humanity's encounter with God. What is valuable in the catechumenal process is that it is long enough and broad enough for all forms of encounter to occur. Its length and breadth open each of us to the richness of the encounter God desires with everyone. The clue to the length and breadth of the catechumenal process lies in the nature of the Christian community offering it. The local congregation, no matter how small, has enough Christian variety in it both to sound the fullness of the Christian call to ministry in God's reign and to provide the support needed by people being formed in the Christian way.

Section 2

The Catechumenate
or
The Preparation of Adults
for Holy Baptism

Purpose: To train and instruct adults in Christian understandings about God, human relationships and the meaning of life in preparation for Holy Baptism

Stage	*Rite*
1. The pre-Catechumenal Period	
Inquirers determine they wish to become Christians and begin their response to the Gospel	Admission of Catechumens Signing with the Cross
2. The Catechumenate	
Participation in corporate worship, the life of prayer, scriptual study, small group life, service to the poor and neglected, and work for a more just society	

Stage   *Rite*

bear fruit as participants grow in Christ

Enrollment of Candidates for Baptism
Sign the Congregation's Register for Baptism

3. Candidacy for Baptism

Public prayer by the congregation and private disciplines of fasting, examination of conscience and prayer

Holy Baptism
Water, dying and rising with Christ

4. Experience the fullness of church life and ministry in the world and gain deeper understanding of the sacraments (mystagogia)

The rites are discussed fully in Chapter 11.

Section 3

The Preparation of Baptized Persons for Reaffirmation of the Baptismal Covenant

Purpose: To prepare mature baptized persons to reaffirm their baptismal covenant and receive the laying on of hands by the bishop; to offer already confirmed persons a time of disciplined renewal; and to incorporate those who are entering a new congregation.

Stage   *Rite*

1. Inquiry

    Story and information sharing so that participants can determine they desire mature formation

                                          The Welcoming of Baptized Christians into a Community

                                          Sign the parish register

2. Deeper Exploration of Faith and Ministry

    Candidates explore the baptismal covenant, biblical reflection,

Stage	*Rite*
corporate worship, the life of prayer and ministry as they grow in Christ	The Calling of the Baptized to Continuing Conversion
	Receive and help impose ashes
3. Immediate Preparation for Reaffirmation	
Candidates explore the Lenten disciplines and their role in ministry to others and share their ongoing experience of conversion	Maundy Thursday Rite for Baptized Persons in Preparation for the Paschal Holy Days
	Candidates receive and share in foot–washing
4. Candidates reaffirm their baptismal covenant at the Easter vigil.	
Presentation of the Candidates to the bishop for the Laying on of Hands, Reception or Commitment to Christian Service during the Great Fifty Days of Easter. They join those just baptized in the post-baptismal instruction.	

Section 4

The Catechumenal Process and Its Liturgies Diocese of Milwaukee

Rites for the Unbaptized	*Stages*	*Rites for the Baptized*
	GATHERING	
	INQUIRY	
Admission of Catechumens —signing with the cross		Welcoming of Baptized Persons to a Community —sign register
	FORMATION IN CHRIST	
Lent I Enrollment of Candidates for Baptism Sign register for baptism		Ash Wednesday Call to Continuing Conversion —remind all of continuing conversion —receive ashes, share in imposing ashes

Rites for the Unbaptized	*Stages*	*Rites for the Baptized*

INTENSIVE PREPARATION
AND
THE RITES OF THE PASCHAL HOLY DAYS

Easter Vigil Holy Baptism		Maundy Thursday Preparation for the Paschal Holy Days —receive foot washing —wash the feet of others
Easter Week Reaffirmation of Baptismal Vows bishop lays on hands		Easter Week Reaffirmation of Baptismal Vows bishop lays on hands

FORMATION IN MINISTRY

A Form of Commitment to Christian Service (when appropriate)		A Form of Commitment to Christian Service (when appropriate)

Section 5

The Preparation of Parents and Godparents for The Baptism of Infants and Young Children

PURPOSE: To deepen the Christian formation of those who will present infants and young children for baptism.

Stage	*Rite*
1. Parents discover the pregnancy, choose godparents and meetings throughout the pregnancy are planned	The Blessing of Parents at the Beginning of the Pregnancy
	Sunday Eucharist after the Prayers of the People and followed by the Peace
2. Remainder of pregnancy and the birth. Reflect on the vocation of marriage,	

Stage   *Rite*

family and
child-bearing and
prayer and worship in
the home

Thanksgiving for the
Birth or Adoption of a
Child

Sign infant with the
cross, announce
baptismal date, and
pray for the child every
Sunday until baptism

3. Preparation for
   baptism by reflection
   on parenthood;
   interpreting the
   Eucharist to the child
   partaking of it in the
   growing years;
   modeling ministry and
   prayer; and introducing
   the child to the story
   of salvation

Holy Baptism

Baptized, signed and
receive Holy
Communion (a few
drops of wine if not
weaned)

4. Parents, godparents
   and congregation carry
   out child's formation in
   salvation history,
   prayer, worship and
   social ministry.

APPENDIX B

Documents from The Milwaukee Pilot Project

Sections

Section 1

Living Our
Baptismal Covenant

An Overview

A Pilot Project of the Diocese of Milwaukee in Collaboration with Nashotah House and the Evangelism Ministries Office [As of December 12, 1987]. (The unbaptized are called "catechumens" and the baptized are called "candidates.")

Overall thesis: During the entry process for newcomers, both unbaptized and baptized, the mission of the church will be strengthened by fostering and intensifying their mature commitment to God as known in Jesus Christ by the power of the Holy Spirit.

Overall purpose: To help participants to make an effective response to the Gospel, build a working Christian world view, and become conscious agents of the reign of God in Jesus Christ in their daily lives (at work, at home, in the community, as citizens, at leisure, and in church life).

I. Gathering

Thesis: Laity and clergy will be involved in contacting and inviting adults to consider or re-examine Christian commitment. The gathering will be an ongoing process.

Those contacted will include:
• Baptized or unbaptized adults and youth (sixteen or older) not affiliated with the church

- Members, age sixteen or older, who were baptized as infants
- New participants
  —who have entered their children in church school
  —who are adults returning to church participation
  —who have sought out the church in a time of crisis or for its sacramental ministries
- Regular members and/or communicants seeking further formation
- Baptized members of other churches seeking membership in the Episcopal Church
- Lapsed members considering reaffirmation of their faith.

II. Inquiry

Thesis: A period of group inquiry will follow initial contacts.

During this period, adults will be given enough information about Christian faith and practice and the life of the local congregation to help them decide whether or not they wish to enter the catechumenal process. Those choosing to enter will have an initial and/or increased understanding of and response to the Gospel in ministry in their daily lives. Inquiry is an ongoing process. Individual consultations begin during this stage.

At the end of this period, one or more sponsors are chosen from the local congregation. The sponsor accompanies the catechumen or the baptized candidate through the stages and liturgies that follow. Catechumens are admitted through the rite provided at a principal Sunday liturgy (not later than Advent I). Candidates are welcomed at a principal Sunday liturgy the following week.

III. Formation in Christ

Thesis: Adults seeking to make or further their mature commitment will be involved in a regular period of preparation including:

• Regular participation in corporate worship
• Development of their personal devotional life
• Involvement in social service and social justice ministry
• Exploration of their own history in light of salvation history
• Exploration of proportionate giving with a serious consideration of tithing
• Small group reflection, in a trusting relationship with the group, on what God is doing in their daily lives—their work, homes, communities, citizenship, leisure, and church life— and how they become accountable for their Christian conduct in their lives.

Individual consultations may occur four or five times during this stage. A year or more of life with the lectionary might be a useful guide for length. The lectionary is the basis of small group reflection and content. Participants are encouraged to experiment with new behavior in spirituality, service, justice, and evangelization. Such experiments—and their learnings from them—are the subject of the individual consultations. They may also be the subject of group discussion if the participant chooses. Group theological reflection on their experiences of ministry normally occurs through the study of Scripture, in prayer, and in worship. Formation in Christ is an ongoing process. Catechumens and baptized candidates continue in it until they, their sponsors, and their catechists determine that they are ready to enter intensive preparation for mature commitment.

At the end of this period, the candidates share in the liturgy of the call to continuing conversion at the principal service on Ash Wednesday. The catechumens are enrolled as candidates for baptism on the First Sunday in Lent. Signs of new behavior

are a key point in the determination of readiness for the enrollment or call for each participant.

IV. Intensive Preparation and Rites of Initiation and Commitment

Thesis: Using appropriate rites from *The Book of Common Prayer*
and *The Book of Occasional Services,* adults seeking to make their
mature faith commitment will be baptized, confirmed, or they
will be received or reaffirm their faith.

During Sunday services, public prayers are offered for the
catechumens and for candidates from *The Book of Occasional Ser-*
vices and the Prayer Book. The catechumens and the baptized
come forward together, with their sponsors, for these prayers
and the laying on of hands. The Lenten disciplines of prayer and
fasting are used to explore ministry more deeply. Sponsors
share in prayer and fasting. The baptized share their ongoing
experience of conversion with the catechumens.

On Maundy Thursday, the baptized candidates are recognized as they share in the foot-washing ritual. At the Easter Vigil,
the catechumens are baptized and the baptized renew their vows
with the congregation. During Easter week, the newly baptized,
with the already baptized candidates, share in a regional gathering for the Reaffirmation of Baptismal Vows and the Laying On
of Hands by the bishop.

V. Formation in Ministry

Thesis: Following initiation or reaffirmation, participants will
reflect on the meaning of the rites for their ministry in the world
and in the church.

By this time, the participants' experience has built their capacity, in the company of their fellow pilgrims, to use the lections
to recognize God's presence and call in their daily lives and in

the Christian community, and to give and receive support in responding to God's presence and call. They probably will want an ongoing support group for ministry for the rest of their lives. The task of this period, then, is to help the participants get settled in such an ongoing group. Frequent use of some form of the Celebration of a New Ministry will express their sense of vocation in their daily places year by year.

Section 2

Congregational Plans

St. Thomas of Canterbury Episcopal Church
Greendale, Wisconsin (average attendance: 175)

Plans for Living Our Baptismal Covenant

I. Gathering

Purpose: To gather the people of our church, those interested in being baptized and confirmed, and those interested in renewing their Christian lives by exploring the baptismal covenant.

Resources: Publicity, questionnaire, parish newsletter.

Dates: Survey during late May and early June. Three ninety-minute meetings, in September.

II. Inquiry

Purpose: To help participants begin to find a deepening understanding of Anglicanism and of the Episcopal Church; to provide an understanding of the community of faith and of the Christian way of life; and to determine the commitment of the participants to later stages of the program.

Resources: "Peter and Paul" (film); the Anglican story—bishop, priest, and people sharing their stories; discussion of parish story using *Sizing Up a Congregation* and *Reshaping a Congregation.*

Dates: Six ninety-minute meetings, in October and November.

III. Formation in Christ

Purpose: To enable participants to form and live, through worship and the community, a personal Christian style of life, and to involve each more fully as active Christians in their daily lives.

Resources: The Gospel of Mark; A Taste of New Wine; The Bible in Today's Church; course plans from St. James' Episcopal Church, Jackson, Mississippi. Sponsors are involved at this stage.

Dates: Nine ninety-minute meetings, November 30 to February 22.

IV. Intensive Preparation and Rites

Purpose: To help participants develop their growing faith in God's community by intensely exploring and daily living of the baptismal covenant.

Resources: Catechism: The Outline of the Faith We Profess, Rothauge; "Introduction to Worship"; the lectionary.

Dates: Five ninety-minute meetings, March 8 to April 5.

V. Formation in Ministry

Purpose: To help participants to move into a conscious and active ministry, providing support as needed.

Resources: Teaching on gifts for ministry, 2 meetings; conscious ministry, 1 meeting; ministry, 1 meeting; and ministry support groups, 1 meeting.

Dates: Five ninety-minute meetings, May 3 to June 7.

St. Francis Episcopal Church
Menomonee Falls, Wisconsin (average attendance: 140)

Proposed Outline for Living Our Baptismal Covenant

I. Gathering

Purpose: To identify and invite people to consider the Christian way.

Method: Advertising in local newspaper, one-on-one contacts, identifying persons who are at a stage in which they are searching for Christ.

Resources: Media; human contact; the catechumenate team; vestry; *Proclamation As Offering Story and Choice,* Schwab and Yon; good listening skills.

Dates: September.

II. Inquiry

Purpose: To provide a free and open atmosphere in which interested people (unbaptized and baptized) can identify where they are on their life's journey, their needs on this journey, and how the Christian faith can respond to those needs.

Resources: What is Anglicanism?, U. Holmes; *Helping Adults to Learn and Grow,* R. Robinson; *Proclamation as Offering Story and Choice,* Schwab and Yon; "The Outline of Faith" in *The Book of Common Prayer; The Three Sisters,* Michael Harper; *The Anglican Tradition,* Michael Marshall; "The St. Francis Story" (film); "What Episcopalians Believe" (videotape).

Dates: October 5 to November 23.

III. Formation in Christ and Intensive Preparation

Purpose: To present the Christian story through the lectionary for those who wish to further explore the Christian way as a possible answer to their needs.

Resources: Living the Good News Bible; "What Episcopalians Believe" (videotape); *The Incarnation,* Urban Holmes; *The Gospel Conspiracy,* Michael Marshall; *Journey in Faith,* Frederick Wolf; "Characteristics of a Helpful Sponsor," J. Westerhoff; "The Catechumenate in Story and Experience," Jerry Ryle; "Basic Questions for Christian Commitment," Evangelism Ministries Office, The Episcopal Church Center; "Living Out Our Baptismal Vows," Kathryn Cayler; "Method in Religious Education and Ministry," J. Dunning.

Dates: Fifteen meetings, December 7 to April 12.

IV. Formation in Ministry

Purpose: To help participants to begin to discover their spiritual gifts and natural talents and to more clearly discern their ministries in the world and in the church. To help participants experience Word and sacrament, using small groups to support their ministry.

Resources: "The Identification of Gifts for Ministry," Anne Mahaffey: resources from Jean Haldane; "A Workshop for Discerning and Empowering Our Gifts for Ministry," Akyol and Plattenburg; "Giftedness Conference," Harrison; Office of Evangelism Ministries.

Dates: Six meetings, Easter season.

St. Peter's Episcopal Church
West Allis, Wisconsin (average attendance: 150)

Plan for Stages of the Catechumenal Process

I. Gathering

Purpose: To select candidates for the catechumenal process.

Dates: Spring and summer.

II. Inquiry

Purpose: To build a sense of community and assess commitment to proceed further.

Resources: Proclamation as Offering Story and Choice, Schwab and Yon.

Date: September 14.

III. Formation in Christ

Purpose: To discover one's relationship with God; to explore one's relationship with God; to confirm one's relationship with God.

Resources: The lectionary using the African model for Bible study; "Case Studies from Church History"; music.

Dates: November 9 to March 8.

IV. Enlightenment

Purpose: To become a sacramental person.

Resources: "Case Studies from Church History"; *Death of a Salesman; Diary of Anne Frank.*

Dates: March 8 to April 18.

V. Formation in Ministry

Purpose: To move into an active ministry in the world.

Resources: Proclamation as Offering Story and Choice, Schwab and Yon

Dates: April 26 to June 7.

St. Andrew's Episcopal Church
Madison, Wisconsin (average attendance: 160)

Proposed Schedule for Living Our Baptismal Covenant

I. Gathering

Purpose: To identify and recruit persons who might wish to explore their baptismal covenant more deeply. This will include those who have not been baptized, newcomers to the community from other Christian traditions, persons who are already established members of the congregation but who have not yet received the Laying on of Hands, and confirmed persons who wish a renewal of their adult preparation for

Christian living or who have not received adequate preparation as adults.

Dates: Small group meetings to determine interest, September 7 to October 5.

II. Inquiry 1: An introduction to the Episcopal Church

Purpose: To introduce some basic material of the Christian church from an Anglican perspective.

Content: Joining with participants from St. Luke's Church, use a format that combines videotapes, lectures, and group discussion to cover five topics: [1] The Importance of Church History; [2] How Episcopalians do Theology; [3] Liturgy/*The Book of Common Prayer;* [4] How Do We Look at Scripture; [5] Authority and the Catechism.

Dates: Five 2-¼ hour meetings, every other week, October 19 to December 14.

III. Inquiry 2: Community Building

Purpose: To encourage participants to commit themselves to the next stage of the program, and to discover the depth of their Christian commitment.

Content: Topics include, "What does it mean to be a Christian?" and "What does it mean to belong to St. Andrew's?" Reflect on first five meetings and prepare for Formation in Christ.

Dates: January 11 and January 25.

IV. Formation in Christ

Purpose: To explore in greater depth the Christian life through instruction, small group story-sharing, and worship together in Christian community.

Content: Using Bible study, lecture presentations, and small group discussions, cover ten topics: [1] Creation/Humanity; [2] Sin; [3] Redemption/Jesus Christ; [4] The Church; [5] Sacraments; [6] Prayer; [7] God/Theology; [8] Christian Living; [9] Last Things/Eschatology; [10] Worship/Holy Week. Participants commented that they "had their questions answered."

Dates: Ten 2 hour meetings, February 1 to April 5

V. Rites of Initiation

Purpose: To lead the participants through the Commemoration of the Passion of Jesus Christ, culminating in the Celebration of the Resurrection at the Easter Vigil.

VI. Formation in Ministry: Gifts and Ministry

Purpose: To encourage each participant to discern those gifts that can be used for ministry to others, both within and outside the church.

Content: Five sessions covering the following topics: [1] Reflection on Holy Week and Easter; [2] Gifts and Ministry, Scripture/ *Book of Common Prayer;* [3] Discerning Spiritual Gifts; [4] Outreach Ministries of St. Andrew's, Presentation of Opportunities; [5] Development of Personal Rule of Life and Concluding Reflection on the Process.

Dates: April 25 to May 31.

St Lukes's Episcopal Church
Madison, Wisconsin (average attendance: 195)

The St. Luke's brochure described their program as "Journey in Faith: A Comprehensive Program of Instruction and Exploration of Christian Tradition and the Development of the Spiritual Life as Found in the Episcopal Church." The process at St. Luke's followed a format similar to that of St. Andrew's, Madison. The two churches held five joint meetings at St. Luke's at the beginning of the inquiry phase, as noted. The first two meetings during Epiphany focused on small group work with reflection techniques for Bible study. This was followed by ten sessions on the same topics covered by St. Andrew's in Formation in Christ, but in a quite different way. At St. Luke's, a brief presentation was followed by significant small group time and then a plenary session. Bible study used the same pattern. Each week a member shared his or her own journey with questions and sharing of similar experiences from all present. These three elements—topic, Bible study, and journey-sharing—were part of each of the ten sessions. Participants commented that they had "learned a new way to think." After Easter, five meetings were devoted to discussing gifts and ministries in the same small group and plenary pattern.

The brochure further listed the expectations of the program as:

- Enjoying learning how our own lives fit into God's plan for his people
- Meeting many of St. Luke's outstanding leaders who will share their faith stories with us
- Become aware of our unique Anglican tradition and heritage as expressed in the Episcopal Church
- Learning practical Christian skills—how to pray, how to worship, how to read Scripture, how to love (even our enemies), how to approach social issues

- Understanding the Bible's central messages and their meaning in our lives
- Becoming more aware of the presence of God in our lives
- Finding our own ministry, our way to serve and promote the mission of the church
- Finding our own place in St. Luke's parish family
- Understanding more deeply the mystery of God's covenant with his people, and with each one of us.

Section 3

Guidelines for Sponsors

St. Francis Church

1. Sponsors must not be spouses, parents, siblings, or children of the candidate, except in unusual circumstances.
2. Candidates must discuss potential sponsors with the priest before contacting the sponsors.
3. Sponsors must be selected and committed by the end of January.
4. Sponsors must attend all sessions with the candidates, beginning with the eighth session, Formation in Christ (Stage Two), and continuing through Formation in Ministry (Stage Four).
5. Sponsors must attend two sponsor-training sessions.
6. Sponsors must meet regularly (at least every other week) with their candidate to:
   Develop a spiritual friendship.
   Assist the candidate in developing a rule of life (which presupposes that the sponsor has one as well).
7. Sponsors are not counselors; they are there to be soul-friends. Genuine care and concern can best be demonstrated by the ministry of presence. Such ministry means:

   Having a regular time together, with a limit on the duration.
   Listening first and not attempting to have all the answers.
   Not trying to be a problem solver, unless the problem relates to issues such as how to pray, study, or become involved in ministry.
   This does not mean one is being a spiritual director.

8. Sponsors need to know to whom they can go for help (priest, lay leaders, team members, etc.).

9. Sponsors need to be willing to make a commitment to continue the relationship with their candidates for one year following their baptism, reception, or confirmation.

Further comments:

• All relationships must involve trust, honesty, and commitment.

• Sponsors will be commissioned early in the program at a regular Sunday service so that the whole congregation will be aware that the Lord is with them and so that the sponsors will know the congregation is supporting them.

Section 4

First Group of Congregations

Milwaukee Pilot Project, 1986–87

Outline of diocesan planning, and training and work of congregation teams:

December 1985
Meeting of clergy and lay leaders from participating congregations to discuss the pilot project and agree to a calendar for implementing the five stages of the catechumenal process.

January to June 1986
Preparation, vestry and parish orientation, selection of resources, recruiting and training of workers; Congregational teams develop plans and calendar for their programs.

April 1986
Two-day Teams Training session on identifying gifts, story-sharing, and models for Biblical reflection.

June 1986
One-day Teams Training session on the Gathering stage; trainer visits each congregation to review overall plans in depth.

June through August 1986
Congregational teams continue with planning, recruiting, and publicity: Prepare for Gathering stage.

September 1986: Gathering Stage Begins.
One-day Teams Training to reflect on experiences in Gathering stage and to prepare for Inquiry stage; Discussion of sponsor

selection, determining readiness for moving to the next stage, and freedom to withdraw at any point.

October 1986: Inquiry Stage Begins.
One-day Teams Training to reflect on Inquiry and prepare for Formation in Christ stage.

November and December 1986
Rites of Admission of Catechumens and Recognition of Baptized Seekers begins the stage of Formation in Christ. Participants continue with regular worship and begin [1] development of personal devotional life; [2] involvement in social service and social justice ministry; and [3] participation in a bi–weekly small group to reflect on experience, share their own stories, and consider tithing and making a financial pledge. Small group meetings use prayers for catechumens according to *The Book of Occasional Services.*

December 1986
One-day Teams Training to continue work on Formation in Christ and to reflect on process so far.

December through February 1987
Participants continue in stage of Formation in Christ.

January 1987
One-day Teams Training reflects on progress in Formation in Christ and prepares for stage of Intensive Preparation and Rites of Initiation and Reaffirmation.

March 1987
First Sunday of Lent, Rite of Enrollment of Candidates for Baptism and Reaffirmation of Baptismal Vows, begins the stage of Intensive Preparation; During Lent at Sunday services, prayers over candidates according to form in *Book of Occasional Services;* One-day Teams Training for Rites of Initiation and Reaffirmation and preparation for fifth stage, Formation in Ministry; Trainer visits sessions in three of the five congregations.

April 1987

Catechumens are baptized at Easter Vigil, baptized join with congregation to reaffirm their baptismal vows, confirmation and reaffirmation with the Bishop during Easter Week; Formation in Ministry begins.

May and June 1987

Formation in Ministry continues.

July 1987

One-day Teams Training for evaluation.

Summer 1987

Congregations evaluate and begin to plan, recruit, and train for the coming year.

Section 5

Second Group of Congregations

Planning Outline for Congregations Beginning the Second Phase (1988–89)

Dates

January 14–16
Diocesan Orientation Conference for teams from congregations

February
• Team building and planning (4–8 hours)
• Consolidating January training
• Story-sharing (10–30 minutes per person)
• Plan vestry and congregational involvement
• Assign resources for study

March
Involve (vestry and) congregation in a survey

April 16
Teams meet at Nashotah House for sharing and problem solving
　　Bring tentative plans for each element of activities listed in Formation in Christ (from LOBC, An Overview)

April 17–May 15
• Teams plan for the fall
• Develop an overall statement of purpose

- How much will we move at the participant's pace? How will we keep in touch with their movement?
- Identify purpose, select resources and leaders, and review liturgy for each stage
- Consider format of entire process; List options and discuss rescheduling and flexibility
- Plan use of sponsors—their recruitment, training, and ongoing support
- Plan gathering in detail—training, schedule, leaders

May 15–31
- Team reviews plans with liaison

May 15
- Teams complete basic planning
- Agree on format
- Agree on procedure for planning each session
- Agree on way to sense and support the spiritual formation of participants and role of sponsors in this process
- Agree on how liturgies will be planned, held, and evaluated for each stage

July and August
- Gathering participants

September, October and November
- Inquiry
Advent I at the latest
- Admission of Catechumens.
Advent II at the latest
- Welcome of the Baptized Candidates

December, January and February
- Formation in Christ

Ash Wednesday/February 17
- Call to Continuing Conversion (for the baptized candidates)
  Lent I
- Enrollment of the Catechumens

  February and March
- Intensive Preparation
  Maundy Thursday

  March 31
- Preparation for the Paschal Holy Days (for the baptized candidates)

  April 2
- Baptism of the Catechumens at the Easter Vigil

  April 3
- Easter

  April 4–10
- (To be set)
- Reaffirmation of vows and laying on of hands for catechumens and candidates

  April, May, June
Formation in Ministry

Planning "rule of thumb": Allow two hours of planning for every hour of group session.

Editor's note: This is a first year plan. As experience is acquired, the plan will be based more and more on the pace of the participants and less and less on the calendar.

PROJECTED PERSONNEL NEEDS FOR A CATECHUMENAL PROCESS

Average Sunday Attendance and Catechumenal Team	Gathering — Prospects, Leaders Response	Inquiry — Participants, Leaders	Formation in Christ — Participants, Leaders	Intensive Preparation and Rites — Participants, Leaders	Formation in Ministry — Participants, Leaders	Total Leaders
FAMILY SIZE Up to 50 att. Catechumenal team - 1 + clergy or 2 + clergy resource	10 Prospects 2-3 Gatherers (may be on catechumenal team) 5-6 Respond	5 Participants 2 Gatherers 2 Catechists (group leaders and may be on catechumenal team)	4-5 Participants 4-5 Sponsors (may have been Gatherers) 2 Catechists	(Same - perhaps)	(Same - perhaps)	Catechumenal team - 1 + clergy or 2 + clergy resource 2-3 Gatherers 4-5 Sponsors 2 Catechists (group leaders)
PASTORAL SIZE 50-150 att. Catechumenal team - 2 + priest or clergy resource	10-25 Prospects 3-6 Gatherers 5-15 Respond	5-15 Participants 2-5 Gatherers 2-6 Catechists	4-12 Participants 4-12 Sponsors 2-6 Catechists	(Same - perhaps)	(Same - perhaps)	Catechumenal team - 2 + clergy 3-6 Gatherers 4-12 Sponsors 2-6 Catechists
PROGRAM SIZE 150-350 att. Catechumenal team - 2-4 + priest	20-40 Prospects 5-10 Gatherers 12-25 Respond	12-30 Participants 4-8 Gatherers 4-8 Catechists	10-25 Participants 10-25 Sponsors 4-8 Catechists	(Same - perhaps)	(Same - perhaps)	Catechumenal team - 2-4 + priest 5-10 Gatherers 10-25 Sponsors 4-8 Catechists

Average Sunday Attendance and Catechumenal Team	Gathering Prospects Leaders Response	Inquiry Participants Leaders	Formation in Christ Participants Leaders	Intensive Preparation and Rites Participants Leaders	Formation in Ministry Participants Leaders	Total Leaders
CORPORATION SIZE						
350 and up Catechumenal team - 4-6 + priest	40-80 Prospects 10-20 Gatherers 20-40 Respond	20-40 Participants 8-18 Gatherers 6-12 Catechists	16-36 Participants 16-36 Sponsors 8-18 Catechists	(Same - perhaps)	(Same - perhaps)	Catechumenal Team - 4-6 + priest 10-20 Gatherers 16-36 Sponsors 8-18 Catechists

Notes: Catechumenal team has a lay leader. Team plans, recruits, trains, supports (and serves in any roles desired).

Gatherers act as participants in Inquiry stage to offer continuing support to those whom they gathered.

Sponsors act as full participants in sessions.

Catechists are projected on basis of 8-10 in a group (made up of participants and gatherers/sponsors) with eight or less preferred. Catechists work in pairs.

Decision not to continue by some is likely as part of movement from stage to stage.

Section 7

Summary

**February 19, 1988, Meeting of Parish Teams of
Second Year Churches**

What Has Gone Well for You in Your Second Year?

- Limited scope of sessions—not trying to cover too much in one session
- Continuity of concerns, prayer within group has encouraged growth
- Flexibility required with different candidates
- This year more experimental, inclusive of parish
- Bonding, community, deeper level in small groups
- Overwhelming positive responses to faith stories
- Gathering questions important—establishes the agenda.

What Are Some of the Rough Spots You Have Encountered?

- Four teenagers out of six participants have created a new situation—team must be sensitive to where the candidates are, adapt to family pressures, shy participants, peer pressures
- Not praying together as a team
- Inquiry stage lacking, did not set a tone of openness
- Could not answer all the questions asked
- Not enough time for team building in the middle—good at first, then stopped, added new people

- Struggle between developing community and conveying information—not enough time for either one
- Not enough time for gathering as a team—story-sharing at the beginning would have helped
- New team members had not been at the Nashotah House meetings—difficult to convey this to new members—discontinuity between team members/years
- Differences in personality/piety/needs for community, sharing
- People on teams not attending meetings
- Relationship with priest could be stronger—rector stepped back
- More advance notice of meetings—at least two months.

What Are Your Expectations for This Second Year? Are They Being Met?

- Expected rector to be less involved—has worked well
- Expected more teaching/intellectual content—not met
- Lay leadership strong—missed priest, but a good resource
- Expected to streamline the program—has worked well
- Expected second year to be like the first year—shocked at how different it is; but has adapted to smaller, younger group
- Expected program to be more accessible because joined with adult class—has worked well.

What Do You Need to Learn in Order to Be Better Prepared?

- Organization skills
- More discipline
- Small group skills
- Adult learning skills
- Gathering process—planning ahead, "How to's"

- Collate information, documentation of process in other parishes
- More frequent sessions to share ideas, resources, and information
- About sponsors
- Team building—times to begin, "How to's."

What Resources Have You Found Helpful?

- Videos from General Seminary concerning personal witness
- Raymond Kemp: *Journey in Faith*
- Gifts for Ministry—panel discussion by parishioners, sharing about how they discovered their gifts, how they use them
- Videos: *Death of a Salesman,* used during Formation in Christ phase; *Workshop on Spiritual Disciplines*

What Resources Do You Need?

- To meet quarterly with the teams

We discussed the practice of gathering for joint services, as we did last year. No consensus was reached, but we agreed to try separate visitations this year. This agreement was made with the understanding that when more parishioners are involved, and the catechumenate is better established in our parishes, a diocesan approach to the confirmation/reaffirmation/baptismal liturgy would be preferable to a number of parochial liturgies.

Editor's Note: Attendance at individual services was small, so this group chose to return to regional services for 1988–1989.

Section 8

A Proposal for Ongoing Support

Congregations Participating in Living Our Baptismal Covenant

The Diocesan Cathechumenal Team recommends the following:

Occasion:
Time now to plan for full growth.

Assumptions:
- Volunteer leaders and consultants with administrative and expense support.
- Accountability to bishop.

Volunteer Leaders:
Availability.
"Insiders" grasp.

Support for First Year Churches:
(a) On-site review of year's plans (May–June).
(b) Five group meetings before transition points:
- Gathering to Inquiry
- Inquiry to Formation in Christ
- Formation to Intensive Preparation and Rites
- Preparation and Rites to Formation in Ministry
- Formation in Ministry to ongoing support for ministry.

Agenda for these meetings:
share experience, skills of team work, leadership of groups,
learning theory, planning, feedback, etc.
(c) Group evaluation of year's work.
(d) Three on-site visits during the working year (during Inquiry,
    Formation in Christ, and Formation in Ministry) for support,
    data-gathering, and problem-solving.
(e) Recruiting (October–November) and orientation (January)
    of next year's churches.

Support for Second Year (and Beyond) Churches:
(a) Two group meetings during Inquiry (probably October) and
    Formation in Christ (probably January) and an evaluation
    meeting. Two group meetings share experience and assess
    progress and needs.
(b) One on-site visit during Formation in Ministry (before eval-
    uation).
(c) For third-year and beyond churches, an annual day-long
    session with a keynote speaker and workshops (May-June).

Team Subgroups:
(a) First-year churches (six to eight people)
(b) Second-year (and beyond) churches (two to eight people).

Team Standards:
(a) Ongoing use of consultants.
(b) Team subgroups plan and train for each activity using
    needed consultants.
(c) Each church is represented by two lay leaders and a priest
    at each group session.

Team Support:
(a) Use of Evangelism Consultants Training personnel—or sim-
    ilar personnel—as consultants.
(b) On-site participation of national staff as local consultants
    assume working roles followed by ongoing consultation by
    national staff for three to five years.

Present Needs:

(a) Bishop to name diocesan catechumenal team and leader.
(b) Meet every four to six weeks as a group.
(c) Present transition team revises this proposal June 17, 6–8 PM or longer, in Dousman.
(d) Leader and administrative assistant meet bi-weekly.
(e) Office space.

APPENDIX C

Resources for Catechesis and Session Plans

Sections

Section 1

Catechesis[1]

Three deliberate (intentional), systematic (related), and sustained (lifelong) processes, which establish, build-up, equip, and enable the community to be Christ's body or presence in the world to the end that all people are restored to unity with God and each other.

I. Christian Formation

A. Definition of the formational process:
   To experience Christian faith and life.
B. Outcomes of the formational process:
   1. To incorporate—to induct persons into the life and spirit of a Christian faith community and to establish their identity as members of Christ's body and church.
   2. To enculturate—to shape persons into an historic community's present understandings of Christian faith, character, and consciousness.
   3. To apprentice—to provide a context in which new members can observe and imitate ways of Christian living foundational to later judgment and ownership.
C. Components of the formational process:
   1. Participation in its rites (rituals and ceremonials).
   2. Environment (what persons see, touch, taste, smell, and hear).
   3. Interrelational experiences.
   4. Behavior observed, supported, and encouraged.

[1]John Westerhoff, "Formation, Education, Instruction," Religious Education, 82, no. 4 (Fall 1987), pp. 582ff.

5. Role models presented (past and present).

6. Organization (how time is structured, what programs are offered).

7. Naming (how language is used, what things are called).

II. Christian Education

A. Definition of the educational process:
   To reflect on experience in the light of Christian faith and life.

B. Outcomes of the educational process:

   1. To humanize—to aid individuation and the development of the human potential for willful life as autonomous persons in the relationship.

   2. To criticize—to engage in a careful analysis, synthesis, and judgment on traditional understandings and ways of life.

   3. To discover—to encourage the freedom to create the new and to produce change.

C. Steps in the educational process:

   1. Name and describe experience and related feelings.

   2. Explore intuitively alternative interpretations, meanings, and possibilities until clear understanding of the inner nature of the experience is achieved.

   3. Express these initial insights, compare and contrast them with corresponding insights in Scripture and tradition, and through rational processes arrive at summary convictions.

   4. Talk about initial implications of these convictions, compare and contrast them with ethical principles and norms of Christian faith, and through rational processes arrive at summary commitments to action(s).

   5. Manifest these commitments in willing action(s) and evaluate their consequences.

III. Christian Instruction

A. Definition of the instructional process:
To acquire knowledge and skills considered necessary and useful to Christian life.

B. Outcomes of the instructional process:
  1. To know—to be knowledgeable of the Scriptures, the tradition (fundamental, constructive, and practical theology) and the community's social and intellectual history.
  2. To use—to be able to interpret Scripture, think historically and theologically, and reflect morally.
  3. To do—to be able to relate to God in ever-deepening and loving ways, and to others, personally and socially, in caring and liberating ways.

C. Steps in the instructional process:
  1. Establish participants and context.
  2. Establish aims and goals.
  3. Establish behavioral and/or process objectives.
  4. Establish instructional activities and resources.
  5. Conduct these activities.
  6. Evaluate.

Section 2

Bible Study and Reflection

An African Model for Bible Study[2]

Source: Lumko Missiological Institute of South Africa via the base communities of South America.

1. Each person shares his or her experiences in the area of their prayer from the session before. (If this is the first session, begin with Step 2.)
2. Read the Gospel slowly (one person out loud).
3. Name the word or phrase that catches your attention (one minute).
4. Each person shares the word or phrase with the group.
5. Read the Gospel again—the opposite sex reads.
6. Name/write: where this passage touches my life today (three to five minutes).
7. Each shares the above: "I . . ."
8. Read the Gospel again.
9. Name/write: from what I have heard and shared what does God want me to do or be this week? How does God invite me to change?
10. Each shares the above: "I . . ."
11. Each person prays for the person on the right (naming what was shared in no. 10), and prays that prayer daily until the group meets again.

---

[2]"An African Model for Bible Study" (New York: The Episcopal Church Center, Office of Evangelism Ministries), October 1986.

Questions for Biblical Reflection[3]

1. What is the context of the passage?
2. What do the words mean?
3. What does it say about God?
4. What does it say about us/me?
5. What are some implications for my:

- work
- home
- community
- citzenship
- leisure time
- church

Developing Questions for Bible Reflection[4]

The following suggested methods were included among the resources for planning prepared by the Reverend A. Wayne Schwab for the Diocese of Milwaukee Pilot Project.

Another method [for small group Bible study] is to read the passage aloud and meditate in silence for 2–5 minutes on (1) What did the passage say? and (2) What did the passage say to me? The leader invites anyone to begin, seeks by all responses to the first question, then responses by all to the second. The group may want to react to any one response. Let them do so. Get back on course by going to the next person once discussion needs on a point have been satisfied. Be sure all get to offer their responses.

This method can be enhanced by increasing the number of questions to five:

(1) What did the passage say?
(2) What might the passage have meant to the hearers in biblical times?

---

[3]Peter Arvedson and Lynde E. May IV, "sharing Resources in Madison, Wisconsin," *Water and Fire,* Summer 1987, pp. 2–3.
[4]A. Wayne Schwab, "Resources for Planning" (Episcopal Church Center, Evangelism Ministries Office, 815 Second Avenue, New York, NY 10017, 1-800-334-7626, or 1-212-867-8400, February 1986, pp. 9–10.

(3) What might the passage mean to hearers today?
(4) How could I pray on the basis of this passage?
(5) How could I live on the basis of this passage?

The questions can be varied still more with this set from Rt. Rev. Mark Dyer, Bishop of Bethlehem.

(1) What does the Scripture say? Listening to the Word of God, meditate on how God is speaking to you.
(2) What do you have to say back to God in relation to the Scripture?
(3) How do you pray about the Scripture? Compose a prayer that engages the Scripture and your personal reflection.
(4) After prayer, how does the Scripture affect your personal life? What are you going to do about it?
(5) After prayer, how does Scripture affect your ministry? What will you do about it?

Prayer is handled by asking each person to name the situation he or she faces for which prayer is desired between now and the next meeting of the group. The group closes with the offering of those prayers by the leaders and/or members. After the Bible reflection at the next session, each person tells what has happened in that area of prayer concern since the last session. Following these reports, each person names the prayers desired during the next interval and the prayers are offered. As the weeks pass, group members will begin to offer ideas and ask questions of one another more often. This free flowing discussion will deepen the accountability already started by the simple reporting of what happened.

The Gospel Story and My Story[5]

This process may be used on Sundays or week nights during the precatechumenate, or it can be used in shortened form when catechumens are dismissed after the liturgy of the Word.

---

[5]Gail C. Jones, *Seeking Life in Christ,* pp. 37–38.

Time: 60–90 minutes

Materials: The Bible and *The Book of Common Prayer*

The session is opened and closed with prayer.

STEP 1 Look up the Gospel reading for the present or following Sunday in the Lectionary—beginning on p. 888 of *The Book of Common Prayer.*

STEP 2 From the Bible, read the Gospel passage out loud.

STEP 3 Each person reads the passage to him/herself

STEP 4 Reflection questions:
• What word/phrase stands out for you?
• What person do you identify with?
• What person is "Church" for you?

STEP 5 Read the passage out loud, again.

STEP 6 Reflection questions:
• What am I being called to live out?
• What is the price I'll pay?
• What is the struggle I'll face?

STEP 7 Summary reflection:
What have I learned or relearned about:
• the Church
• reconciliation
• forgiveness
• grace
• faith
• God
• other
What questions do I have about:
• Christian life
• doctrine
• sacraments
• other

Section 3

Sunday Morning Catechetical Sessions

Catechetical Methods for Sunday Morning Dismissal Sessions[6]

The following methods used in Roman Churches presume that people are dismissed for classes following the Liturgy of the Word and sermon. They have been adapted only slightly to refer to Episcopal liturgical resources.

There are a variety of methods for Sunday morning dismissal sessions—perhaps as many methods as there are creative men and women to develop them. Two methods are listed below which have been used in the United States and Canada.

African Model

1. Attend the Liturgy of the Word with the entire congregation.
2. Gather after the Dismissal [Liturgy of the Word] in a room set apart.
3. Opening prayer options could include: Collect for the Day or other appropriate prayer from *The Book of Common Prayer*, spontaneous prayer; other prayers selected from resources such as *The Book of Occasional Services* or *Lesser Feasts and Fasts*,

---

[6]Karen M. Hinman, North American Forum on the Catechumenate, 5510 Columbia Pike, Suite 310, Arlington, VA 22204, 1-703-671-0330, 1983.

The Oxford Book of Prayer, or *Prayers for Pastors and People.* The purpose of this prayer time is to gather the catechumens and to begin their time together.

4. Read the Gospel (slowly and deliberately). As you read it invite catechumens and candidates to listen for the word or phrase that stands out to them, that speaks to them.
5. One minute of silence.
6. Invite everyone to say the word or phrase that touched them.
7. Read the Gospel again.
8. Tell the group you will now give them three to five minutes of silence to sit with the text. (When you are first starting out, three minutes is adequate. As the group progresses, five minutes is better.) Give them the amount of silent time that you stated you would.
9. Invite catechumens to write: What do I hear in my heart? Where does this passage and today's homily touch my life today?
10. Divide into groups of five people to share experiences. Instruct the groups that they are to share; that is, they are to speak from their experiences using the pronoun "I" (I am . . . I feel . . . I think . . .). Do not preach at others or become didactic. Do not discuss. Do not solve the problems of another. Share your *own* experiences.
11. Read the Gospel again.
12. From what I have heard and shared, what does God want me to do or to be this week? How does God invite me to change? Be concrete and specific. Or ask: What do I take home with me this week?
13. Share this in small groups.
14. Gather the larger group to close with prayer. (Options include: the first or second reading as a prayer, spontaneous petition prayer, shared prayer, or summary prayer).
15. Announcements (if you have any to make) and give the group the readings for the next week.

St. Augustine's Church*

Washington, D.C. (average attendance: 750)

1. Gather for the Liturgy of the Word.
2. Gather after the Dismissal in a room set apart.
3. Opening prayer (same as African Model, read the Gospel at some point during the prayer).
4. Invite the catechumens and candidates to write reflections on the following questions:

What Did You Hear?

Write three thoughts, ideas, phrases, images that struck you in today's readings and homily.

What Does It Mean?

• Why did these words/phrases strike you today? What do they mean for your life?
• Can you recall a time in your life (past or present) when you experienced something similar to the event expressed in today's readings? How do these readings and the homily enlighten or challenge that experience?
• Write three questions that today's readings and sermon raise for you about your life, about your faith, about church . . .

Model developed by Raymond Kemp.

What Does It Cost You to Live This Message?

- List one concrete way you feel called to live this message this week.
- What will help you live this message? What will be the obstacles?
- Divide the entire group into small groups of five or six people. Encourage members to share their reflections.
- Share learnings with the large group. Share any questions that are unresolved.
- Closing prayer (could be the same as the African Model).
- Announcements and give the group the readings for the next week.

Model Developed by Karen Hinman

1. Gather for the Liturgy of the Word.
2. Gather after the Dismissal in a room set apart.
3. Opening prayer. (Same as the preceding two models. Be certain to reread the Gospel.)
4. Right Lobe/Left Lobe reflections
   a. "Journaling" activity
   b. "Imagination" activity
   c. Respond to these questions: What did you hear? What does it mean? What does it cost?
   d. Raise questions about the meaning of life, church, faith as raised by the Sunday readings.
5. Allow time for small group sharing.
6. Allow time for large group feedback.
7. Catechesis from the homily: an issue or topic prepared ahead of time on questions that have surfaced prior to the session, or on a theme raised by the lectionary or the liturgical year.
8. Closing prayer (same as in the preceding two methods).
9. Announcements and time to give the group next week's readings.

Section 4

Story-sharing

Sharing Our Spiritual Journey[7]

Our own personal history, particularly that part of our story that tells how we came to our present religious understanding, is important to us for a number of reasons. We need to take some time to write that history down, and we need to keep adding to it as we remember more events. Then as our journeys bring us to new experiences, we will come to know more about ourselves. Moreover, if we are able to share that story, or some parts of it, in a group where others are sharing their stories, too, we find support, enrichment, and affirmation for who we are.

Being part of a story-sharing group not only affirms us as individuals; it also makes us part of a very special kind of learning community. To an initial sharing of the journey that brought us to this group, we continue to add stories of our everyday experiences. As we have new learnings about Scripture, as well as our own theologies, we have new insight into both our own stories and our present experiences.

The story-sharing group is an essential part of the catechumenal process since it brings us into a uniquely religious mode of learning. Very few secular systems use a way of learning as effective as ours.

Simply put, we learn from one another. The Bible contains the history of the lives and works of those who sought a relationship with God in agreement with the covenant established by our Creator from the beginning, and renewed again and again

---

[7]Designed by Rev. Canon Thomas J. McElligott, February 1988, Indianapolis, IN.

through time in people's lives. It offers us stories of people's spiritual journeys; it offers us interpretations of the meaning of those stories. As we learn from those ancient stories, so we learn from one another all the time. When we are intentional about it, as in a story-sharing group, we learn more effectively. We learn about how God is among us and acting in our lives. We learn that when we dare to allow it, God will direct us and empower us in ways we never dreamed possible.

The Value of Story-Sharing

Almost any group in the church will be willing to enter into the story-sharing experience. The rewards are great—affirming and enlightening. There are several things about the story-sharing experience that are of note:

1. We rarely have an opportunity to tell our stories without interruption. In story-sharing, we can tell as much or as little as we wish, or nothing at all.
2. Listening is a rewarding experience. We find out how much we are all alike.
3. By telling and listening, we enter into the caring relationship that is basic to our ministries of pastoral care.

How to Begin

There are many ways to begin story-sharing. When a group first gathers, leaders need to provide a setting where people can tell their spiritual histories. The following are ways to help people organize and recount that story:

1. Think of events in your life that were turning points for you in your understanding of your spiritual nature.
2. Think of persons in your life from whom you learned something about the importance of religion, God, or your spiritual nature. When you remember these people, you will probably remember the lesson you learned from them at a crucial time in your life.

3. Think of dates when things happened. It may help you to draw a horizontal line on a page. Then put dates on the line and the incidents that occurred.

When people have had time to remember and reflect on their stories, allow an ample, but defined, amount of time for each member of the group to tell their story—as much or as little as they want to share. Reflection is held until everyone's story has been told.

The more people practice recalling their stories, the easier it will become. If they are encouraged to write things down as they recall them, they will remember more of their stories. People's stories will be reshaped as new things happen. New events from their histories will become important, and their self-understandings will grow.

Keeping the Story Going

Remember that one's individual story is, in a real sense, a part of the history of God's people, those who are in covenant with God. And as one lives more and experiences more and learns more about one's life in relation to Scripture and theology, one adds to one's personal story. Write it out. Share it with others in a Story–Sharing Group.

A Turning Point[8]

This discussion model allows one to reflect on one's life and especially those times of change and transition. Begin by allowing time for people to make notes of their responses. Divide into pairs and allow each person ten minutes to share what they wrote. This might be used as part of the discerning process of persons preparing for the intense preparation of Stage Three.

---

[8]"A Turning Point" (New York: The Episcopal Church Center, Evangelism Ministries Office) December 1986. Adapted from the North American Forum on the Catechumenate.

1. Choose an event when you were called from the old and into the new that was a turning point in your life.
2. Name the feelings involved for you.
3. What did you leave/let go of/turn from?
4. What did you find/gain/turn to?
5. To what did you die?
6. How did you come to new life?
7. Who journeyed with you?
8. Is there a biblical event like yours?

When the group reassembles, share how the experience went for them. The leader can point out questions 3–5 are Exodus-like and questions 5–7 reflect Good Friday, Easter and Pentecost (the Church).

Section 5

Critical Reflection

Praxis Method of Critical Reflection[9]

[*The following is an excerpt from an article on catechetical method for the catechumenal process by James B. Dunning.*

Another method . . . which I especially recommend to you is the praxis method of critical reflection developed by Thomas Groome in *Christian Religious Education* (Harper & Row), chapters 9 and 10. Like all praxis, this must be practiced in order to plumb its possibilities.

The method flows from praxis to praxis. That term is not an effort to be esoteric. As Groome explains, there is a disastrous split in our thinking between theory and practice. We "apply theory to practice." For the Greeks, praxis meant reflection in the midst of action, listening to the "vibes," with antennae out, hearing the signs from the people, the event, the signs of the times in the very midst of our acting.

We Americans are doers, actors, but often without reflection. Groome gives us a method of five movements to help us unite this needed reflection to our deeds. The goal in a sense is to self-destruct the five separate movements by becoming so adept at connecting Tradition to our lives that we don't need five steps.

The five movements are simple.

What are you doing?
Why do you do that?
What have Christians done and why have they done it?
Let's talk about it.
Now, what are you going to do?

---

[9]James B. Dunning, "Method is the Medium is the Message: Catechetical Method in the RCIA" (New York: William H. Sadlier, Inc., 1982), pp. 3–4. Reprinted by permission, the North American Forum on the Catechumenate.

Let's go back over those. The first movement asks about your present praxis. Groome also uses the language, "What is your story?" What is your past and present experience?

The second movement asks the "why" question. This is critical, literally critical. We do what Americans often do not do; we critique why we do what we do—our values, our vision. This gets at our assumptions (theological, psychological, sociological, cultural, etc.) and our hopes (what consequences do we expect from what we do?).

The third movement asks about the Christian story and vision. This is the place, perhaps, for dialogical lecture which taps our Tradition in response to what was heard (or not heard) in the first two movements. My understanding is that Tradition can be taken in the broadest sense—any source which responds to the person who has shared his or her story, although recognized Judaeo-Christian Tradition should always be part of that.

Fourth, let's talk about it. Put Story into dialogue with my story; Vision of the Gospel into dialogue with my vision. Questions might be, What did you hear in Tradition which affirms you? What challenges you? How does the Christian Story add to your story? Where do you agree or disagree? Where can you relate? What seems nonsense to you?

Fifth, how does this reflection flow into your future praxis? This is key. Groome suggests that the model is the Incarnation in which Word becomes not theory but flesh. Christianity was first called "the Way" because people saw they were called to practice the Good News preached.

[*For further information concerning the process and examples see: Thomas H. Groome, <u>Christian Religious Education</u>* [10]*, pp. 184–232. In addition to reviewing the stages, Groome describes the process in action in a variety of settings. Also see this article by James Dunning for examples of how the method is applied in the catechumenal process.*]

---

[10]Thomas H. Groome, *Christian Religious Education: Sharing Our Story and Vision* (San Francisco: Harper & Row, 1980).

Section 6

Session Plans: Jackson, Mississippi

The Catechumenate Process of St. James' Church (average attendance: 650)[11]

An Outline of Weekly Meetings:

The Inquiry Period
1 Introduction
2 Telling your Story (a group process)
3 Clergy and Catechists tell their stories
4 Stories (continued)
5 The Story of Anglicanism
6 The Story of the Parish and tour
7 The Story of the Prayer Book
8 The Story of Jesus
9 The Story of the Church and its responsibilities for justice and peace
10 The Story of the Diocese told by the Bishop.

The Rite of Admission to the Catechumenate
Those to be baptized are admitted as catechumens. Those who are baptized but seek confirmation and renewal of Baptismal vows are recognized as candidates.

The Catechumenate Period
1 The Bible and its authority
2 Creation

---

[11]"An Outline of Weekly Meetings," *Water and Fire,* Fall 1985, p. 3.

3 Sin
4 Judgement
5 Redemption
6 The God of Love
7 Jesus reveals the love of God
8 Who I am in the light of God's love
9 God's love and our sin
10 A Theology of Prayer

The Rite of Enrollment
Those to be baptized are enrolled as candidates to be baptized. Those seeking Confirmation and renewal of Baptismal vows are recognized as making a deeper commitment in their faith at this point in the process of conversion in their lives.

The Enlightenment Period
1 Confronting Evil: The Temptation of Jesus, Lent I, Cycle A Lections
2 Personal Sin, Prayer and the way of purification, Lent II
3 For what do you thirst? Our longings rise out of longing for God. Lent III
4 Through sin we have become blind. Jesus brings sight and light. Lent IV
5 From death to life; from unconsciousness to consciousness, unbinds us and let us go. Lent V
6 The Way of the Cross and the Way of Conversion. Passion Sunday.

The Easter Vigil and Holy Baptism and The Renewal of Baptismal Vows

Those not baptized are baptized. Those seeking confirmation renew their Baptismal vows and support the candidates for Baptism.

The Mystagogia Period
1 Reflection on the Easter Vigil and the Paschal Mystery
2 The Ministry of the Church from birth to death (Pastoral Offices)
3 The journey of faith and Christian Disciplines
4 Discovering your gifts
5 Sharing your Gifts in the Community
6 Giving your Gifts in the world

The Rite of Confirmation and the Renewal of Baptismal Vows

Ideally this would be done at the Easter Vigil. The Bishop comes after Easter, however, usually on or near Pentecost. Thus the laying-on-of-hands carries the aspect of empowerment for ministry.

The Process of the Catechumenate

[The following are excerpts from "An Outline" of the cate-chumenal process of St. James' Episcopal Church, Jackson, MS. Additional details are supplied by excerpts from articles written in *Water and Fire,* a newsletter for sharing resources and experiences with the catechumenal process. They describe the cate-chetical method for each stage of the process as practiced in one congregation.]

The sessions are varied in method from a lecture format to experiential processes that involve the participant intellectually and emotionally. It is important, however, to note that this is not a program or a series of classes. It is a process that happens day to day. The meetings of the group are only a part of the process of study, prayer, worship, activity and reflection. Because of the nature of the process it is necessary to be flexible in the construction of sessions. Regular contact with participants through questionnaires, interviews and contact through sponsors keeps catechists and clergy aware of group and individual process.[12]

THE INQUIRY PERIOD

This period which takes ten to twelve sessions is based on storytelling. Participants tell their own stories and then clergy and catechists tell theirs. The story of the parish is shared by founding members and the story of the Anglican Church is rehearsed. Finally the Christian story is told. At each session ten to fifteen minutes are given to the leader of some aspect of the church's ministry such as Christian outreach or music to introduce his or her program in the parish. Some reading in a very basic inquirer's class book is assigned along with some Bible reading and prayer assignments. It is during this time, too, that information concerning the customs and ceremonies of the church are shared. A tour of the church, the sacristy and other facilities is taken. This is a time for general information to be given and it is an opportunity to orient the newcomers to worship and to the life of the parish.[13]

In this particular church, the inquiry period coincides with the beginning of the church school in September and continues throughout the fall, culminating on the first Sunday of Advent with the visit of the bishop. During the months of September and October, the inquirers are joined by individual sponsors and trained catechists, each of whom will work closely with a group of four inquirers and their sponsors. This process includes not only weekly Sunday morning sessions led by clergy and lay people; it extends to informal gatherings for hospitality and community building. In small discussions and in the larger group, there is time for sharing personal and religious stories, asking questions and exploring new ways of being part of the

---

[12]"The Process of the Catechumenate, St. James' Church, Jackson, Mississippi, An Outline," c. 1984, p. 7. [Referred to hereafter as "An Outline."]
[13]"An Outline," p. 1.

Body of Christ. Throughout the three months, regular reading assignments are made; daily devotional readings in Scripture are suggested; other booklets, charts and prepared materials are made available. Each Inquirer is invited to meet with one of the priests for an in-depth interview before the decision is made to continue the journey in faith.[14]

THE PERIOD OF THE CATECHUMENATE

It is during this period [of the catechumenate] that catechists play a particularly important role, as, in group discussions, in small groups and in the larger community, they interpret the word and the church's teaching to the catechumens and candidates and encourage and enable them to search the scriptures. In the Catechumenate at St. James', there is a careful balance between clerical and lay leadership. During each of the hour sessions of the Catechumenate Period, a priest presides and introduces the subject, engages the whole group in discussion, assigns topics for reflection, then summarizes and makes a concluding, comprehensive statement. The priest's comments may be theoretical, historical, doctrinal or personal.

The focus of the discussion moves from the priest leading the whole group to smaller table groups of eight to ten. For each table there is a catechist, trained in theological study and group process. Actually, any of the twelve catechists are qualified to lead the whole group (and on occasion they do fill in for the clergy); many of them have completed Education for Ministry: Theological Education by Extension, directed by the University of the South. Others are currently enrolled in EFM or are engaged in some other course of theological or Biblical study. Each catechist is provided with a detailed outline of each session and suggested points for reflection. The catechists meet with the

---

[14]Rev. Anne Broad Stevenson, "The Inquiry Period: One Church's Model," *Water and Fire,* Fall 1986, pp. 7–8.

clergy team several times during the year to discuss the material and their role as mentors.

The role of the sponsor continues to be crucial during the Catechumenate Period. Whereas the catechist is responsible for a table and its group process, sponsors are directly responsible for their candidate or catechumen. For many of those journeying toward baptism and/or confirmation, the period of the Catechumenate can be a time of questions and of confrontation with other views of Scripture and ways of believing and living out those beliefs. In those cases where the sponsor took seriously his or her responsibilities, their relationship with their candidate or catechumen was one of growing trust and communication.[15]

THE ENLIGHTENMENT PERIOD

This period begins with the Rite of Election on the first Sunday in Lent. This period prepares catechumens and candidates for Easter eve when baptism and the renewal of vows (the center of the catechetical process) are made. Thus the theme of this period is, "What is baptismal faith?" The cycle A lectionary readings form the basis for answering that question (1) by choosing Old Testament passages that have to do with God's relationship to the people who discerned his presence in their midst from generation to generation, (2) by choosing epistle passages that underline the effects of participation in the baptismal community, and (3) by selecting gospel pericopes (passages probably existing alone in the period of oral transmission) that present Jesus and his message at the center of baptismal faith. While the catechumen period is devoted more to the church's teachings about creation, sin, judgment and redemption, this period concentrates on the preparation of mind, heart and spirit for the Easter eve experience of and later reflection on the Paschal Mystery. The scrutinies (rites of healing) may be used

---

15. Stevenson, "The Period of the Catechumenate," *Water and Fire.*

on the 3rd, 4th, and 5th Sundays in Lent to ritualize the purification process of this period.[16]

THE MYSTAGOGICAL PERIOD

It is during this period that catechumens and candidates reflect upon the Paschal Mystery as experienced in the Liturgy of the Easter Vigil. The death/life cycles of life are identified and Christ's gift of eternal life is explored in terms of experience, response, and commitment. The process of this period is to lead the new Christians into a deeper awareness of new life in himself or herself and to heighten his or her awareness of the particular gift that he or she has been given in life. It follows then to identify avenues by which he or she will continue to grow and be nurtured in the faith. It also involves an identification of personal gifts to offer for the ministry of the community to the world. Life in Christ is a gift and in order to grow and become full, it is shared in relationship to him and his church in service to all humankind. This is the theme of this period and its conclusion is on Pentecost when the bishop comes for the service of Confirmation. Among all the meanings the church has given this sacramental act, in this context it becomes, at least, the laying on of hands for the empowerment for ministry.[17]

[*For further detail on the presentations and discussions, assigned readings, and texts for Bible study, the "Outline" is available from St. James' Episcopal Church.*]

Editor's note: St. Jame' tends to refer to the catechumenal process as the "Catechumenate." Since they refer to both the baptized and unbaptized, their usage departs from that set forth in The Book of Occasional Services.

---

[16]"An Outline," p. 3.
[17]"An Outline," pp. 5–6.

Section 7

Session Plans:
Milwaukee Pilot Project

St. Luke's (average attendance: 195) and St. Andrew's (average attendance: 160) Episcopal Churches, Madison, WI[1]

During the intensive period of preparation and reflection, the two congregations followed a similar basic outline with some specific variations.

Session 1   Humanity
Session 2   Sin
Session 3   Redemption
Session 4   Church
Session 5   Sacraments
Session 6   Prayer
Session 7   God
Session 8   Last Things
Session 9   Christian Personality

SESSION PLANS FOR ST. LUKE'S, MADISON

Each session was divided into three parts.

1. Faith Story by a parish leader, starting with the rector, with time for reaction and comment.

---

[1]Arvedson and May, "Sharing Resources in Madison, Wisconsin," *Water and Fire* (Summer 1987), pp. 2–3.

2. Small group discussion based on Frederick and Barbara Wolf, *Journey in Faith,* followed by large group summation.
3. Bible study using the Gospel for the following Sunday.

SESSION PLANS FOR ST. ANDREW'S, MADISON

1. Opening Devotion (5 min.)—an appropriate Psalm
2. Reflection on Sunday's Gospel (20 min.)—using the African method of Bible Study
3. Presentation on the Topic by the Rector (60 min.)

   Break (10 min.)

4. Small group discussion, to formulate questions on topic (15 min.)
5. Discussion of Questions from small groups (15 min.)
6. Compline, reading next Sunday's Gospel (10 min.)

St. Francis Episcopal Church, Menomonee Falls (average attendance: 140)

Session		
Session	1	Human Nature
Session	2	Sin
Session	3	Jesus Christ
Session	4	The Church
Session	5	The Bible
Session	6	Sacraments: Baptism, Confirmation, Holy Eucharist
Session	7	Sacraments: Holy Matrimony, Holy Orders, Reconciliation, Unction
Session	8	Corporate (Liturgical) Worship
Session	9	Personal Prayer
Session	10	God the Father
Session	11	God the Holy Spirit
Session	12	Christian Personality (Ethics)
Session	13	"The Last Things"
Session	14	Where are we now?

Two hour sessions had a varied format each week to include Bible study, small group discussion, case studies, and presentations. Resources used were:

The Episcopal Church Center, *In Dialogue,* and *Proclamation as Offering Story and Choice;*

Frederick and Barbara Wolf, *A Journey in Faith;* Lyman Coleman, *The Serendipity Bible Study Book;* Walter Wink, *Transforming Bible Study;*

"What Anglicans Believe" by Verna Dozier, a videotape; "An Outline of the Faith" from *The Book of Common Prayer.*

EXAMPLES OF THREE SESSIONS

SESSION 1: Sin

PURPOSE: To assist participants in seeing how sin invades our lives and how we, on our own, are unable to conquer it.

PROCESS:

   5 Minute Introduction, welcome, review of previous session

   30 Minute Bible study:

Matthew 3:13–17 using "The African Model," 20 minutes in small groups; 10 minutes in plenary group.

   45 Minute Small group exercise:

   Use the exercise for the session on "Sin" from *Journey in Faith.* Present the story to the plenary group; divide into small groups for discussion of questions concerning the story; return to plenary group for reports on small group discussions.

   20 Minute Presentation by leader:

   1. The nature of sin as defined in the "Outline of the Faith."

   2. Discussion of ineffective ways we try to deal with sin on our own (fight it, resolutions, flight, run away from it, deny it, say it doesn't matter, or just give up because that's the way I am).

   3. What we need is help from beyond ourselves. . . . A Savior.

   5 Minute Wrap-up; prayer circle.

SESSION 2: The Church
PURPOSE: To identify the church as the primary place we
encounter Jesus Christ
PROCESS:
    5 Minute Welcome, introduction to session
    15 Minute Review of previous session
    30 Minute Bible Study:
Matthew 4:12–23 using "Questions for Biblical Reflection," 20
minutes in small groups; 10 minutes in plenary group.
    55 Minute Group exercise
    15 Minutes: On three sheets of newsprint, leader(s) place the
following headings:

    1. Helps me to clearly see myself.
    2. Forgives me and gives me power and courage to live my
life.
    3. Gives direction and meaning to my life.
As they write each of the above, leader(s) give a personal wit-
ness/reflection on a moment in their lives when they have experienced one of these life-renewing moments.
    15 Minute: Divide into small groups and invite participants to
share instances in their lives when they experienced moments of
life renewal that fit into the categories listed on the newsprint;
leaders keep them informed of time so each participant has
opportunity to share.
    10 Minutes: Feedback to large group; leader asks if any wish
to share their discussion.
    15 Minutes: Summary by one leader. Note that we usually
experience such life-renewing moments through relationships
with others. Spend a few moments reflecting on how it is
through such relationships that we experience the redeeming
action of Christ. Also, note that the church is one place where
such relationships can and should occur. Stress some of the
misconceptions about the nature of the church. Refer to the
section on the church in the "Outline of Faith," *BCP.*
    15 Minutes: Questions and answers; wrap-up; prayer circle.

SESSION 3: Christian personality (ethics)
PURPOSE: To help participants apply their Christian faith
to life situations.
PROCESS:
  30 Minute Bible Study: John 4:5–42
  60 Minutes: Small Group Exercise:

  1. Participants have been asked to submit a case study/personal experience that involves a Christian ethical question. Some examples received are:
  a. The bank informs you $10,000 has been deposited into your account. You know it is not yours. What do you do?
  b. You are at a party with a friend (the driver), who has had too much to drink. [Submitted by a teenager.]
  c. Someone with whom you work has a history of sexually abusing children and now is in a position that involves working with children. The supervisor does not know this person's history. What do you do?
  2. Participants are divided into small groups. Each group is given a case study selected from those submitted. They have twenty minutes to develop a response to the situation and a defense on the basis of their Christian faith.
  3. Reassemble the plenary group. Each group has five minutes to present its case study, its resolution, and its defense. Allow time for discussion after each case.
  15 Minute Wrap-up: Time for questions and answers led by clergy/lay leader. Prayer circle.

St Peter's Episcopal Church
West Allis (average attendance: 150)

[*The lesson plans designed by the team at St. Peter's, West Allis, are described by the catechists in a paper they wrote reflecting on their first year with the process.*]

[We decided] to view the catechumenal experience as a *process* and not as a program . . . This would include reducing the scope of the course. We would use experimental methods and move away from the traditional confirmation class approach. The catechumenal process would be led by the laity. The rector would serve only as a resource person. The sponsors would be an integral part of all catechetical sessions. Finally, we decided to schedule the catechumenal sessions during the Sunday morning Christian education tour.

On I Advent, our inquirers enrolled during our Sunday services. It was in these services that a sponsor was assigned to our one catechumen and to each candidate. In a sense, the enrollment liturgy introduced our catechumen, the candidates, and their sponsors to the wider parish community. With the first stage, we formed small groups composed of two candidates, or our catechumen, their sponsors, and two table leaders. Each group read the appointed Sunday lessons and reflected on how the Gospel of Christ touched their daily lives and how they could respond to the Good News. During each session, the entire catechumenal community was "held up" to the Lord in the chapel by our Prayer Support Group. At the end of each session, we formed a prayer circle. Prayers were offered, a catechist (a committee member or table leader) laid hands on our catechumen and on each candidate in silent prayer. During this period, we learned more about God and each other through a process we did not completely understand. The Holy Spirit seemed to be guiding us because what was happening was good.

St. Peter's Episcopal Church, West Allis

CATECHUMENAL RETREAT SCHEDULE

GOOD FRIDAY:

7:00 PM - Stations of the Cross	Church
7:45 PM - Meeting & Set-up	Downstairs

8:15 PM - Meditation—Prodigal Son
        Heavy Silence   Church
9:00 PM - Meditation—Renunciations
        Heavy Silence   Church
9:45 PM - Tenebrae Service
        Light Silence   Church
10:45 PM - Confessions with Fr. Jay
        Spiritual Direction with Deacon
        Fiona
        Light Silence

HOLY SATURDAY:

8:00 AM - Good Saturday Liturgy   Church
8:30 AM - Breaking of the Fast   Downstairs
9:00 AM - Service of Opening (*Ephphatha*)   Church
9:15 AM - Reading of the *Story of Euphemius* Downstairs
9:30 AM - Break
9:45 AM - Meditation—Zacchaeus
        Discussion   Downstairs
10:30 AM - Meditation—Baptismal Affirmations
        Group Discussion of Affirmations Downstairs
12:15 PM - Dismissal of Catechumens   Church
        Parabaptismal Liturgy for Candi-
        dates   Church

[*The following is a narrative description of the retreat written by the convener and catechist at St. Peter's.* [19]]

The final preparation of the catechumenal community for Easter was an overnight retreat which began with Stations of the Cross on Good Friday evening. This was followed by a period of silence during which a meditation on the Prodigal Son was given by the rector. A second meditation on the Baptismal renunciations, [*BCP*, p. 302] was given by our seminarian. A

---

[19]Jelinek and Tapper, "Our Journey Into the Unknown," p. 4.

special Good Friday Tenebrae service, compiled by the rector ended the day's devotions. We journeyed from the cross to the tomb.

The Liturgy for Holy Saturday was read in the morning followed by the rite of *Ephphatha,* "Service of Opening," which included a reading from Mark 7:31–37. The rector, touching the ears and mouth of each candidate, exclaimed: "Ephphatha, be opened by the Grace of Christ. Listen to the Word of God and proclaim the faith he teaches you for his praise and glory." Our catechumen's ears and mouth were anointed at this rite. We then listened to the reading of an account of a Fourth Century baptism of a boy, Euphemius. The group next heard and discussed two meditations on the story of Zacchaeus and the Baptismal Affirmation [*BCP,* p. 302–30]. The catechumen was dismissed, and the candidates, sponsors, and team then participated in a closing liturgy, each person went to the altar, dipped a hand into a bowl of water, crossed himself/herself and prayed, "I, (Name), have been baptized; grant me grace to remain faithful." In doing so we symbolically recalled our own baptism.

Section 8

Preparation for the Rites of Admission and Enrollment and Reflection on Them

The Rites of Admission and Enrollment can be enhanced by preparation. All the participants—catechumens, their sponsors, liturgist, and celebrant—meet for about two hours to consider what has been going on in their journeys. The rites are varied slightly as appropriate to reflect whatever emphases are needed.

To prepare for admission, all may reflect on a turning point in their lives (see the discussion model in Appendix C, Section 4). Potential catechumens and sponsors pair up for about forty minutes to share their turning point experiences. If this approach has been used before, suggest that each person select a recent turning point, which can be a minor or a major one. Catechumens formulate brief expansions on the answer "Life in Christ," which reflect their specific journeys at this point. When the group regathers, all share their expansion. The presenter and celebrant lead all to help each potential catechumen to be succinct, to reflect their own particular journey, and to preserve appropriate privacy.

The liturgist then briefs the participants on meaningful ways to carry out the actions that will be used. Pairs of candidates and sponsors stand at different places in the aisles so that everyone in the congregation is close to at least one pair. The celebrant may stand directly in front of each catechumen as "What do you seek?" is asked. Each catechumen answers, practicing the specific elaboration planned. Similar procedures will be thought of as experience with the rite progresses.

For some, this preparation may seem too much like a rehearsal. Some of the rite may lose meaning just because it is practiced and the candidate knows what is coming. The purpose, however, is to carry on the rite meaningfully rather than correctly. A further purpose of the preparation is for those leading the rite to become more familiar with the participants' stories so that they can reflect them in the rite.

At the first session after the rite, the liturgist can guide reflection on the rite. First the catechumens, then sponsors, then presenter, then celebrant, share something of their experience of the rite. All others present then share their own experience of the rite. Congregations reflecting in this way—when time can be found for them to do so—find that reflection increases everyone's sense of meaning in the rite and sense of power bestowed during it.

A similar preparation is offered for enrollment. Here the sharing between catechumen and sponsor might be on what has happened for each during this stage. Each might answer, "How is God calling me now?" and, "How am I responding to God's call now?" When God calls, a price has to be paid. What price has been, is being, or will be paid? Catechumens may also name and share their "growing edges"—those areas of spiritual development on which they are now working and will need help in the near future. They may also share a particular area of discipline and fasting that they will undertake for Lent, taking care that they name its relevance to their daily lives. The liturgist recommends actions that will enhance the rite; for example, some informal words by the sponsor on what they have seen happening in the life of the catechumen. The sponsors say aloud the name of their catechumen and sign the book also.

The underlying principle involved in such preparation for and reflection on the rites is that the rites are testimonies to growth in faith and living. Catechumens are moving through the rite to the next stage because they have moved ahead in their believing and living. The catechumenal team has seen this growth and rejoices in it. The preparation helps participants to see more clearly their own growth and so offer thanksgiving for what has been received and pray more earnestly for help in the growth that lies ahead.

Section 9

Preparation for and Reflection on the Rites for the Baptized

These rites can also be enhanced by preparation. The preparation centers on the journeys of the baptized and the articulation of where they are now. All the principals share in the preparation.

The "turning point" reflection used at the Admission of Catechumens also works well as preparation for The Welcoming of Baptized Christians Into a Community. The response to the question, "What do you seek?" can be expanded to reflect each person's pilgrimage.

A sharing between candidate and sponsor of their growth since the Welcoming and of their present "growing edges" in faith and living can be valuable preparation for the Calling of the Baptized to Continuing Conversion. At the rite, the sponsor can certify to the congregation something of the candidate's growth, while speaking generally to keep a sense of privacy.

Preparation for the Maundy Thursday Rite of Preparation for the Paschal Holy Days can center on an exchange between candidate and sponsor concerning what they are learning about being served and serving. As the candidates' feet are washed and then wash the feet of others, their sponsors can stand beside them, praying silently for their needs to grow in being served and serving.

The liturgist, joined by others where possible, thinks through the rite's actions so that their meaning is heightened and the congregation participates as much as possible. The liturgist's proposals are practiced during the preparation.

As with the rites for the catechumens, these rites grow in meaning by reflecting on what happened to the participants sharing them.

As with the unbaptized, the whole of the preparation and reflection should ensure that the candidate and the catechumenal team are aware of the candidate's growth in faith and living. This awareness brings both joy and seriousness to the catechumenal process.

Section 10

A Catechumenal Plan for a Family-Size Congregation

Gathering: Early to mid-Pentecost (June through September)
- Preparation of all members for sharing this flyer with friends and neighbors.
- Prayers for friends and neighbors with invitations to Sunday services and congregational activities.

Inquiry: Late Pentecost (October and November)
- Four sessions with inquirers and sponsors looking at one's initial attraction to the Christian faith.
- What do I seek?
- Why am I here? What brought me to this point in my life?
- What are my hopes and desires?
- Decision whether or not to continue.

Formation in Belief and Practice: Advent, Christmas, and Epiphany
- Admission of Catechumens: Advent I—Signing with the Cross.
- The Welcoming of Baptized Christians Into a Community/the Affirming of Seekers of Deeper Commitment to the Baptismal Covenant: Advent II—Signing or initialing the Baptismal Register.
- Weekly sessions with catechumens, candidates and sponsors.

- The Sunday Gospels using the African Bible study method.
- The sacramental way of nurture in the faith.
- Individual spirituality.
- Small group life.
- Community service project.
- Pursuing alleviation of poverty with local, state or national representatives.
- Discussion of stewardship, proportionate giving and tithing.

Intensive Preparation and the Rites of the Paschal Holy Days:
Lent, Holy Week and Easter

- The Calling of the Baptized to Continuing Conversion: Ash Wednesday—candidates receive the ashes first and help administer them to others.
- Enrollment of Candidates for Baptism: Lent I—sign the Register of Catechumens.
- Laying on of hands for silent prayer by all at Sunday services.
- Gifts for ministry in one's daily places—work, home, community, citizenship, leisure and church.
- Maundy Thursday Rite of Preparation for the Paschal Holy Days—the already baptized receive foot washing first and then help wash the feet of others.
- Easter Vigil with Holy Baptism for the Catechumens.
- Easter Week for Reaffirmation of Baptismal Vows with the Bishop—for both groups.

Formation in Ministry: Easter season

With sponsors, all explore Christian ministry now at work, home, community, citizenship, leisure, and church.

Form of Commitment to Christian service—when appropriate as the newly baptized or strengthened choose to express their commitment to ministry in one (or more) of their specific daily places and ask the support of their Christian brothers and sisters.

With appreciation to the Reverend William Cooper and the catechumenal team of St. John's, Essex, NY who have developed a similar procedure.

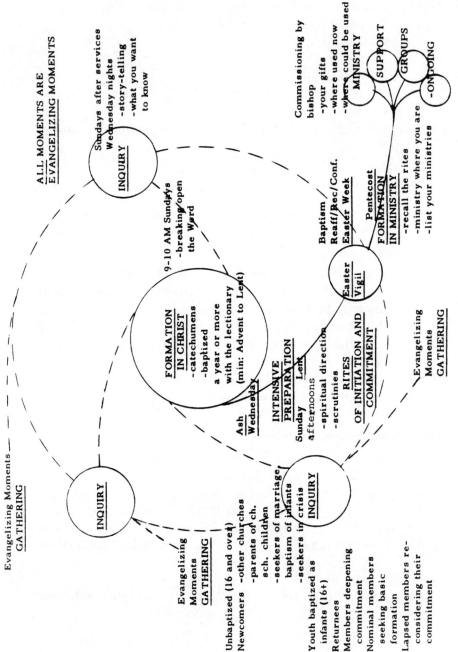

ALL MOMENTS ARE
EVANGELIZING MOMENTS

Evangelizing Moments
GATHERING

INQUIRY
Sundays after services
Wednesday nights
-story-telling
-what you want
to know

INQUIRY

FORMATION
IN CHRIST
-catechumens
-baptized
a year or more
with the lectionary
(min: Advent to Lent)

9-10 AM Sundays
-breaking open
the Word

INTENSIVE
PREPARATION
-spiritual direction
-scrutinies
Ash Sunday
Wednesday Lent
afternoons

RITES
OF INITIATION AND
COMMITMENT

Easter
Vigil

Baptism
Reaff/Rec/Conf.
Easter Week
Pentecost

FORMATION
IN MINISTRY
-recall the rites
-ministry where you are
-list your ministries

Commissioning by
bishop
-your gifts
-where used now
-where could be used

MINISTRY
SUPPORT
GROUPS
-ONGOING

INQUIRY

Evangelizing
Moments
GATHERING

Unbaptized (16 and over)
Newcomers -other churches
-parents of ch.
sch. children
-seekers of marriage
baptism of infants
-seekers in crisis

Youth baptized as
infants (16+)
Returnees
Members deepening
commitment
Nominal members
seeking basic
formation
Lapsed members re-
considering their
commitment

A Cathechumenal "Flow-Chart" for a Large Congregation

Section 12

Design and Evaluation: Short- and Long-Range Plans

Whenever we *plan* to do a program, a lesson, a conference, a meeting, or any kind of event, it is important to plan it as carefully as we can, so that the outcome will be as satisfactory as we hope it will be. Moreover, if we plan well, the plan itself makes the perfect tool for evaluating the outcome of the event. You may already have a very satisfactory planning method of your own. All the better. Always, *write your plan,* keeping track of every detail.

DATA. You need to know *who* wants to learn or do *what, when* and *where.* Data concerning who and what is to be learned or done are key. Allow enough time to get this information accurately and plan what questions you will ask to get it. The *place* you will be able to work in as well as the working space it offers. *How many* clients can you be sure of? *How much* will it *cost,* who will *pay?* Can you do the work alone or do you need others to help you? You may already have much of the information you need; be sure you try to think of everything.

ANALYZE. Knowing what you know, is it feasible for you to proceed further? Does any aspect of the data present a problem that needs solution before you proceed? Do you understand the purpose and goals of the event.

PURPOSE. The purpose needs to be as clear a statement as you (and your team) are able to make about the outcome you hope for, as a result of the event you plan to offer. Example:

"To enable teachers to plan their lessons more effectively." A test question for a purpose is "In order that what might happen?" If you can go further with it, the purpose is not clear. Moreover, the purpose should promise only what you really believe you can do. The purpose should be easily understood by the student or client, so they can decide whether they wish to go into the event you have planned. The purpose takes a long time to work out (longer if you have a team), but it is well worth the time, because you will be more accurate in reaching your goal.

PLAN. This is the general statement of how to propose to carry out your purpose. Example: "Give a theory lecture on lesson planning, give a printed set of guidelines to the students, let them practice writing a plan, individually. Gather in small groups to criticize each other's work. Gather in the large group to share learnings and general dialogue on the subject."

THEME. Plans can be enhanced and made more interesting by deciding to work around a *theme.* Example: "Ways we can act out the tumbling of the walls at Jericho." Themes help to highlight the idea we want to teach. Use you imagination.

PROCEDURE. At every step of the plan, time everything, assign responsibilities, include every detail. Example:

SATURDAY OF THE DAILY SCHEDULE:
8:00 AM Breakfast
9:00 AM Whole group meets in Room A. Lecture (by Charles), assignments of tasks, questions.
10:00 AM Small groups for critique. (Ed will check rooms for supplies needed. We all will visit the groups.)

EVALUATE. Using the plan that you develop from these guidelines, as soon as possible after the event has been completed go through each item of the plan, step by step. What worked, what did not work, how can you make it better the next time you do it? Even more important questions are: What was happening between and within the participants? What questions or issues seem to be emerging? How is the leadership team working together?

Section 13

St. Paul's Church, Indianapolis

Materials Introducing a Catechumenal Process for Corporation-Size Churches

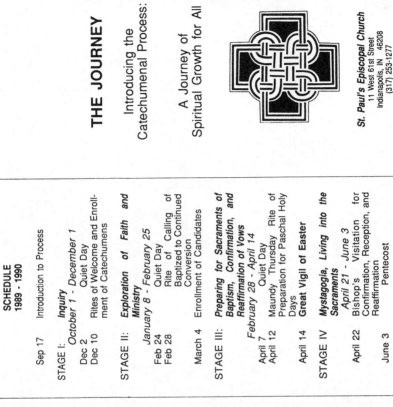

THE JOURNEY

Introducing the
Catechumenal Process:

A Journey of
Spiritual Growth for All

St. Paul's Episcopal Church
11 West 61st Street
Indianapolis, IN   46208
(317) 253-1277

SCHEDULE
1989 - 1990

Sep 17   Introduction to Process

STAGE I: *Inquiry*
            October 1 - December 1

Dec 2   Quiet Day
Dec 10   Rites of Welcome and Enroll-
            ment of Catechumens

STAGE II: *Exploration of Faith and
            Ministry*

            January 8 - February 25

Feb 24   Quiet Day
Feb 28   Rite of Calling of
            Baptized to Continued
            Conversion

March 4   Enrollment of Candidates

STAGE III: *Preparing for Sacraments of
            Baptism, Confirmation, and
            Reaffirmation of Vows*
            February 28 - April 14

April 7   Quiet Day
April 12   Maundy Thursday Rite of
            Preparation for Paschal Holy
            Days

April 14   **Great Vigil of Easter**

STAGE IV   *Mystagogia, Living into the
            Sacraments*
            April 21 - June 3

April 22   Bishop's Visitation for
            Confirmation, Reception, and
            Reaffirmation

June 3   Pentecost

THE CONGREGATION'S JOURNEY

While the participants engage in individual journeys, the process itself is a time of growth for all members of the congregation.

* We as a congregation offer this process for spiritual enrichment both to one another and to the whole community.

* It is process representing the fullness of ministry in the Episcopal Church. Lay persons and clergy share leadership. Parish clergy and the Bishop of the Diocese take their roles in the liturgies of the process.

* THE JOURNEY has a central place in the life of the whole congregation. Through the liturgies, participants both witness to the congregation and serve as representatives of the congregation, making public their commitment to enter each stage and engage in a journey of faith. Each stage is celebrated with an appropriate rite through the seasons of the Christian Year: in Advent, on Ash Wednesday, on Maundy Thursday, at the Great Vigil of Easter, in Eastertide, and at Pentecost.

The interest and support of every member of St. Paul's is an important and valued part of THE JOURNEY. We all share this ministry--one we can offer to all our members and to all who come to us seeking to be followers of Jesus Christ.

THE JOURNEY offers me a chance to reassess my personal relationship with God in fellowship with other members of my parish.
-- John Bowman

As one newly baptized, I thought THE JOURNEY would simply be the logical "next step" in my Christian education—perhaps an academic program leading to Confirmation. While I hope to be confirmed through my participation in THE JOURNEY, I now realize this will be time to learn how God acts among us and within us.
-- Anne Robinson

I want to explore ways in which I can live out the vows of my baptismal covenant . . . (and) I want to do that in community with fellow Christians.
-- Derrick Harding

As a newcomer to St. Paul's, THE JOURNEY offers me a unique opportunity to know parish members beyond Sunday morning coffee. More importantly, it enables me to explore the authority given to me at my baptism as a member of Christ's body, and how that exploration empowers me to understand my life and work as ministry.
-- Emily Puckett

My journey in faith makes me aware that THE JOURNEY is important in bringing new depth of spirituality to my life.
-- Julia Collins

At its heart, THE JOURNEY is meant to be a process that touches us and enables each one of us to grow spiritually. It is an invitation to positive change --to become more fully what we can be as Christians, both as individuals and as members of a congregation.

THE JOURNEY is called a catechumenal process. Yet it differs markedly from that concept of "catechism" many of us may have. Rather than instruction, it is a process of discovery and growth and change. It is to help us put the promises of our baptisms into action and integrate them into all aspects of our lives.

THE INDIVIDUAL'S JOURNEY

THE JOURNEY begins with a period of time for inquiry that is open to all--baptized and unbaptized, youth and adult.

Lasting approximately ten weeks, this first Inquiry Stage is a time when we can come together to:

* Share our personal histories or stories. Happy or sad, simple or complex, each one of us has a story to tell. We are always free to tell as much or as little as we like. The telling offers one a unique opportunity to look at one's own life, to listen to the story of another's, and to talk together about how each of us has come to know God. The simplest thing to say about this process is that those who have done so (in training workshops at St. Paul's) have found it very rewarding.

* Reflect on our stories in light of the stories of the Bible. Like the people we meet in Scripture, we are being shaped by our relationship to God. Through our Bible study, we are able to learn more about who we are as Christians.

* Examine the possibilities for our lives. We examine our spiritual gifts and our natural, or God-given, talents in light of our baptismal promises.

* Learn more about the Christian Faith. Using The Book of Common Prayer and other resources, we explore how Christian faith is expressed in the traditions of the Episcopal Church.

Most of all, the period of the Inquiry Stage is meant to create an atmosphere of trust, support and fellowship, so participants can freely decide whether or not to commit themselves to entering into the next stage of a disciplined exploration of Christian living.

Those who do decide to continue will participate in the first of several public liturgical celebrations marking the four stages of THE JOURNEY. From Advent through Pentecost, THE JOURNEY will lead its participants into:

* study of scripture
* practice of prayer
* theological reflection
* service to the community
* intensive observance of Lenten disciplines
* reflection on the baptismal covenant
* study of the sacraments

While the "process" of THE JOURNEY may come to a close, our journey in faith is unending. Through the process, it is hoped participants will be able to discern and enact their own purpose as followers of Christ.

THE JOURNEY

Late Pentecost

STAGE I   INQUIRY
Content: - Sharing our own stories of our life journey
- learning about and discerning the Christian life through scripture and the catechism of the <u>Book of Common Prayer</u>
- prayer, worship, Christian service

Adults will meet for "Inquirers Class Sessions"
Young people preparing for confirmation will begin with a retreat and continue with regular meetings

Advent I

RITE I   Welcoming into the Community
This rite marks the formal beginning of The Journey and of the Catechumenate.
- Enrollment of Catechumens (unbaptized adults and older youths)
- Welcoming of Baptized Christians into Community
- Commissioning of Sponsors

Advent through Epiphany

STAGE II   Exploration of Faith and Ministry
Content: - scripture, especially the lectionary
- prayer
- ministry and service
- theological reflection

Adults will be involved in some form of ministry or service. Sessions will use the lectionary as a text and provide time for theological reflection on experience of ministry
Young people will be engaged in some ministry in the community and reflect on their experiences in sessions.

Ash Wednesday and Lent I

RITE II   Enrollment and Calling
These rites mark entry into a Lenten time of intensive preparation and discipline.
- Admission of Candidates for Baptism
- Calling of Baptized to Continuing Conversion

---

*Portions of "The Journey" appearing on pages ooo and ooo may be reproduced by a congregation for its own use. Reproduction other than this purpose, without written permission, is prohibited.

Lent

STAGE III   **Preparing for the Sacrament of Holy Baptism and Affirmation of Baptismal Vows**
Content: - Lenten disciplines of prayer, fasting and examination
- reflection on the Lenten gospel readings
- deepening the call to conversion and to Christian witness and service
- reflection on the Baptismal Covenant

Both adults and young people will use the Lenten Season to reflect on the meaning of the Baptismal Covenant. Opportunities for retreats will be offered.

Holy Week

RITE III   **Maundy Thursday Rite of Preparation for Paschal Holy Days**
The Baptized complete their Lenten disciplines in preparation for their celebration of Easter and renewal of Baptismal Vows

EASTER   **The Great Vigil of Easter**
Holy Baptism and Reaffirmation of Baptismal Vows

Easter Season

BISHOP'S VISITATION
During the 50 Days of Easter, the Bishop will administer laying on of hands for candidates for confirmation, reception, or reaffirmation of Baptismal vows

Stage IV   **The Mystagogia - Living into the Paschal Mystery**
Content: - time to reflect on the baptismal promises
- focus on living out the Christian life
- study of the sacraments
- discerning one's own specific Christian ministry or service

Pentecost

Celebration of the Fullness of the Corporate Life and Witness of the Church as We Are Sent out by the Holy Spirit for Evangelism and Service

- A celebration emphasizing that those who have journeyed together through this process are ready to take their places in the congregation, and in the larger community of the Body of Christ. Sponsors introduce their candidates to the congregation.

THE JOURNEY:

A CATECHUMENAL PROCESS

FORMATION FOR CHRISTIAN

LIFE AND MINISTRY

St. Paul's Episcopal Church
10 West 61st Street
Indianapolis, IN   46208

Fall, Late Pentecost

STAGE I: Inquiry

Advent

RITE I: *Welcoming into the Community*

STAGE II: Exploration of Faith and Ministry

Lent

RITE II: *Enrollment and Calling*

STAGE III: Preparing for the Sacrament of Holy Baptism and the Reaffirmation of Baptismal Vows

RITE III: *Maundy Thursday Rite of Preparation for Paschal Holy Days*

The Great Vigil of Easter

STAGE IV: The Mystagogia, Living into the Paschal Mystery

Bishop's Visitation: Confirmtion, Reception, and Reaffirmation

Pentecost

As a Christian community, we are to be a place where people can find sustenance, healing, support, and care. We are to be a place where the Gospel is proclaimed and God's love is manifest. We are to be a place where our human story is given new meaning in God's story. We are to be a place where all are welcomed and loved in God's name. **THE JOURNEY** is an organized process for welcoming, supporting, and caring for people and for providing a place where the human story and God's story can be heard and told. The process is not an end or a solution. It is an imperfect way of offering ourselves to be companions to one another on our Christian journeys.

THE JOURNEY is open to all persons, baptized or unbaptized, who want to enter a process of exploration and growth. Divided into four stages, each stage marked by an appropriate rite. At the center are the initiatory sacraments of baptism, confirmation, reception, reaffirmation, and baptismal renewal. Beyond these sacramental celebrations is a process to form people of faith as they strive to live in their daily places as followers of Jesus Christ.

THE JOURNEY is a process of formation to prepare and support persons for living according to the vows and promises of Christian Baptism. It is modeled on an early Church pattern for initiating Christians through a four-stage process that provided ritual, instruction, practical experience and study, spiritual guidance, and nurture. A similar process is becoming increasingly credible in our contemporary world where forming Christians in the midst of secular, pluralistic society presents new challenges for our Churches.

In the third and fourth centuries, persons wanting to become Christian would participate in a lengthy preparation process, often as long as three years, before being baptized. The initiatory sacraments of baptism, confirmation and first communion were administered to candidates at the Great Vigil of Easter. Persons preparing for baptism were called *catechumens*, meaning "hearers of the Word." During their time of formation, they were sponsored by members of the community, and were given guidance and training for becoming Christians, especially for living as Christians.

Although modeled after early church practice of "the catechumenate," **THE JOURNEY** is not only for those who are unbaptized. Since formation for Christian living is a life-long pilgrimage, this program is for:

- persons baptized as infants who want to make mature public affirmation of their faith
- persons seeking out the church for marriage or for baptism of a child
- newcomers from other churches
- persons returning to the church from another church or denomination
- active members seeking to deepen their commitment
- nominal members seeking basic Christian formation
- lapsed members reconsidering their Christian commitment.

Persons reaffirming their commitment, renewing their vows, or seeking to deepen their understanding of faith need formation, just as do persons preparing for baptism. **THE JOURNEY** provides this nurture.

At its heart, **THE JOURNEY** is about conversion. The language of our baptismal covenant presumes we are growing into our faith and ministry. In our Baptismal Covenant, we vow to "continue" and to "persevere" and to "seek" and to "strive." The language presumes we are growing and being transformed. Such Christian transformation is conversion, an essentially human experience of growth and change.

Conversion takes place when one confronts a growing sense of restlessness and separation, when one's world of meaning is challenged or rendered worthless. It is followed by an "in-between" stage marked by disorientation and disillusionment and an intense desire for something distant and unknown. It is resolved when one experiences rebirth and finds new life and renewed purpose. This experience of separation, disillusionment, and renewal -- or of death, burial, and resurrection - lies at the very heart of human experience. It also is at the very heart of the Christian experience. Jesus endured this in his crucifixion, death, and resurrection; we too endure it when we are plunged into the water of baptism and raised to new life in Christ. It forms the heart of our Christian pilgrimage.

THE JOURNEY is one way that we, the community of St. Pauls, can offer support to persons in this process of Christian growth and conversion.

THE JOURNEY
Youth Track

A Journey of
Spiritual Growth for Young Persons

The Catechumenal Process
leading
toward Baptism,
Confirmation,
and Reaffirmation

St. Paul's Episcopal Church
11 West 61st Street
Indianapolis, Indiana   46208
(317) 253-1277

1989 - 1990 SCHEDULE

Sept. 17	Orientation program for parents and youth.

STAGE I: **Inquiry**
(September 24 - December 3)

Sept. 24	10:15am-12:15pm
Oct. 7-8	Retreat at Hickory Hill
Oct. 22	Meeting 10:15am-12:15pm
Nov. 12	Meeting 10:15am-12:15pm
Nov. 19	Meeting 10:15am-12:15pm
Dec. 2	Quiet Morning
Dec. 10	Rites of Welcome and Enrollment of Catechumens

STAGE II **Exploration of Faith and Ministry**
(January 8 - February 25)

Feb. 24	Quiet Morning
Feb. 28	Rite of Calling of Baptized to Continued Coversion
March 4	Enrollment of Candidates

STAGE III **Preparing for Sacraments of Baptism, Confirmation, and Reaffirmation of Vows**
(February 28 - April 14)

April 7	Quiet Morning
April 12	Maundy Thursday Rite of Preparation for Paschal Holy Days
April 14	**Great Vigil of Easter**

STAGE IV **Mystagogia, Living into the Sacraments**
(April 21 - June 3)

April 22	Bishop's Visitation for Confirmation, Reception, and Reaffirmation
June 3	Pentecost

The Journey is a program and process of learning, discovery, and reflection upon our journey as followers of Christ. The Youth Track is offered to persons in 9th-12th grade who wish to explore and grow in their spiritual identity and pilgrimage. **The Journey** is an invitation to more fully become what we are as young Christians, to reflect upon and practice the life and ministry given to us in Christ.

The Journey begins with a period of inquiry which is open to all, baptized and unbaptized, confirmed and unconfirmed. For those who desire to be baptized and/or confirmed, this program is the catechumenal process which prepares one for those Sacraments.

Lasting until early December, the inquiry stage is a time of:
Sharing our personal histories and stories,
Reflecting upon our stories in light of the stories of the Bible,
Learning more about the Christian faith, and
Examining the possibilities for our lives.

Most of all, the inquiry stage is that period where we create a community of trust, support, and friendship so participants can choose whether to move further into the process towards Baptism and/or Confirmation.

Those who decide to continue in the process after the inquiry stage will participate in the first of several public liturgical celebrations which mark the movement from stage to stage in **The Journey**. From Advent through Pentecost, **The Journey** leads persons into a deeper study of scripture, practice of prayer, theological reflection, service to the community, observance of Lenten disciplines, reflection on the Baptismal Covenant, and study of the sacraments.

The Journey is rooted in the life of the congregation which offers, supports, and celebrates this program for one another and the community throughout the year. In addition to the Youth Track, many members of the congregation will be participating in **The Journey** themselves on the Adult Track. Each person also who chooses to move deeper in the process at Stage II will be given a sponsor, a member of the parish who will walk along with them throughout the year.

The Journey offers an opportunity for adolescents to begin a life-long process of discernment, reflection, and action as followers of and witnesses to Christ.

JOURNEY WITH ME.

APPENDIX D

Texts of Rites for the Unbaptized and for the Baptized[1]

Sections

---

[1]Included by permission of The Church Hymnal Corporation

Section 1

The Preparation of Adults for Holy Baptism: The Catechumenate

Concerning the Catechumenate

The catechumenate is a period of training and instruction in Christian understandings about God, human relationships, and the meaning of life, which culminates in the reception of the Sacraments of Christian Initiation.

The systematic instruction and formation of its catechumens is a solemn responsibility of the Christian community. Traditionally, the preparation of catechumens is a responsibility of the bishop, which is shared with the presbyters, deacons, and appointed lay catechists of the diocese.

Principles of Implementation

1. A catechumen is defined as an unbaptized adult. These rites are appropriate for use only with such persons.
2. During the period of the catechumenate, the context of catechesis is a continual reflection on Scripture, Christian prayer, worship, and the catechumen's gifts for ministry and work for justice and peace. These elements are more or less a part of each catechetical session.

3. The principal curriculum for each catechetical session is reflection on the respective readings of the Sunday Eucharistic Lectionary as these illumine the faith journey of catechumens, sponsors, and catechists.

4. The catechetical methodology of the catechumenal and baptismal rites is: experience first, then reflect. As the catechumen journey from inquiry to baptism, there is formation of an ability to discern God's activity in the events of one's life. It is recommended that the services not be discussed prior to their celebration. It is appropriate that sponsors be well prepared for their ministry in the respective services and to guide and support their catechumen during the celebration.

5. The catechumenate exists throughout the year in the parish, and persons may enter at any time. The catechumenate is of undetermined length for each catechumen. The appropriate time for the call to Candidacy for Baptism is discerned by sponsors, catechists, and clergy on behalf of the local congregation. Baptism of catechumens is normally reserved for the Great Vigil of Easter.

6. Since the catechumenate is ecclesial formation for the ministry of the baptized, it is appropriate that the catechists be representative of the diversity of the local congregation.

7. It is appropriate for those catechumens baptized at the Great Vigil of Easter to join the ministry of sponsor or catechist for new catechumens at the conclusion of the Great Fifty Days.

The Catechumenate is marked by three stages.

Stage 1. The Pre-catechumenal Period. To this stage belongs inquirers' classes with sufficient preparation to enable persons to determine that they wish to become Christians. It is a time during which those who have been initially attracted to the Christian community are guided to examine and test their motives, in order that they may freely commit themselves to pursue a disciplined exploration of the implications of Christian living.

Stage 2. The Catechumenate. Entry into the catechumenate is by a public liturgical act (which may take place for individuals or groups at any time) at the principal Sunday liturgy. Normatively, the act includes signing with the cross. To this stage belong regular association with the worshiping community, the practice of life in accordance with the Gospel (including service to the poor and neglected), encouragement and instruction in the life of prayer, and basic instruction in the history of salvation as revealed in the Holy Scriptures of the Old and New Testaments. This stage will vary in length according to the needs of the individual. For those persons who, although unbaptized, already possess an understanding and appreciation of the Christian religion, it might be relatively short.

Each person to be admitted a catechumen is presented by a sponsor who normally accompanies the catechumen through the process of candidacy and serves as sponsor at Holy Baptism.

Admission to the catechumenate is an appropriate time to determine the name by which one desires to be known in the Christian community. This may be one's given name, a new name legally changed, or an additional name of Christian significance.

From the time of admission, a catechumen is regarded as part of the Christian community. For example, a person who dies during the catechumenate receives a Christian burial.

Stage 3. Candidacy for Baptism. To this stage belongs a series of liturgical acts leading up to baptism. These ordinarily take place on a series of Sundays preceding one of the stated days for baptism, and involve public prayer for the candidates, who are present at the services as a group, accompanied by their sponsors. When the sacrament of Holy Baptism is administered at Easter, enrollment as a candidate normally takes place at the beginning of Lent; when baptisms are planned for the Feast of the Baptism of Our Lord, the enrollment takes place at the beginning of Advent.

In addition to these public acts, this stage involves the private disciplines of fasting, examination of conscience, and prayer, in order that the candidates will be spiritually and emotionally ready for baptism. It is appropriate that, in accordance with ancient custom, the sponsors support their candidates by joining them in prayer and fasting.

A fourth period immediately follows the administration of Holy Baptism. In the case of persons baptized at the Great Vigil, it extends over the Fifty Days of Easter. This period is devoted to such activities, formal and informal, as will assist the newly baptized to experience the fullness of the corporate life of the church and to gain a deeper understanding of the meaning of the Sacraments.

The bishop, the bishop's representative, or the rector (or priest-in-charge) of the congregation should preside at the rites of Admission and Enrollment.

It should be noted that the rites and prayers which follow are appropriate for use only with persons preparing for baptism. Validly baptized Christians present at instruction classes to deepen their understanding of the faith, including members of other Christian bodies preparing to be received into the Episcopal Church, are under no circumstances to be considered catechumens. The same is true of persons preparing to reaffirm their baptismal vows after having abandoned the practice of the Christian religion, since "The bond which God establishes in Baptism is indissoluble" (*BCP,* p. 298).

Preparation of Adults for Holy Baptism: The Catechumenate

Admission of Catechumens

The admission of catechumens may take place at any time of the year, within a principal Sunday liturgy.

After the sermon (or after the Creed) the Celebrant invites those to be admitted as catechumens to come forward with their sponsors.

The Celebrant then asks the following question of those to be admitted. If desired, the question may be asked of each person individually.

What do you seek?

Answer Life in Christ.

The Celebrant then says,

Jesus said, "The first commandment is this: Hear, O Israel: the Lord our God is the only Lord. Love the Lord your God with all your heart, with all your soul, and with all your strength. The second is this: Love your neighbor as yourself. There is no other commandment greater than these." Do you accept these commandments?

Answer I do.

Celebrant Do you promise to be regular in attending the worship of God and in receiving instruction?

Answer I do.

Celebrant Will you open your ears to hear the Word of God and your heart and mind to receive the Lord Jesus?

Answer I will, with God's help.

The Celebrant then addresses the sponsors.

Will you who sponsor *these* persons support *them* by prayer and example and help *them* to grow in the knowledge and love of God?

Sponsors I will.

Those to be admitted kneel. The sponsors remain standing, and place a hand upon the shoulder of the one they are sponsoring, while the Celebrant extends a hand toward them and says

May Almighty God, our heavenly Father, who has put the desire into your hearts to seek the grace of our Lord Jesus Christ, grant you the power of the Holy Spirit to persevere in this intention and to grow in faith and understanding.

People Amen.

Each of those to be admitted is presented by name to the Celebrant, who, with the thumb, marks a cross on the forehead of each, saying

N., receive the sign of the Cross on your forehead and in your heart, in the Name of the Father, and of the Son, and of the Holy Spirit.

People Amen.

The Sponsors also mark a cross on the foreheads of their catechumens. The catechumens and sponsors then return to their places.

The Liturgy continues with (the Creed and) the Prayers of the People, in the course of which prayer is offered for the new catechumens by name.

If any of the catechumens, after consultation with the celebrant, wishes to renounce a former way of worship, an appropriately worded renunciation may be included immediately following the first question and answer.

During the Catechumenate

During this period, and continuing through the period of Candidacy, formal instruction is given to the catechumens. At the conclusion of each session, a period of silence is observed, during which the catechumens pray for themselves and for one another. Sponsors and other baptized persons present offer their prayers for the catechumens. The instructor then says one or two of the following or some other suitable prayers, and concludes by laying a hand individually on the head of each catechumen in silence. It is traditional that this act be performed by the instructor, whether bishop, priest, deacon, or lay catechist.

1

O God, the creator and savior of all flesh, look with mercy on your *children,* whom you call to yourself in love. Cleanse *their hearts* and guard *them* as *they prepare* to receive your Sacraments that, led by your Holy Spirit, *they* may be united with your Son, and enter into the inheritance of your sons and daughters; through Jesus Christ our Lord. *Amen.*

2

O God of truth, of beauty, and of goodness, we give you thanks
that from the beginning of creation you have revealed yourself
in the things that you have made; and that in every nation,
culture, and language there have been those who, seeing your
works, have worshiped you and sought to do your will. Accept
our prayers for *these* your *servants* whom you have called to know
and love you as you have been perfectly revealed in your Son
Jesus Christ our Redeemer, and bring *them* with joy to new birth
in the waters of Baptism; through Jesus Christ our Lord. *Amen.*

3

O God of righteousness and truth, you inaugurated your victory
over the forces of deceit and sin by the Advent of your Son: Give
to *these catechumens* a growing understanding of the truth as it is
in Jesus; and grant that *they,* being cleansed from sin and born
again in the waters of Baptism, may glorify with us the greatness
of your Name; through Jesus Christ our Lord. *Amen.*

4

O God, in your pity you looked upon a fallen world, and sent
your only Son among us to vanquish the powers of wickedness.
Deliver *these* your *servants* from slavery to sin and evil. Purify *their*
desires and thoughts with the light of your Holy Spirit. Nourish
them with your holy Word, strengthen *them* in faith, and confirm
them in good works; through Jesus Christ our Lord. *Amen.*

5

Look down in mercy, Lord, upon *these catechumens* now being
taught in your holy Word. Open *their* ears to hear and *their hearts*
to obey. Bring to *their minds their* past sins, committed against
you and against *their* neighbors, that *they* may truly repent of
them. And in your mercy preserve *them* in *their* resolve to seek
your kingdom and your righteousness; through Jesus Christ our
Lord. *Amen.*

6

Drive out of *these catechumens,* Lord God, every trace of wickedness. Protect *them* from the Evil One. Bring *them* to the saving

waters of Baptism, and make *them* yours for ever; through Jesus Christ our Lord. *Amen.*

7

Lord Jesus Christ, loving Redeemer of all, you alone have the power to save. At your Name every knee shall bow, whether in heaven, on earth, or under the earth. We pray to you for *these catechumens* who *seek* to serve you, the one true God. Send your light into their *hearts,* protect *them* from the hatred of the Evil One, heal in *them* the wounds of sin, and strengthen *them* against temptation. Give *them* a love of your commandments, and courage to live always by your Gospel, and so prepare *them* to receive your Spirit; you who live and reign for ever and ever. *Amen.*

8

Most merciful God, behold and sustain *these catechumens* who *seek* to know more fully: Free *them* from the grasp of Satan, and make *them* bold to renounce all sinful desires that entice *them* from loving you; that, coming in faith to the Sacrament of Baptism, *they* may commit *themselves* to you, receive the seal of the Holy Spirit, and share with us in the eternal priesthood of Jesus Christ our Lord. *Amen.*

9

Lord God, unfailing light and source of light, by the death and resurrection of your Christ you have cast out hatred and deceit, and poured upon the human family the light of truth and love: Look upon *these catechumens* whom you have called to enter your covenant, free *them* from the power of the Prince of darkness, and number *them* among the children of promise; through Jesus Christ our Lord. *Amen.*

10

Stir up, O Lord, the *wills of these catechumens,* and assist *them* by your grace, that *they* may bring forth plenteously the fruit of good works, and receive from you a rich reward; through Jesus Christ our Lord. *Amen.*

Enrollment of Candidates for Baptism

The enrollment of candidates for Baptism at the Great Vigil of Easter normally takes place on the First Sunday in Lent. For those preparing for Baptism on the Feast of our Lord's Baptism, it takes place on the First Sunday of Advent.

The large book in which the names of the candidates for Baptism are to be written is placed where it can easily be seen and used.

After the Creed, the catechumens to be enrolled are invited to come forward with their sponsors.

A Catechist, or other lay representative of the congregation, presents them to the bishop or priest with the following or similar words

I present to you *these catechumens* who *have* been strengthened by God's grace and supported by the example and prayers of this congregation, and I ask that *they* be enrolled as *candidates* for Holy Baptism.

The Celebrant asks the sponsors

Have they been regular in attending the worship of God and in receiving instruction?

Sponsors They have. (*He* has.)

Celebrant Are *they* seeking by prayer, study, and example to pattern *their lives* in accordance with the Gospel?

Sponsors They are. (*He* is.)

The Celebrant asks the sponsors and congregation

As God is your witness, do you approve the enrolling of *these catechumens* as *candidates* for Holy Baptism?

Answer We do.

The Celebrant addresses the catechumens

Do you desire to be baptized?

Catechumens I do.

The Celebrant then says

In the Name of God, and with the consent of this congregation, I accept you as *candidates* for Holy Baptism, and direct that your *names* be written in this book. God grant that *they* may also be written in the Book of Life.

The candidates then publicly write their names in the book; or, if necessary, someone else may write the names. Each name is said aloud at the time of the writing. The sponsors may also sign the book.

The candidates remain together at the front of the church while the Deacon, or other person appointed, leads the following litany:

In peace let us pray to the Lord, saying "Lord, have mercy."

For *these catechumens,* that *they* may remember this day on which *they were* chosen, and remain for ever grateful for this heavenly blessing, let us pray to the Lord.
Lord, have mercy.

That *they* may use this Lenten season wisely, joining with us in acts of self-denial and in performing works of mercy, let us pray to the Lord.
Lord, have mercy.

For *their* teachers, that they may make known to those whom they teach the riches of the Word of God, let us pray to the Lord.
Lord, have mercy.

For *their* sponsor(s), that in *their* private *lives* and public action *they* may show to *these candidates* a pattern of life in accordance with the Gospel, let us pray to the Lord.
Lord, have mercy.

For *their families* and friends, that they may place no obstacles in the way of *these candidates,* but rather assist *them* to follow the promptings of the Spirit, let us pray to the Lord.
Lord, have mercy.

For this congregation, that [during this Lenten season] it may abound in love and persevere in prayer, let us pray to the Lord.
Lord, have mercy.

For our Bishop, and for all the clergy and people, let us pray to the Lord.
Lord, have mercy.

For our President, for the leaders of the nations, and for all in authority, let us pray to the Lord.
Lord, have mercy.

For the sick and the sorrowful, and for those in any need or trouble, let us pray to the Lord.

Lord, have mercy.

    For ———, let us pray to the Lord.

Lord have mercy.

    For all who have died in the hope of the resurrection, and for all the departed, let us pray to the Lord.

Lord, have mercy.

    In the communion of [——— and of all the] saints, let us commend ourselves, and one another, and all our life to Christ our God.

To you, O Lord our God.

    Silence.

    The Celebrant says the following prayer with hands extended over the candidates

    Immortal God, Lord Jesus Christ, the protector of all who come to you, the life of those who believe, and the resurrection of the dead: We call upon you for *these* your *servants* who *desire* the grace of spiritual rebirth in the Sacrament of Holy Baptism. Accept *them,* Lord Christ, as you promised when you said, "Ask, and it will be given to you; seek, and you will find; knock, and it will be opened to you." Give now, we pray, to those who ask, let those who seek find, open the gate to those who knock; that *these* your *servants,* may receive the everlasting benediction of your heavenly washing, and come to that promised kingdom which you have prepared, and where you live and reign for ever and ever. *Amen.*

    The candidates then return to their places and the Liturgy continues with the Confession of Sin or with the Peace.

During Candidacy

On the Sundays preceding their baptism, the candidates attend public worship with their sponsors, and both the candidates and sponsors are prayed for by name in the Prayers of the People. (When Eucharistic Prayer D is used, however, it is appropriate that the names be inserted at the place provided in that prayer.)

    In addition, the following prayers and blessings may be used immedi-

ately before the Prayers of the People, especially on the Third, Fourth, and Fifth Sundays in Lent (or, the Second, Third, and Fourth Sundays of Advent). When these prayers are used, the candidates and sponsors are called forward. The candidates kneel or bow their heads. The sponsors each place a hand upon the shoulder of their candidate.

The Celebrant then calls the people to prayer in these or similar words

Let us pray in silence, dearly beloved, for *these candidates* who *are* preparing to receive the illumination of the Holy Spirit in the Sacrament of Baptism.

All pray in silence.

The Celebrant says one of the following prayers:

Lord God, in the beginning of creation you called forth light to dispel the darkness that lay upon the face of the deep: Deliver *these* your *servants* from the powers of evil and illumine *them* with the light of your presence, that with open eyes and glad hearts *they* may worship you and serve you, now and for ever; through Jesus Christ our Lord. *Amen.*

or this

Lord Christ, true Light who enlightens every one: Shine, we pray, in the *hearts* of *these candidates,* that *they* may clearly see the way that leads to life eternal, and may follow it without stumbling; for you yourself are the Way, O Christ, as you are the Truth and the Life; and you live and reign for ever and ever. *Amen.*

or this

Come, O Holy Spirit, come; come as the wind and cleanse; come as the fire and burn; convict, convert, and consecrate the minds and hearts of *these* your *servants,* to *their* great good and to your great glory; who with the Father and the Son are one God, now and for ever. *Amen.*

The celebrants lays a hand on the head of each candidate in silence.

The Celebrant then adds one of the following blessings:

May Almighty God bestow upon you the blessing of his mercy, and give you an understanding of the wisdom that leads to salvation; through Christ our Lord. *Amen.*

or this

May Almighty God keep your steps from wandering from the way of truth, and cause you to walk in the paths of peace and love; through Christ our Lord. *Amen.*

or this

May Almighty God nourish you with true knowledge of the catholic faith, and grant you to persevere in every good work; through Christ our Lord. *Amen.*

The candidates and sponsors return to their places and the Liturgy continues.

Additional Directions:

1. When there are catechumens who are candidates for baptism at the Great Vigil of Easter, it is appropriate in any year with the consent of the Bishop to use the Sunday lectionary for Year A during Lent and the Great Fifty Days of Easter.
2. In parishes where catechumens are dismissed from the Sunday Eucharist, it is appropriate that this take place following the sermon. The celebrant should send them forth from the Assembly with a blessing and commission to study the Word they have received. Catechumens should be accompanied from the Assembly by their sponsors and catechists to the place for the catechetical session.
3. It is appropriate that the Apostles' (or Nicene) Creed be given to the Candidates for Baptism on the Third Sunday in Lent and the Lord's Prayer be given to them on the Fifth Sunday in Lent following the "Prayers for the Candidates for Baptism" on those Sundays.

Section 2

Preparation of Baptized Persons for Reaffirmation of the Baptismal Covenant

Concerning Reaffirmation of Baptismal Vows

This series of rites and stages of preparation employs a process similar to that of the catechumenate to prepare mature baptized persons to reaffirm their baptismal covenant and receive the laying on of hands by the bishop. It is also appropriate for already confirmed persons who wish to enter a time of disciplined renewal of the baptismal covenant and for those who have transferred into a new congregation.

It is important to note, however, that this is not the catechumenate, which is appropriate only for the unbaptized. In some congregations, it may be desirable, due to limited resources, for catechumens and the previously baptized to attend meetings together during each stage. Care should be taken, however, to underscore the full and complete Christian membership of the baptized. For this reason, the rites of the catechumenate are not appropriate for them. During meetings, prayers offered for the baptized should acknowledge their baptism. Good examples of such prayers are found in the weekday collects for the Great Fifty Days of Easter in *Lesser Feasts and Fasts.* When they join the catechumens in their meetings, the baptized may appropriately be considered as assisting the catechists.

There are three stages of preparation and formation, each

concluding with a rite as a transition. A final period after the third rite leads to the Reaffirmation of the Baptismal Covenant at the Easter Vigil and the presentation of the candidate to the bishop for Confirmation, Reception, or Commitment to Christian Service during the Great Fifty Days of Easter. Throughout, the candidate is valued by the community as a living example of our common need to reexamine and reaffirm our baptismal covenant, and as a model of conversion.

Lastly, the rites attempt to make full use of the existing symbolic language of the liturgy, through the use of actions and physical symbols as well as words.

Stage One. A period of inquiry designed for story-sharing and to give persons enough information about Christian faith and practice and the life of the local community so they may determine if they wish to enter a disciplined period of mature formation in the story of God's saving deeds, prayer, worship, and service. At the conclusion of this period, one or more sponsors are chosen from the local congregation.

Rite One Page 135
The Welcoming of Baptized Christians Into a Community

Stage Two. This is a longer period during which those being formed, along with the sponsors, catechists, and other members of the community engage in deeper exploration of faith and ministry.

This formation period is based on a pattern of experience followed by reflection. The baptized persons explore the meanings of baptism and the baptismal covenant, while discerning the type of service to which God calls them in the context of the local community. The sponsors and catechists in turn train and support them in that service and help them to reflect theologically on their experience of ministry through the study of Scripture, in prayer, and in worship. Substantial periods of time are spent doing ministry and reflecting on it with catechists and sponsors.

Baptized candidates take part in the Eucharist, including the reception of Holy Communion, unless prevented by penitential discipline.

This rite may also be used to welcome baptized persons who are transferring from another congregation of the Church.

Rite Two Page 137
The Calling of the Baptized to Continuing Conversion

Stage Three. This is a stage of immediate preparation for Reaffirmation of the Baptismal Covenant at the Easter Vigil. The candidates focus on the Lenten disciplines and their role in ministry to others. In their group meetings, candidates for reaffirmation share their on-going experience of conversion—especially with those catechumens who are preparing for baptism—and explore more deeply the life of prayer and ministry.

Rite Three Page 140
Maundy Thursday Rite for Baptized Persons in Preparation for the Paschal Holy Days

The baptized reaffirm their baptismal covenant at the Easter Vigil. It is appropriate for them to join those baptized at the same Vigil in the post-baptismal catechesis during the Great Fifty Days of Easter. If the bishop was not present at the Vigil, the baptized are presented to the bishop for the laying on of hands, preferably during the Great Fifty Days as appropriate.
Preparation of Baptized Persons for Reaffirmation of the Baptismal Covenant

The Welcoming of Baptized Christians Into a Community
This rite is used as the principal Sunday Eucharist. It is provided for baptized persons who have been inquiring about life in the community and for those baptized persons who are transferring from another congregation of this Church. Those who wish to pursue a disciplined exploration of the

implications of Christian living are recognized by the community and welcomed to begin this process.

During the Prayers of the People, those about to be welcomed are prayed for by name.

After the Prayers of the People, the senior warden or other representative of the community presents the baptized to the celebrant with these or other words:

N., We present to you these persons (or *N., N.,*) who are baptized members of the Body of Christ and we welcome them to our community as they undertake a process of growth in the meaning of their baptism.

Celebrant (to each baptized person) What do you seek?
Answer Renewal of my life in Christ.
Celebrant In baptism, you died with Christ Jesus to the forces of evil and rose to new life as members of his Body. Will you study the promises made at your baptism, and strive to keep them in the fellowship of this community and the rest of the Church?
Answer I will, with God's help.
Celebrant Will you attend the worship of God regularly with us, to hear God's word and to celebrate the mystery of Christ's dying and rising?
Answer I will, with God's help.
Celebrant Will you join us in our life of service to those who are poor, outcast, or powerless?
Answer I will, with God's help
Celebrant Will you strive to recognize the gifts that God has given you and discern how they are used in the building of God's reign of peace and justice?
Answer I will, with God's help.
Celebrant (to the congregation) Will you who witness this new beginning keep *(N., N.)* in your prayers and help them, share with them your ministry, bear their burdens, and forgive and encourage them?
People We will, with God's help.
Celebrant (to the congregation) Will you who witness this new beginning keep *(N., N.)* in your prayers and help them, share with

them your ministry, bear their burdens, and forgive and encourage them?

People We will, with God's help.

The new members remain standing. The sponsors place a hand on their shoulders.

Celebrant (extending both hands toward the baptized) Blessed are you, our God, our Maker, for you form us in your image and restore us in Jesus Christ. In baptism, *N., N.,* were buried with Christ and rose to new life in him. Renew them in your Holy Spirit, that they may grow as members of Christ. Strengthen their union with the rest of his Body as they join us in our life of praise and service; through our Savior, Jesus Christ, who lives and reigns with you and the Holy Spirit, now and for ever.

All Amen.

In full view of all, the baptized write their names in the church's register of baptized persons. The deacon or a sponsor calls out the names as they are written.

Celebrant Please welcome the new members of the community.

People We recognize you as members of the household of God. Confess the faith of Christ crucified, proclaim his resurrection, and share with us in his eternal priesthood.

The service continues with the Peace. It is appropriate for the new members to greet as many of the faithful as possible. Some may also read the lessons, present the Bread and Wine, and perform other liturgical functions for which they have been previously qualified.

The Calling of the Baptized to Continuing Conversion

This rite is used at the principal service on Ash Wednesday. In it, baptized persons who have been exploring the implications of their baptismal covenant and are preparing to reaffirm it at the coming Easter Vigil are recognized as examples of conversion for the congregation in its journey towards Easter.

After the Blessing of the Ashes and before their imposition, the senior warden or other representatives of the congregation presents the baptized to the celebrant with these or other words:

N., We present to you *N., N.,* who have been growing in an understanding of their call as Christians among us and now desire to undertake a more intense preparation to renew their baptismal covenant this coming Easter.

Celebrant Have they studied the promises made at their baptism and strived to keep them in fellowship with this community and the rest of the Church?

Sponsors: They have.

Celebrant Have they attended worship regularly to hear God's word and to celebrate the mystery of Christ's dying and rising?

Sponsors They have.

Celebrant Have they joined us in our life of service to those who are poor, outcast, or powerless?

Sponsors They have.

Celebrant Have they strived to recognize the gifts that God has given them and to discern how they are to be used in the building up of God's reign of peace and justice?

Sponsors They have.

Celebrant (to the baptized) Will you strive to set an example for us (and especially for those among us who are preparing for baptism) of that turning towards Jesus Christ which marks true conversion?

Answer We will, with God's help.

Celebrant (to the sponsors) Will you accompany these candidates in their journey to conversion and help them renew their commitment to Christ?

Sponsors We will, with God's help.

In full view of the congregation, the candidates kneel or bow their heads. Their sponsors stand behind them and place a hand on their shoulders.

Celebrant (extending both hands towards the candidates) Blessed are you, our God, our Maker, for you faithfully call us to return to you and do not abandon us to our own selfishness. You have given N., N., to us as examples of our reliance on you. Renew your Holy Spirit in them that they may lead us in our turning back to you as they prepare to celebrate with us Christ's passage from death to life, who lives and reigns with you and the Holy Spirit, one God, now and for ever.

Answer Amen.

The candidates stand.

Celebrant Receive ashes as a symbol of repentance and conversion and show us by your example how to turn to Christ.

The Celebrant imposes ashes on the candidates using the words of imposition on page 265 of The Book of Common Prayer.

The candidates join the celebrant in imposing ashes on the congregation. The second Preface of Lent is used.

During the Lenten season, the candidates are prayed for by name at the Prayers of the People, separately from any catechumens.

Maundy Thursday Rite of Preparation for the Paschal Holy Days

This rite is used at the principal service on Maundy Thursday. In it, baptized persons who have been preparing for reaffirmation of their baptismal covenant at the Easter Vigil are further recognized as members so they may join the community in its Paschal celebration.

When this rite is used, the appropriate Gospel is John 13:1–15. Before the foot-washing ceremony, the candidates for reaffirmation and their sponsors stand before the celebrant in full view of the congregation.

Celebrant (to the candidates and their sponsors) N., N., you have been setting an example for us of that true turning to God which lies at the heart of our Christian calling. Tonight we welcome you to join us as disciples of Jesus Christ by imitating his example and dedicating ourselves to service among us in this community. Christ Jesus came among us not to be served but to serve. Tonight we wash your feet as a sign of the servanthood to which Christ has called us and we ask you in turn to join us in this symbol of our discipleship. *N., N.,* are you prepared to join us in our life of service?

Candidates We are prepared.

The service continues with a rite of contrition, beginning on page 450 of The Book of Common Prayer with the words, "Now in the presence of Christ . . .," omitting the confession of particular sins ("Especially . . ."). The celebrant lays a hand on each while saying the first form of absolution ("Our Lord . . . who offered . . .").

The candidates' feet are washed. When all are ready, the celebrant distributes basins, ewers, and towels to the candidates, saying to each:

Celebrant May Christ strengthen you in the service which he lays upon you.

The candidates in turn wash the feet of other members of the congregation.

The service proceeds immediately with the Peace. It is appropriate to use Eucharistic Prayer D, including in it intercessions for the Church and for the world.

Section 3

The Preparation of Parents and Godparents for the Baptism of Infants and Young Children

Concerning the Service

This process is designed to deepen the Christian formation of those who present infants and young children for baptism. Its division into stages—each concluding with a rite—parallels the form of the catechumenate. It is essential, however, that these persons be distinguished from the catechumens except when they may be themselves preparing for baptism, and therefore catechumens.

Stage One. This stage begins as soon as the parents discover the pregnancy. In consultation with the pastor, they choose godparents. The godparents must be baptized persons and at least one a member of the local community. A schedule of meetings throughout the pregnancy is planned. This is a brief stage, leading shortly to the first rite.

Rite One.
The Blessing of Parents at the Beginning of the Pregnancy

In order to more strongly indicate the role of the father, during "The Blessing of a Pregnant Woman" (*BOS,* p. 153), the following changes should be made, in addition to changing the title. (If the father is not present or not involved, the rite follows the form for a woman, omitting the father's name in the prayers.)

In the opening prayer, the father's name as well as the mother's is used, and "they" replaces "she."

After the fourth petition is added:

Blessed are you, our God. May *N.* and *N.,* along with their child's godparents, *N.* and *N.* (and *N.* and *N.,* their other children), find their faith deepened and their ministry strengthened as they prepare for this child's birth and baptism. Amen.

This rite takes place at the Sunday Eucharist after the Prayers of the People. It is followed by the Peace.

Stage Two. This period consists of the remainder of the pregnancy and the time of birth. During this stage, the parents, their other children, and the godparents meet regularly with one or more catechists to deepen their formation in salvation history, prayer, worship, and social ministry. Its educational pattern is one of experience followed by reflection. In their daily lives, participants find ample resources for reflection upon the ways in which their own baptismal covenant is being lived within their vocation of marriage, family and child-bearing. They also explore prayer and worship in the home as an extension of the liturgy of the church and in the context of the Church Year, and they grow in an understanding of the household as a domestic manifestation of the people of God whose life together is part of the history of salvation.

If a parent is a catechumen, this process takes place within the catechumenate. A baptized spouse may serve to sponsor the catechumen.

Rite Two
Thanksgiving for the Birth or Adoption of a Child

This rite is found in The Book of Common Prayer (pages 439–445). Of the final prayers, the prayer "For a child not yet baptized" (page 444) is appropriate. The celebrant signs the infant with the cross and announces the date of the baptism.

Henceforth the child is prayed for by name at the Prayers of the People, until the baptismal day.

Stage Three. In this period of preparation for baptism, the parents and godparents continue to meet with the catechist(s). Couples or individuals who have raised children in the church may be helpful as resources or catechists, as may be others who have completed this process previously. The experience of parenthood furnishes new challenges to faith and ministry upon which reflection will be fruitful. The process of family life, sharing in the congregation's life of worship, and ministry to others will find new shape with the advent of the new child.

This is also a time to explore more fully the responsibilities that the parents and godparents will accept at the baptism. They explore topics such as: the best way to interpret the meaning of the Eucharist to a child partaking of it in his or her growing years; how to model ministry and prayer for the growing child; and ways of introducing the child to the story of salvation. The role of the godparents is also more fully developed.

Rite Three
Holy Baptism (BCP, p. 299)

In accordance with The Book of Common Prayer, this will take place on a major baptismal day at a principal service of worship. The infant will be signed (with chrism, if desired) and may receive Holy Communion (in the form of a few drops of wine if the child is not yet weaned).

After this, the parents, godparents and congregation have the responsibility of carrying out the child's formation in salvation history, prayer, worship, and social ministry. Childhood and adolescence will be a time of formation and exploration of the mysteries of the faith, moving towards the goal of reaffirmation of the baptismal covenant at a mature age.

Those who lead this preparation process should include laity and clergy. Deacons have a special role as leaders of servant ministry, as do those who have reared children in the church, even if they seem to have had little success. Whenever possible, the bishop should preside over the rites and take part in the teaching. The bishop will also preside at the baptism whenever possible.

Adaptation for Special Circumstances
Deferred Baptism
In the case of young children, the parents may, in consultation with the pastor of the congregation, determine to defer baptism until the child is old enough to go through the catechumenate. In such case, parents go through the same process during the pregnancy and birth, but the stages conclude not with baptism but with the admission of the child to the catechumenate (page 115). The parents and godparents should receive ongoing support in the formation of the child.

Other Adaptations
When parents present a child for baptism without having gone through this process beginning at pregnancy, the first and second stages above are combined. The first rite is dropped and the second rite is the enrollment of the child as a candidate for baptism (adapted to circumstances). After a final period of preparation (perhaps along with adult candidates), the child is baptized.

It is important to acknowledge that, if a difficulty arises during the course of the pregnancy, the godparents and catechists are the primary ministers. If the pregnancy is terminated by miscarriage, or if the baby is stillborn, these persons continue to support and assist the parents in dealing with such an event.

It should be noted that a baby with congenital deficiencies (including mental or learning disabilities) should be baptized.

In cases where it seems necessary to perform an emergency baptism, the sponsoring group supports the parents. If the infant survives, the formative period may continue and the formal celebration of the baptism takes place on a major baptismal day.

APPENDIX E

Resources by Subject

ANGLICANISM

The Anglican Study Series. Wilton, CT: Morehouse-Barlow, 1979–83:
> Booty, John E., Owen C. Thomas, and William J. Wolf, *The Spirit of Anglicanism.*
> Borsch, Frederick H., ed., *Anglicanism and the Bible.*
> Elmen, Paul, ed., *The Anglican Moral Choice.*
> Holmes, Urban T. III, *What is Anglicanism?*
> Vogel, Arthur A., ed., *Theology in Anglicanism.*
> Wolf, William J., *Anglican Spirituality.*
Booty, John. "The Drama of Anglicanism." Cincinnati, OH: Forward Movement Publications, 1986.
——. *What Makes Us Episcopalians?* Wilton, CT: Morehouse-Barlow, 1982.
"The Churches Teaching Series." New York: Seabury Press, 1979.
Bennett, Robert A., and O. C. Edwards, *The Bible for Today's Church.*
Booty, John E., *The Church in History.*
Brill, Earl H., *The Christian Moral Vision.*
Holmes, Urban T. III, and John H. Westerhoff III, *Christian Believing.*
Hosmer, Rachel, and Alan Jones, *Living in the Spirit.*
Norris, Richard A., *Understanding the Faith of the Church.*
Price, Charles P., and Louis Weil, *Liturgy for Living.*
Readings in the History of the Episcopal Church. Robert W. Pritchard, ed. Wilton, CT: Morehouse-Barlow, 1986.
Sydnor, William. *Looking at the Episcopal Church.* Wilton, CT: Morehouse-Barlow, 1980.
Tucker, Beverly D. and William H. Swatos Jr. *Questions on the Way: A Catechism Based on the Book of Common Prayer.* Cincinnati, OH: Forward Movement Publications, 1987.

HISTORY OF CHRISTIAN INITIATION AND FORMATION: PRIMARY SOURCES

Ambrose. *On the Sacraments and On The Mysteries.* T. Thompson, trans. London: S.P.C.K., 1950.
Augustine. *Confessions.* New York: Penguin Books, 1961.

———. "De catechizandis rudibus," in *The First Catechetical Instruction*. J. P. Christopher, trans. Ancient Christian Writers, no. 2. Westminster, MD: Newman Press, 1946.

Egeria's Travels to the Holy Land. Revised Edition. John Wilkinson, trans. Jerusalem: Ariel Publishing House, 1981.

Hippolytus: A Text for Students. Geoffrey J. Cumin, ed. Bramcote, Notts.: Grove Books, 1976.

St. John Chrysostom, Baptismal Instructions. Paul W. Harkins, trans. Westminster, MD: The Newman Press, 1963.

Kiefer, Ralph A. "Christian Initiation: The State of the Question," in *Made, Not Born*. South Bend, IN: University of Notre Dame Press, 1976.

Whitaker, E. C. *Documents of the Baptismal Liturgy*. 2nd Ed. London: S.P.C.K., 1970.

The Works of Saint Cyril of Jerusalem. Vol. 2. Leo P. McCauley and Paul W. Harkins, trans. Washington, DC: Catholic University Press, 1970.

Yarnold, Edward J. *The Awe-Inspiring Rites of Initiation*. Slough, Great Britain: St. Paul Publications, 1972.

HISTORY OF CHRISTIAN INITIATION AND FORMATION: SECONDARY SOURCES

Djarier, Michel. *A History of the Catechumenate*. New York: Sadlier Press, 1979.

———. *The Rites of Christian Initiation: Historical and Pastoral Reflections*. New York: Sadlier Press, 1979.

A Faithful Church: Issues in the History of Catechesis. John H. Westerhoff and O. C. Edwards, eds. Wilton, CT: Morehouse-Barlow, 1981.

Finn, Thomas M. *The Liturgy of Baptism in the Baptismal Instructions of St. John Chrysostom*. The Catholic University of America Studies in Christian Antiquity Series, no. 15. Washington, DC: The Catholic University of America Press, 1967.

Made, Not Born: New Perspectives on Christian Initiation and the Catechumenate. Papers from the Murphy Center for Liturgical Research. South Bend, IN: University of Notre Dame Press, 1976.

Merriman, Michael W., ed. *The Baptismal Mystery and the Catechumenate*. New York: The Church Hymnal Corporation, 1990.

Riley, Hugh M. *Christian Initiation: A Comparative Study of the Interpretation of the Baptismal Liturgy in the Mystagogical Writing of Cyril of Jerusalem, John Chrysostom, Theodore of Mopsuestia, and Ambrose of Milan*. Catholic University of American Studies in Christian Antiquity Series, no. 17. Washington, DC: Catholic University of America Press, 1974.

Initiation and Catechumenal Process

Brooks, Robert J. "Faith of our Fathers." *The Living Church* (January 11, 1981): 9–10.

———. "Imaging the Story of Jesus Through Baptism." *The Christian Ministry* (July 1987): 5–10.

———. "Reflections on the Adult Catechumenate and Baptism in the Episcopal Church." *Open* (May 1986): 15–18.

Catechumenate, a monthly journal. Chicago: Liturgy Training Publications.

Catholic Update, a monthly newsletter. Cincinnati: St. Anthony Messenger Press.

"Christian Initiation." *Ministry Development Journal,* no. 7. 1985.

"Diocesan Guidelines for Christian Initiation and Confirmation." *Open* (June 1984): 6–8.

Eastman, A. Theodore. *The Baptizing Community: Christian Initiation and the Local Congregation.* New York: The Seabury Press, 1982.

Hatchett, Marion J. *Commentary on the American Prayer Book.* New York: The Seabury Press, 1980.

Hinman, Karen M. *How to Form a Catechumenal Team.* Chicago: Liturgy Training Publications, 1986.

Lambert, Jay. "Forming Christians: A Model for the Catechumenate:" *The Living Church* (June 7, 1987): 8–9.

Liska, Martha. "A Companion in Christ." *Water and Fire* (Fall 1986).

Merriman, Michael, W. "The Liturgy in the Easter Season." *Open* (March 1987): 16–19.

"A Parish Customary for Christian Initiation: The Guidelines for Christian Initiation at St. John's Church in Olympia, Washington." *Water and Fire* (Fall 1985).

Stevick, Daniel B. *Adult Baptism: Getting Back to the Beginning.* Clues 7, Papers on Renewal and Evangelism. Cincinnati, OH: Forward Movement Publications, 1984.

———. *Baptismal Moments: Baptismal Meaning.* New York: The Church Hymnal Corporation, 1987.

———. *Holy Baptism.* Supplement to Prayer Book Studies 26. New York: The Church Hymnal Corporation, 1973.

Liturgy

The Book of Common Prayer and Administration of the Sacraments and Other Rites and Ceremonies of the Church. New York: The Church Hymnal Corporation, 1979.

The Book of Occasional Services, 2nd edition. New York: The Church Hymnal Corporation, 1988.

The Great Vigil of Easter: A Commentary; Celebrating Redemption—the Liturgies of Lent; Holy Week, and the Great Fifty Days, Christian Initiation—A Theological and Pastoral Commentary on the Rites. Washington, DC: Associated Parishes, 1977.

Lesser Feasts and Fasts together with The Fixed Holy Days. 3rd Ed. New York: The Church Hymnal Corporation, 1980.

The Oxford Book of Prayers. George Appleton, ed. New York: Oxford University Press, 1985.

Prayers for Pastors and People. Carl G. Carlozzi, ed. New York: The Church Hymnal Corporation, 1984.

PRAYER AND SPIRITUAL DIRECTION

Canham, Elizabeth. *Praying the Bible.* Cowley Publications, 1987.

Dunnan, Maxie. *The Workbook on Spiritual Disciplines.* Nashville, TN: The Upper Room, 1984.

Edwards, Tilden H. *Spiritual Friend: Reclaiming the Gift of Spiritual Direction.* New York: Paulist Press, 1980.

Fenhagen, James C. *Invitation to Holiness.* San Francisco: Harper & Row, 1987.

———. *More Than Wanderers: Spiritual Disciplines for Christian Ministry.* New York: The Seabury Press, 1985.

———. *Mutual Ministry: New Vitality for the Local Church.* San Francisco: Harper & Row, 1986.

Leech, Kenneth. *True Prayer: An Invitation to Christian Spirituality.* San Francisco: Harper & Row, 1980.

Mitchell, Lionel L. *A Theological Commentary on the Book of Common Prayer.* Wilton, CT: Morehouse-Barlow, 1985.

Russell, Joseph P. *Daily Prayer and Bible Study with the BCP.* Cincinnati, OH: Forward Movement Publications, 1986.

———. *The Daily Lectionary, A Weekly Guide for Daily Bible Reading.* Vol. 1–4. Cincinnati, OH: Forward Movement Publications, 1987–88.

Sprague, Minka Shura. *One to Watch, One to Pray: A Devotional Introduction to the Gospel.* Wilton, CT: Morehouse-Barlow, 1985.

Thornton, Martin. *Spiritual Direction.* Cambridge, MA: Cowley Press, 1984.

Weil, Louis. *Gathered to Pray: Understanding Liturgical Prayer.* Parish Life Source Books. Cambridge, MA: Cowley Publications, 1986.

RESOURCES AVAILABLE IN PHOTOCOPIED FORM FROM THE
EPISCOPAL CHURCH CENTER
815 SECOND AVENUE, NEW YORK, NY 10017
(800)334-7626 OR 1-212-867-8400:

from Evangelism Ministries Office:
"An African Model for Bible Study: Alternate." October 1986.
Cayler, Kathryn M. "Living Out Our Baptismal Vows," 1983.
"Choosing to be Christian Ministers," 1985.
Harrison, Anne. "Giftedness Conference," 1984.
Jelinek, Albert J. and Rosemarie Tapper. "Our Journey into the Unknown,"
    1987.
Kiblinger, Charles. "The Process of the Catechumenate at St. James' Church,
    Jackson, Mississippi." Jackson: St. James' Church, 1984.
"Living Our Baptismal Covenant: Diocese of Milwaukee, Resources for Plan-
    ning," February 1986.
May, Lynde E. IV. "Leadership Style and the Catechumenal Process," 1987.
McElligott, Ann E.P. *Evangelism With the Poor,* 1986.
———. *Faith Development and Evangelism,* 1987.
Plattenburg, George and Sherrill Akyol. "A Workshop for Discerning and
    Empowering Our Gifts for Ministry," c. 1978.
Rothauge, Arlin J. *Catechism: The Outline of the Faith We Profess.* Clues 4, Papers
    on Renewal and Evangelism. Cincinnati, OH: Forward Movement Pub-
    lications, 1982.
Ryle, Jerry. "The Catechumenate in Story and Experience: A Roman Catholic
    Setting," 1986.
Schwab, A. Wayne. "A Visit to Three Churches in a Catechumenal Process,"
    June 1987.
———. "Changed Lives," June 1987.
———. "Resources for Planning," February 1986.
———. "Using a Catechumenal Process for Christian Initiation," June 1987.
"Six Weekly Sessions in Ministry Formation," 1986.
Sullivan, Mark. "No Bolts of Lightning," A Catechumenal Process in a Pas-
    torial Size Congregation, 1985.
"A Turning Point," December 1986.
Weil, Louis. "Christian Initiation and Ministry," 1988.
Westerhoff, John. "Characteristics of a Helpful Sponsor," February 1986.

THE FOLLOWING TITLES ARE AVAILABLE FROM EPISCOPAL
PARISH SERVICES, THE EPISCOPAL CHURCH CENTER, NEW
YORK, NY 10016, (800)223-2337, EXT. 437-8.

"Do This for the Remembrance of Me," #50 319V (VHS), #50-319B (Beta II),
1985.
Rothauge, Arlin, J., *Reshaping a Congregation for a New Future,* #56-8602, 1985.
———, *Sizing Up a Congregation for New Member Ministry,* #56-8801, 1983.
Russell, John P. and John D. Vogelsang. *In Dialogue: An Episcopal Guide for Adult
Bible Study,* 1986.
Schwab, A. Wayne. *Handbook for Evangelism,* 1989.
Schwab, A. Wayne and William Yon. *Proclamation as Offering Story and Choice,*
1988.
From The Office of Stewardship Development:
Kelshaw, Terrence, *Three Streams, One River, A Biblical Understanding of Steward-
ship;* and Terence McCabe, *A Leader's Manual,* 1987.
Reed, Ronald. *The Steward's Count. A Theological Essay on Stewardship,* 1987.

RESOURCES AND REPRINTS AVAILABLE IN PHOTOCOPY FORM
FROM THE NORTH AMERICAN FORUM ON THE
CATECHUMENATE,
5510 COLUMBIA PIKE, SUITE 310, ARLINGTON, VA 22204,
(703)671-0330:

Dunning, James B. "Dynamics of Evangelization in the Catechumenate,"
c. 1982.
———. "Method is the Medium is the Message: Catechetical Method in the
RCIA." 1982.
———. "Methods in Religious Education and Ministry," c. 1982.
———. The RCIA Journey: From Emmaus to South Carolina to San Antonio."
Winona, MN: St. Mary's Press, 1983–84.
———. "What Happens After 'Christ Among Us'?" c. 1983.
———. "Words of the Word: Evangelization, Catechesis, and the Catechume-
nate," c. 1982.
Hinman, Karen M. "Catechetical Method: A Model for Sunday Catechetical
Sessions," 1983.

RESOURCES FOR SMALL GROUPS:

Berry Institute, "Conference on Growing the Church Through Small
Groups"; offered twice a year; Fuller Theological Seminary, Pasadena,
CA 91182, (800) 235-2222 Ext. 5315.

Hestenes, Roberta, "Building Community Through Small Groups," Media Services, Fuller Theological Seminary, Pasadena, CA 91182. Videotape.

Neighborhood Bible Studies Inc.; small group study guides; Box 222, Dobbs Ferry, NY 10522.

"Powerhouse of Prayer" Workshop leading to small prayer groups, Anglican Fellowship of Prayer, P. O. Box M, Winter Park, FL 32790, (407) 628-4330.

Serendipity House; current catalogue. Box 1012, Littleton, CO 80160, (800) 525-9563.

THE RITE OF CHRISTIAN INITIATION OF ADULTS:

Becoming a Catholic Christian: A Symposium on Christian Initiation. Organized and directed by Christiane Brusselmans. William J. Reedy, ed. New York: Sadlier Press, 1979.

Dunning, James B. *New Wine: New Wineskins: Pastoral Implications of the Rite of Christian Initiation of Adults.* New York: Sadlier Press, 1981.

Kavanagh, Aidan. *The Shape of Baptism: The Rite of Christian Initiation.* New York: Pueblo Publishing Company, 1978.

Kemp, Raymond B. *A Journey in Faith: An Experience of the Catechumenate.* New York: Sadlier Press, 1979.

SESSION PLANNING:

Bennett, Boyce M. *Bennett's Guide to the Bible: Graphic Aids and Outlines.* New York: The Seabury Press, 1979.

Coleman, Lyman. *The Serendipity Bible Study Book.* Grand Rapids, MI: Zondervan Publishing House, 1986.

Dozier, Verna. *Equipping the Saints.* Washington, DC: Alban Institute, 1981.

Dunning, James B. *Ministries: Sharing God's Gifts.* Winona, MN: St. Mary's Press, 1980.

Jones, Gail C. *Seeking Life in Christ: A Manual for Developing a Process for Christian Initiation Including the Catechumenate in Your Congregation.* Resource Center, Diocese of Olympia, P. O. Box 12126, Seattle, WA 98102.

The Journal of General Convention, 1988. New York: The Episcopal Church Center, 1989.

Mahaffey, Anne Carter. "The Identification of Gifts for Ministry." April 1986. Available from Anne Carter Mahaffey, 6004 Rodes Court, Louisville, KY 40222.

The Prayer Book Guide to Christian Education. Wilton, CT: Morehouse-Barlow, 1987.

272 APPENDIX E

Russell, John P. and John D. Vogelsang. *In Dialogue: An Episcopal Guide for Adult Bible Study.* New York: The Episcopal Church Center, 1986.

Vos, Nelvin. *Seven Days a Week: Faith in Action.* Philadelphia: Fortress Press, 1985.

Wink, Walter. *Transforming Bible Study: a leader's guide.* Nashville, TN: Abingdon Press, 1980.

Theory of Catechetical Formation:

Warren, Michael. "Religious Formation in the Context of Social Formation." *Religious Education* 82, no. 4 (Fall 1987): 515–528.

Westerhoff, John. "Formation, Education, Instruction." *Religious Education* 82, no. 4 (Fall 1987): 578–591.

Willimon, William H. "Making Christians in a Secular World." *The Christian Century,* October 22, 1986, 914–917.

Glossary

Baptism. The sacramental rite of sharing in the death and resurrection of Jesus Christ and entering full life in the Body of Christ, the church, and its mission.

Baptismal Covenant. The commitment made by Christians at their baptism (and in the case of infants, made for them by their sponsors) to believe the historic creeds of the church; to continue in the apostles' teaching and fellowship; the breaking of bread; prayer; resisting evil and continuing repentance; to proclaim the Good News of God in Christ; to serve Christ in all persons; and to work for justice and peace among all people.

Baptismal Reaffirmation.[1] A public reaffirming of the Covenant and promises of one's baptism before the bishop. It may take the following forms:

1. CONFIRMATION: A baptismal reaffirmation accompanied by the laying-on-of-hands (and chrismation) by the bishop. The rite is for those baptized in the Episcopal Church or in some other church at an early age who have reached the time in their lives when they wish to make their first public affirmation of the Christian faith in the presence of the bishop.

2. RECEPTION: A baptismal reaffirmation made by an adult from another Christian tradition who was baptized with water in the name of the Trinity and, at some point, made a full mature affirmation of their Christian faith, and who wishes to be received "into the fellowship of this Communion."

---

1. Copyright 1989 St. Paul's Episcopal Church, Indianapolis, IN.

3. REAFFIRMATION: A baptismal reaffirmation before the bishop made by a person who has been previously made a mature public affirmation of faith and desires to do so again for significant reasons, to mark a spiritual turning point in his/her life.

Body of Christ. The whole Christian Church whose members are incorporated into Christ's life through baptism. Beginning with the first Pentecost, the Body of Christ—his Church—became the visible vehicle for his redemptive presence and action on earth.

Candidate. A participant in the catechumenal process. Either a baptized person seeking deeper Christian commitment and a reaffirmation of baptismal vows, or an unbaptized person whose catechumenal journey will culminate in initiation into the Body of Christ through baptism.

Catechesis. The experiences offered to participants in the catechumenal process, both those persons seeking baptism and people moving toward reaffirmation of their baptismal vows. It is based on a Greek work meaning to "sound in the ear" and suggests the centrality of God's word and our discernment of it.

Catechist. A lay or ordained person who participates in the education of people seeking baptism or reaffirmation of their baptismal vows.

Catechumen. An unbaptized participant in the Christian initiation process known as the catechumenate. The catechumen, above all, listens for the Word of God spoken in Jesus Christ.

Catechumenal Process. Describes, in the Episcopal Church, the various ways in which adults are prepared for baptism or reaffirmation of baptismal vows. The process is marked by rites prescribed in *The Book of Occasional Services.*

Catechumenate. The period of instruction and experience set aside by a congregation for adults seeking baptism.

Church Year. In the Episcopal Church, as in some other Christian bodies, the Church or Christian Year consists of two cycles based on a commemoration of the events in the life and ministry of Jesus Christ. The first of the cycles is dependent on Easter Day, which is movable; the second is based on the fixed date of Christmas, December 25.

Commitment (Christian). The involvement of baptized persons in the life and work and spirit of the church. The catechumenal process is seen as one way of helping people make Christian commitments.

Companion. One of several designations (including sponsor) for a congregation member who moves through the catechumenal process with a person seeking baptism or reaffirmation of baptismal vows.

Confirmation. In the Episcopal Church, the rite wherein one baptized as an infant expresses mature commitment to Jesus Christ in the baptismal covenant and receives strength from the Holy Spirit through prayer and the laying on of hands by the bishop.

Congregation. In the Episcopal Church, the name given a group of baptized Christians worshiping and ministering in mission together as members of the Body of Christ.

Conversion. For Christians, the experience of becoming a Christian and of taking up a new life by following Jesus Christ as Lord and Saviour.

Convert. One who adopts a faith and the way of life set down by that faith. By extension, a person who moves toward a new religious commitment or who moves from no defined religious position to a committed religious position.

Corporate Life. In Christian usage, life in the Body of Christ; life as a committed member of a Christian congregation in mission.

Daily Places. The places and the contexts we move in as we live out our daily lives: our homes, our jobs, our schools and colleges, our communities, our citizenship, our leisure time, and our church communities. The mandate for committed Christians is that they witness to their faith in all the daily places of their lives.

Discern, Discernment. In Christianity, the act of seeing or recognizing the presence of God in the world and in our daily lives. Discernment is seen as an important element in the deepening of Christian formation.

Evangelism. The act of carrying the Good News or Gospel of Christ to all and doing what one can to help others receive it and commit themselves to Jesus Christ and his mission.

Evangelist. In the modern Anglican/Episcopal tradition, any lay or ordained person who consciously proclaims the Good News of the Gospel and enables response to it.

Evangelization. Often used interchangeably with evangelism, it implies a process as well as a decision, and a social as well as a personal context. In this resource, it applies, in particular, to the way a congregation acts out its mission as a baptizing and catechumenal community.

Formation. In Christianity, experiences that form or shape the faith of individuals allowing them to realize, more fully, the meaning of that faith in their lives and in the lives of others. The catechumenal process is a means of deeper Christian formation.

Gathering. One way of describing the stage when a congregation sponsoring the catechumenal process begins to identify people, baptized and unbaptized, who might wish to participate and invites them to do so.

Gospel. The good news and meaning of the story of Christ's life, death and resurrection and his risen life among us in today's world.

Initiation (Christian). Entry into the death and resurrection of Jesus Christ and into full life in the Body of Christ, the church, and its mission.

Initiatory Rites. Essentially, baptism, confirmation or reaffirmation, and Eucharist. Originally these three rites occurred together at the time of initiation. Baptism is normally administered as part of the Eucharist in today's Episcopal Church. Confirmation and reaffirmation occur in the presence of the bishop.

Inquirer.   A person deciding whether or not to enter the catechumenal process by entering its first stage for information
and exploration.

Inquirers' Class.   A widely used name for preparation for reaffirmation of the baptismal covenant that usually suggests a
content-centered, lecture-based, intellectual and relatively
short series of sessions.

Inquiry.   A generic name given to the first stage of the catechumenal process wherein a person seeks information
about and exploration of the Christian faith so as to decide
whether to enter the second stage or not. In the Milwaukee
Pilot Project, the second stage of the catechumenal process
was called Inquiry.

Ministry.   Any action which serves others in Jesus Christ.

Mission.   Describes the ways in which Christian people live out
their baptismal covenant individually and together. "The
mission of the church is to restore all people to unity with
God and each other in Christ" (BCP, p. 855).

Mystagogia.   A study of or knowledge of the mysteries, a term
for the Christian sacraments of baptism and eucharist; often
used for the final stage of the catechumenal process in
which participants reflect on the meaning of the initiatory
rites for their day to day living.

Parish.   Another name for a Christian congregation.

Paschal Mystery.   Derived from *pesach,* the Hebrew word for
Passover. The angel of death "passed over" the Israelite's
homes sparing their children, but the children of the Egyp-
tians died. The following night Moses and the Israelites
escaped from Egypt and slavery (Exodus 11 and 12). The
escape at the Red Sea, and the covenant with God at Sinai
are the center of Israel's deliverance and designation as
God's people. For Christians, deliverance comes in the
death and resurrection of Jesus Christ. From Good Friday
to Easter, Jesus "passed over" from death to life. The Holy
Week Easter story and its rites are the Paschal Mystery or
Mysteries. Mystery here is used in the sense of something

that is so rich that its meaning can never be exhausted. The catechumenal process by which one moves more deeply into the death and resurrection of Jesus Christ is thus centered in and reaches its climax in the observance of Maundy Thursday, Good Friday, and Easter.

Pentecost. The day—ending the Great Fifty Days of Easter—when the church celebrates the gift of the Holy Spirit to the apostles empowering them for ministry in Christ's name.

Personal Faith Journey. The experience of the individual moving through the stages of the catechumenal process; the process of Christian formation, informed by discernment of God's presence in our lives and in the world.

Pre-Catechumenate. The first stage, a stage of inquiry, for the unbaptized in the catechumenal process.

Reception. For one baptized in another communion, the rite of reaffirming one's baptismal covenant in the presence of a bishop and receiving the laying on of hands.

Rites and Stages. In this resource, stages are the steps in the catechumenal process and the rites are the liturgies used to mark the end of one stage and the beginning of the next.

Spiritual Direction. The guidance offered people in their religious journey. In the catechumenal process, it is offered to assist participants to grow in individual and corporate spirituality and to assess their readiness to move to the next stage.

Sponsor. A person chosen and trained by a congregation engaged in the catechumenal process to accompany and help a participant through the process. Sponsors present candidates for baptism and reaffirmation to the congregation.

Story-Sharing. The sharing by participants in the catechumenal process of their stories of God's action in their lives and their growing understanding of what that action might mean in the context of the whole Christian story.

Bibliography

"An African Model for Bible Study: Alternate." October 1986. New York: Evangelism Ministries Office, The Episcopal Church Center.

Ambrose. *On the Sacraments and On the Mysteries.* T. Thompson, trans. London: S.P.C.K., 1950.

The Anglican Study Series. Wilton, CT: Morehouse-Barlow, 1979–1983:
Anglicanism and the Bible, Frederick H. Borsch, ed.
What is Anglicanism? Urban T. Holmes III.
The Spirit of Anglicanism, John E. Booty, Owen C. Thomas, and William J. Wolf.
Anglican Spirituality, William J. Wolf, ed.
Theology in Anglicanism, Arthur A. Vogel, ed.
The Anglican Moral Choice, Paul Elmen, ed.

Arvedson, Peter and Lynde E. May IV. "Sharing Resources in Madison, Wisconsin." *Water and Fire* (Summer 1987).

Augustine. *Confessions.* New York: Penguin Books, 1961.

———— "De catechizandis rudibus," in *The First Catechetical Instruction.* J.P. Christopher, trans. Ancient Christian Writers, no. 2. Westminster, MD: Newman Press, 1946.

Bailey, Kenneth. *Jesus the Theologian, New Testament Themes, Jesus Interprets His Own Cross, A Clear View of Jesus' Birth, Inauguration,* and *Inspiration in the Bible.* Harvest Communications, 900 Washington Blvd, Wichita, KS, 67211 (316) 652-9900. Videotapes.

Becoming a Catholic Christian: A Symposium on Christian Initiation. Organized and directed by Christiane Brusselmans. William J. Reedy ed. New York: Sadlier Press, 1979.

Bennett, Boyce M. *Bennett's Guide to the Bible: Graphic Aids and Outlines.* New York: The Seabury Press, 1979.

Berry Institute, "Conference on Growing the Church Through Small Groups," (offered twice a year) Fuller Theological Seminary, Pasedena, CA 91182 (800) 235-2222 Ext. 5315.

The Blue Book—Reports of Committees, Commissions, Boards and Agencies of the General Convention of the Episcopal Church. New York: The Episcopal Church Center, 1988.

Boerma, Conrad. *The Rich, the Poor and the Bible.* Philadelphia: Westminster Press, 1980.

The Book of Common Prayer and Administration of the Sacraments and Other Rites and Ceremonies of the Church. New York: The Church Hymnal Corporation, 1979.

The Book of Occasional Services. 2nd ed. New York: The Church Hymnal Corporation, 1988.

Booty, John. "The Drama of Anglicanism." Cincinnati, OH: Forward Movement Publications, 1986.

———. *What Makes Us Episcopalians?* Wilton, CT: Morehouse-Barlow, 1982.

Brooks, Robert J. "Faith of Our Fathers." *The Living Church* (January 11 1981): 9–10.

———. "Imaging the Story." *The Living Church* (January 11, 1981): 7–9.

——— "Imaging the Story of Jesus Through Baptism." *The Christian Ministry* (July 1987): 5–10.

——— "Reflections on the Adult Catechumenate and Baptism in the Episcopal Church." *Open* (May 1986): 15–18.

Brotherhood of St. Andrew, *Articulating Our Faith.* Ambridge, PA, 1988.

Brown, Raymond E. *The Churches the Apostles Left Behind.* New York: Paulist Press, 1984.

Canham, Elizabeth. *Praying the Bible.* Cambridge, MA: Cowley Publications, 1987.

Catechumenate, a monthly journal. Chicago: Liturgy Training Publications.

"Catechumenate Retreat Schedule." See Appendix C.

Catholic Update, a monthly newsletter. Cincinnati: St. Anthony Messenger Press.

Cayler, Kathryn M. 1983. "Living Out Our Baptismal Vows." New York: Evangelism Ministries Office, The Episcopal Church Center.

"Choosing to be Christian Ministers." 1985. New York: Evangelism Ministries Office, The Episcopal Church Center.

"Christian Initiation." *Ministry Development Journal,* no. 7. The Episcopal Church Center, 1985.

The Church's Teaching Series. New York: Seabury Press, 1979.
  Liturgy for Living, Charles P. Price and Louis Weil.
  Understanding the Faith of the Church, Richard A. Norris.
  The Bible for Today's Church, Robert A. Bennett and O. C. Edwards.
  The Church in History, John E. Booty.
  Christian Believing, Urban T. Holmes III and John H. Westerhoff III.
  The Christian Moral Vision, Earl H. Brill.
  Living in the Spirit, Rachel Hosmer and Alan Jones.

Coleman, Lyman. *The Serendipity Bible Study Book.* Grand Rapids, MI: Zondervan Publishing House, 1986.

The Confessions of St. Augustine. F. J. Sheed, trans. New York: Sheed and Ward, 1943.

"Diocesan Guidelines for Christian Initiation and Confirmation." *Open* (June 1984): 6–8.

"Do This for the Remembrance of Me." New York: Communications Office, The Episocpal Church Center, 1985. Film/video.

Dozier, Verna. *Equipping the Saints.* Washington, DC: Alban Institute, 1981.

———. "What Anglicans Believe." Word, Inc., 7300 Imperial, Box 2518, Waco, TX 76202 (800) 433-3327. Videotape.

Dujarier, Michel. *A History of the Catechumenate.* New York: Sadlier Press, 1979.

————. *The Rites of Christian Initiation: Historical and Pastoral Reflections.* New York: Sadlier Press, 1979.

Dunnan, Maxie. *The Workbook on Spiritual Disciplines.* Nashville, TN: The Upper Room, 1984.

Dunning, James B. c. 1982. "Dynamics of Evangelization in the Catechumenate." Arlington, VA: North American Forum on the Catechumenate.

————. 1982. "Method is the Medium is the Message: Catechetical Method in the RCIA." Arlington, VA: North American Forum on the Catechumenate.

————. c. 1982. "Methods in Religious Education and Ministry." Arlington, VA: North American Forum on the Catechumenate.

————. *Ministries: Sharing God's Gifts.* Winona, MN: St. Mary's Press, 1980.

————. *New Wine: New Wineskins: Pastoral Implications of the Rite of Christian Initiation of Adults.* New York: Sadlier Press, 1981.

————. "The RCIA Journey: From Emmaus to South Carolina to San Antonio." Winona, MN: St. Mary's Press, 1983–84.

————. c. 1983. "What Happens After 'Christ Among Us'?" Arlington, VA: North American Forum on the Catechumenate. photocopy.

————. c. 1982. "Words of the Word: Evangelization, Catechesis, and the Catechumenate." Arlington, VA: North American Forum on the Catechumenate.

Eastman, A. Theodore. *The Baptizing Community: Christian Initiation and the Local Congregtaion.* New York: The Seabury Press, 1982.

Edwards, Tilden H. *Spiritual Friend: Reclaiming the Gift of Spiritual Direction.* New York: Paulist Press, 1980.

Egeria's Travels to the Holy Land. Revised Edition. John Wilkinson, trans. Jerusalem: Ariel Publishing House, 1981.

A Faithful Church: Issues in the History of Catechesis. John H. Westerhoff and O. C. Edwards, eds. Wilton, CT: Morehouse-Barlow, 1981.

Fenhagen, James C. *Invitation to Holiness.* San Francisco: Harper & Row, 1987.

———. *More Than Wanderers: Spiritual Disciplines for Christian Ministry.* New York: The Seabury Press, 1985.

———. *Mutual Ministry: New Vitality for the Local Church.* San Francisco: Harper & Row, 1986.

Finn, Thomas M. *The Liturgy of Baptism in the Baptismal Instructions of St. John Chrysostom.* The Catholic University of America Studies in Christian Antiquity Series, no. 15. Washington, DC: The Catholic University of America Press, 1967.

The Great Vigil of Easter: A Commentary; Celebrating Redemption—the Liturgies of Lent, Holy Week, and the Great Fifty Days; Christian Initiation—A Theological and Pastoral Commentary on the Rites. Alexandria, VA: Associated Parishes, 1977.

Goetchius, Eugene V. N. and Charles P. Price. *The Gifts of God.* Wilton, CT: Morehouse-Barlow, 1984.

Groome, Thomas H. *Christian Religious Education: Sharing Our Story and Vision.* San Francisco: Harper & Row, 1980.

Harrison, Anne. 1984. "Giftedness Conference." New York: Evangelism Ministries Office, The Episcopal Church Center.

Hatchett, Marion J. *Commentary on the American Prayer Book.* New York: The Seabury Press, 1980.

Hestenes, Roberta. "Building Community Through Small Groups," Media Services, Fuller Theological Seminary, Pasadena, CA 91182. Videotape.

Hinman, Karen M. *How to Form a Catechumenate Team.* Chicago: Liturgy Training Publications, 1986.

———. 1983. "Catechetical Method: A Model for Sunday Catechetical Sessions." Arlington, VA: North American Forum on the Catechumenate.

Hinman, Karen M. and Joseph P. Sinwell. *Breaking Open the Word of God.* New York: Paulist Press, 1986.

Hippolytus: A Text for Students. Geoffrey J. Cumin, ed. Bramcote, Notts.: Grove Books, 1976.

In God's Image. Twelve sessions on Stewardship, Atlanta: Diocese of Atlanta, Department of Stewardship, 1987.

Jelinek, Albert J. and Rosemarie Tapper. "Our Journey into the Unknown." New York: Evangelism Ministries Office, The Episcopal Church Center, 1987.

Jones, Gail C. *Seeking Life in Christ: A Manual for Developing a Process for Christian Initiation Including the Catechumenate in Your Congregation.* Resource Center, Diocese of Olympia, P.O. Box 12126, Seattle, WA, 98102, 1987.

Journal of the General Convention, 1985. New York: The Episcopal Church Center, 1985.

The Journal of General Convention, 1988, New York: The Episcopal Church Center, 1989.

Kavanagh, Aidan. *The Shape of Baptism: The Rite of Christian Initiation.* New York: Pueblo Publishing Company, 1978.

Keifer, Ralph A. "Christian Initiation: The State of the Question," in *Made, Not Born.* South Bend, IN: University of Notre Dame Press, 1976.

Kelshaw, Terrence, *Three Streams, One River, A Biblical Understanding of Stewardship;* and Terence McCabe, *A Leader's Manual.* New York: Office of Stewardship Development, The Episcopal Church Center, 1987.

Kemp, Raymond B. *A Journey in Faith: An Experience of the Catechumenate.* New York: Sadlier Press, 1979.

Kiblinger, Charles. "The Process of the Catechumenate at St. James' Church, Jackson, Mississippi." Jackson: St. James' Church c. 1984.

Lambert, Jay. "Forming Christians: A Model for the Catechumenate." *The Living Church* (June 7, 1987): 8–9.

Leech, Kenneth. *True Prayer: An Invitation to Christian Spirituality.* San Francisco: Harper & Row, 1980.

Lesser Feasts and Fasts together with The Fixed Holy Days. 3rd Ed. New York: The Church Hymnal Corporation, 1980.

LeVerdiere, Eugene. *The Infancy Narratives.* Kansas City, MO:

National Catholic Reporter Publishing Co., 1984. Audio cassettes.

Lewinski, Ron. *A Guide for Sponsors.* Chicago: Liturgy Training Publications, 1986.

———. *Welcoming the New Catholic.* Chicago: Liturgy Training Publications, 1983.

Liska, Martha. "A Companion in Christ." *Water and Fire* (Fall 1986).

"Living the Good News." Adult Lectionary Curricula. Denver, CO: Living the Good News. Published quarterly.

"Living Our Baptismal Covenant: Diocese of Milwaukee, Resources for Planning." February, 1986. New York: Evangelism Ministries Office, The Episcopal Church Center.

McCauley, Leo P. and Harkins, Paul W., trans. *The Works of Saint Cyril of Jerusalem.* Washington, DC: Catholic University Press, 1970.

Made, Not Born: New Perspectives on Christian Initiation and the Catechumenate. Papers from the Murphy Center for Liturgical Research. South Bend, IN: University of Notre Dame Press, 1976.

Mahaffey, Anne Carter. "The Identification of Gifts for Ministry." April 1986. Available from Mahaffey, 6004 Rodes Court, Louisville, KY 40222.

May, Lynde E. IV. "Leadership Style and the Catechumenal Process." New York: Evangelism Ministries Office, The Episcopal Church Center, 1987.

McElligott, Ann E. P. *Evangelism With the Poor.* New York: Evangelism Ministries Office, The Episcopal Church Center, 1986.

———. *Faith Development and Evangelism.* New York: Evangelism Ministries Office, The Episcopal Church Center, 1987.

McElligott, Thomas J. "Sharing Our Spiritual Journey." February 1988. Indianapolis, IN.

Merriman, Michael, ed. *The Baptismal Mystery and the Catechumenate,* New York: The Church Hymnal Corporation, 1990.

———. "The Liturgy in the Easter Season." *Open* (March 1987): 16–19.

"Methods for Bible Study and Reflection." See Appendix C, Section 2.

"Methods for Critical Reflection." See Appendix C, Section 5.

"Methods for Story-Sharing." See Appendix C, Section 4.

"Methods for Sunday Morning Catechetical Sessions." See Appendix C, Section 3.

Mitchell, Lionel L. *A Theological Commentary on the Book of Common Prayer.* Wilton, CT: Morehouse-Barlow, 1985.

Neighborhood Bible Studies, Inc.; Small group study guides; Box 222, Dobbs Ferry, NY 10522.

"An Outline of Faith." The Book of Common Prayer and Administration of the Sacraments and Other Rites and Ceremonies of the Church. New York: The Church Hymnal Corporation, 1979.

"An Outline of Weekly Meetings." *Water and Fire* (Fall 1985).

The Oxford Book of Prayers. George Appleton, ed. New York: Oxford University Press, 1985.

"A Parish Customary for Christian Initiation: The Guidelines for Christian Initiation at St. John's Church in Olympia, Washington." *Water and Fire* (Fall 1985).

Plattenburg, George and Sherrill Akyol. c. 1978. "A Workshop for Discerning and Empowering Our Gifts for Ministry." New York: Evangelism Ministries Office, The Episcopal Church Center.

Powerhouse of Prayer, Workshop leading to small groups, Anglican Fellowship of Prayer, 1988.

The Prayer Book Guide to Christian Education. Wilton, CT: Morehouse-Barlow, 1987.

Prayers for Pastors and People. Carl G. Carlozzi, ed. New York: The Church Hymnal Corporation, 1984.

Proclamation 3 and 4: Series A, B, and C. Philadelphia: Fortress Press, 1989.

Readings in the History of the Episcopal Church. Robert W. Prichard, ed. Wilton, CT: Morehouse-Barlow, 1986.

Reed, Ronald. *The Steward's Count. A Theological Essay on Steward-ship.* New York: Office of Stewardship Development, The Episcopal Church Center, 1987.

Riley, Hugh M. *Christian Initiation: A Comparative Study of the Inter-pretation of the Baptismal Liturgy in the Mystagogical Writing of Cyril of Jerusalem, John Chrysostom, Theodore of Mopsuestia, and Ambrose of Milan.* Catholic University of American Studies in Christian Antiquity Series, no. 17. Washington, DC: Catholic University of America Press, 1974.

Rothauge, Arlin J. *Catechism: The Outline of the Faith We Profess.* Clues 4, Papers on Renewal and Evangelism. Cincinnati, OH: Forward Movement Publications, 1982.

———. *Reshaping a Congregation for a New Future.* New York: The Office of Congregational Development, The Episcopal Church Center, 1985.

———. *Sizing Up a Congregation for New Member Ministry,* The Episcopal Church Center, 1983.

Rowthorn, Anne. *The Liberation of the Laity.* Wilton, CT: More-house-Barlow, 1986.

Russell, Joseph P. *Daily Prayer and Bible Study with the BCP.* Cin-cinnati, OH: Forward Movement Publications, 1986.

———. *The Daily Lectionary, A Weekly Guide for Daily Bible Reading,* vol. 1–4. Cincinnati, OH: Forward Movement Publica-tions, 1987–88.

———. *Sharing Our Biblical Story.* Minneapolis: Winston Press, 1979.

Russell, Joseph P. and John D. Vogelsang. *In Dialogue: An Episco-pal Guide for Adult Bible Study.* New York: The Episcopal Church Center, 1986.

Ryle. Jerry. "The Catechumenate in Story and Experience: A Roman Catholic Setting." Evangelism Ministries Office, The Episcopal Church Center. 1986.

St. John Chrysostom, Baptismal Instructions. Paul W. Harkins, trans. Westminster, MD: The Newman Press, 1963.

Schwab, A. Wayne. "A Visit to Three Churches in a Catechumenal Process." New York: Evangelism Ministries Office, The Episcopal Church Center. June 1987.

———. "Changed Lives." New York: Evangelism Ministries Office, The Episcopal Church Center. June 1987.

———. *Handbook for Evangelism.* New York: Evangelism Ministries Office, The Episcopal Church Center. rev. 1989.

———. "Resources for Planning." New York: Evangelism Ministries Office, The Episcopal Church Center, February 1986.

———. "Using a Catechumenal Process for Christian Initiation." New York: The Evangelism Ministries Office, The Episcopal Church Center. June 1987.

Schwab, A. Wayne and William A. Yon. *Proclamation as Offering Story and Choice.* New York: Office of Evangelism Ministries, Education for Mission and Ministry, The Episcopal Church Center. 1988.

Serendipity House. Current Catalog. Box 1012, Littleton, CO 80160 (800) 525-9563.

"Session Plans: Jackson, Mississippi." See Appendix C, Section 6.

"Session Plans: Milwaukee Pilot Project." See Appendix C, Section 7.

"Six Weekly Sessions in Ministry Formation." New York: Evangelism Ministries Office, The Episcopal Church Center, 1985.

Sprague, Minka Shura. *One to Watch, One to Pray: A Devotional Introduction to the Gospels.* Wilton, CT: Morehouse-Barlow, 1985.

Stevenson, Anne Broad. "The Inquiry Period: One Church's Model." *Water and Fire,* Fall 1986.

———. "The Period of the Catechumenate." *Water and Fire* Summer 1987.

Stevick, Daniel B. *Adult Baptism: Getting Back to the Beginning.* Clues 7, Papers on Renewal and Evangelism. Cincinnati, OH: Forward Movement Publications, 1984.

————. *Baptismal Movements: Baptismal Meaning.* New York: The Church Hymnal Corporation, 1987.

————. *Holy Baptism: Supplement to Prayer 26.* New York: The Church Hymnal Corporation, 1973.

Sullivan, Mark. "No Bolts of Lightning." A Catechumenal Process in a Pastoral Size Congregation. New York: Evangelism Ministries Office, The Episcopal Church Center, 1985.

Sydnor, William. *Looking at the Episcopal Church.* Wilton, CT: Morehouse-Barlow, 1980.

Thornton, Martin. *Spiritual Direction.* Cambridge, MA: Cowley Press, 1984.

Tucker, Beverly D. and William H. Swatos Jr. *Questions on the Way: A Catechism Based on the Book of Common Prayer.* Cincinnati, OH: Forward Movement Publications, 1987.

"A Turning Point." New York: Evangelism Ministries Office, The Episcopal Church Center. Adapted from the North American Forum on the Catechumenate, December 1986.

Vos, Nelvin. *Seven Days a Week: Faith in Action* Philadelphia: Fortress Press, 1985.

Warren, Michael. "Religious Formation in the Context of Social Formation." *Religious Education* vol. 82, no. 4, Fall 1987, pp. 515–528.

Weber, Hans-Reudi. *Experiments with Bible Study.* Geneva: World Council of Churches, 1983.

Weil, Louis. *Gathered to Pray: Understanding Liturgical Prayer.* Parish Life Source Books. Cambridge, MA: Cowley Publications, 1986.

————. "Christian Initiation and Ministry." New York: Evangelism Ministries, The Episcopal Church Center, 1988.

Westerhoff, John. "Characteristics of a Helpful Sponsor." New York: Evangelism Ministries Office, The Episcopal Church Center, February 1986.

————. "Formation, Education, Instruction." *Religious Education* 82, no. 4, Fall 1987, pp. 578–591.

Whitaker, E. C. *Documents of the Baptismal Liturgy.* 2nd Ed. London: S.P.C.K., 1970.

Willimon, William H. "Making Christians in a Secular World." *The Christian Century* (October 22 1986), pp. 914–917.

Wink, Walter. *Transforming Bible Study: A Leader's Guide.* Nashville, TN: Abingdon Press, 1980.

Wolf, Frederick. *Journey in Faith.* Wilton, CT: Morehouse-Barlow, 1982. Out of Print.

Yarnold, Edward J. *The Awe-Inspiring Rites of Initiation.* Slough, Great Britain: St. Paul Publications, 1972.